Bringing the World to MISSISSIPPI

THE UNIVERSITY OF SOUTHERN MISSISSIPPI SYMPHONY ORCHESTRA

1919-2010

Bringing the World to MISSISSIPPI

THE UNIVERSITY OF SOUTHERN MISSISSIPPI
SYMPHONY ORCHESTRA
1919-2010

www.upress.state.ms.us
The University Press of Mississippi is a member of the Association of American University Presses.

Manufactured in China
First edition 2010

∞

Library of Congress Cataloging-in-Publication Data
Montague, Rebecca Smart.
Bringing the world to Mississippi : The University of Southern Mississippi Symphony Orchestra 1919–2010 / by Rebecca Smart Montague. — 1st ed.
p. cm.
Includes bibliographical references and index.
ISBN 978-1-61703-016-1 (cloth : alk. paper) 1. University of Southern Mississippi. Symphony Orchestra—History. 2. Orchestra—Mississippi—Hattiesburg—History. I. Title.
ML28.H32U654 2010
784.206'076218—dc22 2010038549
British Library Cataloging-in-Publication Data available

ACKNOWLEDGEMENTS

It was just seven months ago that Jay Dean approached me about writing a history of the Southern Miss orchestra. Immediately thereafter, he overwhelmed me with mountains of materials—photographs, concert programs, and reams of dusty documents that had collected in the orchestra office, university archives, and numerous other locations on campus for over ninety years. What fun we had going through them all together! I'm deeply indebted to Jay, both for entrusting this project to me and for gathering all the research materials so that I could "just" sit down to write! Thank you, Jay.

Whitney Miller Coll, in the Office of University Communications, patiently and ably served as graphic designer. Most of the photographs were taken over the years by the talented Danny Rawls of the Southern Miss Photo Services department, and I am also grateful for images provided by the university's archives and alumni association, by Michael Lopinto, and by our local newspaper, *The Hattiesburg American.*

I also thank Amy Giust for the beautiful painting which inspired the book's cover and layout and Stanley Hauer who edited an early draft. Special thanks to all the story contributors. I so enjoyed listening to your favorite symphony memories.

Finally, I am grateful to all the conductors, faculty members, and student musicians who have shared their gifts of music and who developed this fine student orchestra into one that rivals any university orchestra anywhere.

-Rebecca Smart Montague

STATE OF MISSISSIPPI
OFFICE OF THE GOVERNOR

HALEY BARBOUR
GOVERNOR

June 1, 2010

Dear Fellow Mississippians,

It gives me great pleasure to write this letter for the centennial book on the history of The University of Southern Mississippi Symphony Orchestra. The remarkable accomplishments by this musical organization certainly merit a publication devoted to its long history.

Mississippi, the birthplace of America's music, is greatly enriched by this orchestra's performances throughout our state. The Southern Miss Symphony Orchestra indeed raises the level of cultural opportunities available to the people of Mississippi, an achievement I was pleased to personally and formally recognize by presenting this organization with the 2009 Governor's Award for Leadership in the Arts.

Frequently, the student musicians trained at Southern Miss reward us by performing with other orchestras and events throughout the state and in the surrounding region. Our state, of course, also benefits from the marvelous internationally known guest artists this organization regularly brings to Mississippi and the national attention that accompanies these celebrity performances. The many performances by this orchestra are an important part of our state's musical fabric, as well as meaningful cultural contributions to our economy and international image. These efforts for our citizens are very much appreciated.

I look forward to my next opportunity to hear this fine orchestra that continues to bring the world to Mississippi.

Sincerely,

Haley Barbour
Governor

POST OFFICE BOX 139 • JACKSON, MISSISSIPPI 39205 • TEL (601) 359-3150 • FAX (601) 359-3741 • www.governorbarbour.com

Haley Barbour
GOVERNOR
STATE OF MISSISSIPPI

mississippi arts commission
support inspire enrich

Malcolm White
EXECUTIVE DIRECTOR OF THE
MISSISSIPPI ARTS COMMISSION

Dear Fellow Music Lovers:

Quite by accident, I was introduced to classical music in 1971 in the basement of the old library at Mississippi State University. Although I ultimately graduated from The University of Southern Mississippi, at Mississippi State I often retreated to the library basement in lieu of attending Spanish class, where I was performing miserably. I dallied away the daylight by randomly selecting records that were unfamiliar to me and came face to face with Mozart's Piano Concerto No. 21. I was smitten and soon found myself adding other classics to my collection that was,heretofore, built on Frank Zappa, The Allman Brothers, John Coltrane, Merle Haggard, and Fats Domino.

When I came to the Mississippi Arts Commission in 2005, I was delighted to begin a more detailed association with orchestras, and I soon observed that many of the faces were the same. I recognized many of the same players in the Meridian Symphony, the Mississippi Symphony, and the Gulf Coast Symphony. As I explored the source of this phenomenon, all roads led me to USM.

When Jay Dean arrived at USM in 1988 and began recruiting musicians, he found only four high school string programs in the state. From there, he searched across state lines without much more success. While conducting in Mexico City, he discovered talented students interested in auditioning to come to the United States and began holding annual auditions in Mexico City. So began the journey of the USM Symphony Orchestra's recruitment efforts in Latin America, Spain, China, Taiwan, Bulgaria, Russia, Canada, Romania, and Hungary.

The orchestral communities in Mississippi and throughout the Gulf South owe a debt of gratitude to the USM orchestra. This successful program increases the depth of Mississippi's musician pool, and none of the region's orchestras would have the quality we enjoy today without this resource.

Paradoxically, my discovery of classical music in the basement at Mississippi State was life-changing, but not completing that Spanish class and developing this second language has put me at a serious disadvantage in communicating with many of these gifted musicians. The language of music will have to suffice.

Sincerely,

Malcolm White
Executive Director

"If in the after-life there is not music,
we will have to import it."

Domenico Cieri Estrada

501 north west street suite 1101a woolfolk building jackson. mississippi 39201 t: 601-359-6030 tdd: 800-582-2233 f: 601-359-6008 www.arts.state.ms.us

THE OFFICIAL STATE AGENCY FOR THE ARTS

THE UNIVERSITY OF SOUTHERN MISSISSIPPI

Office of the President

118 College Drive #5001
Hattiesburg, MS 39406-0001
Tel: 601.266.5001
Fax: 601.266.5756
president@usm.edu

Dear Friends of the University,

You are in for a treat as you turn the pages through 90 years of concerts, operas, and musical theatre productions brought to us by the Southern Miss Symphony Orchestra and Opera. *Bringing the World to Mississippi*, published during our university's Centennial Celebration, commemorates the history of an outstanding symphony orchestra, opera and musical theatre program within a distinguished school of music.

I could not have been more pleased in January 2010 when Southern Miss launched the year-long celebration of its 100th anniversary with the orchestra's spectacular concert featuring world famous operatic soprano, Renée Fleming. It was a night to be remembered! In years to come when we all reflect on the exciting events of our centennial year, I'm sure that this special performance by The University of Southern Mississippi Symphony Orchestra will be chief among them.

The University of Southern Mississippi, in 100 years, has catapulted from a local teachers' college to a nationally known research university. In many ways, the orchestra's development from a small ensemble into an international organization performing with the premier classical musicians of our time echoes our university's growth.

As president, I commend our orchestra conductors, music faculty members, and the thousands of students who have performed with the orchestra over its 90-year history. As a native Mississippian who graduated from Southern Miss, I am particularly proud of this orchestra's many accomplishments.

I hope you will enjoy reliving this musical history as much as I have.

Sincerely yours,

Martha D. Saunders
President

Martha D. Saunders
PRESIDENT
THE UNIVERSITY OF SOUTHERN MISSISSIPPI

THE UNIVERSITY OF SOUTHERN MISSISSIPPI
CENTENNIAL SYMPHONY ORCHESTRA

The Southern Miss Symphony Orchestra would not have achieved its current status were it not an integral part of The University of Southern Mississippi School of Music. The School of Music has a longstanding international reputation for musical excellence and is recognized for its eminence in musical artistry, education, and community service. Serving students from the United States and around the world, the school maintains a strongly diverse student population. It is the only doctoral degree-granting School of Music in Mississippi and is one of only twenty-eight comprehensive doctoral degree-granting Schools of Music among the more than five hundred members of The National Association of Schools of Music.

The School of Music provides a wealth of opportunities for the professional and artistic growth of students. Ensembles host important guest artists and have been featured at numerous national conventions. Faculty members perform at major venues all over the world and teach at international festivals and conferences every year. The school has a strong record of placing its graduates into competitive jobs and graduate programs and has trained many of this nation's finest music educators and performers.

Bringing the World to MISSISSIPPI

THE UNIVERSITY OF SOUTHERN MISSISSIPPI
SYMPHONY ORCHESTRA
1919-2010

CONTENTS

PREFACE

On January 29, 2010, before a capacity crowd of 2,360 people, internationally renowned soprano Renée Fleming performed with The University of Southern Mississippi Symphony Orchestra at Thalia Mara Hall in Jackson, Mississippi. This stellar concert, presented in conjunction with Mississippi Opera's sixty-fifth anniversary, was the university's inaugural Centennial Celebration event and the pinnacle performance in more than two decades' work by Director of Orchestral Activities Jay Dean to present superb orchestral programming on par with any university orchestra in the world.

Ms. Fleming's masterful performance was preceded in recent years by programs featuring globally acclaimed virtuosos including Itzhak Perlman, Yo-Yo Ma, Sir James Galway, Joshua Bell, Nadja Salerno-Sonnenberg, and Plácido Domingo. Other popular celebrity artists who have performed with The University of Southern Mississippi Symphony Orchestra include Doc Severinsen, Ray Charles, Ricky Skaggs, Charley Pride, The Pointer Sisters, Sandi Patty, Dionne Warwick, and Patti LaBelle.

The university's 2010 celebration of its centennial birthday presented the perfect occasion to reflect on the origins of the oldest orchestra in Mississippi. This under-funded ensemble in one of the nation's poorest states overcame numerous obstacles as it evolved into an accomplished orchestra of student musicians representing fifteen countries and benefiting from the rare opportunity to perform with the finest musicians in the world.

A student musician once remarked, upon hearing his conductor announce the upcoming performance of one of these famous artists, "Dr. Dean, we bring the world to Mississippi!" With a nod to this young man, and in appreciation for the many musicians—celebrity, student, faculty, and community—who have performed with The University of Southern Mississippi Symphony Orchestra during the first ninety years of its existence, I pay homage in the following pages to an orchestra which matured from a humble, short-lived, ten-piece ensemble in 1913 into a superior student orchestra and musical ambassador "Bringing the World to Mississippi."

–Rebecca Smart Montague

MISSISSIPPI NORMAL COLLEGE ORCHESTRA, 1920

Bringing the World to
MISSISSIPPI

The Beginning 1919-1963

THE FIRST ORCHESTRA AT THE UNIVERSITY OF SOUTHERN MISSISSIPPI—THEN MISSISSIPPI NORMAL COLLEGE--WAS ORGANIZED IN 1913 AND WAS A MODEST, SHORT-LIVED ENSEMBLE THAT DID NOT PLAY TRADITIONAL ORCHESTRAL LITERATURE AND WAS FORMED TO ACCOMPANY THE SCHOOL'S CHOIR.

1.

Its conductor, Lorena Tomson, who would remain on the music faculty until 1922, established the true orchestral predecessor of The University of Southern Mississippi Symphony Orchestra in 1919 with an orchestra consisting of eleven musicians.

Ms. Tomson was followed in 1922 by conductor Margaret Gillard, under whose direction the orchestra grew to fifteen musicians, including the addition of three brass players. Hazel Horton Read then conducted the small orchestra for two years, followed by Madeleen Armstrong's tenure of two years.

No records confirm the existence of an orchestra for the next few years–perhaps the founding musicians graduated. In 1930, State Teachers College, as Mississippi Normal College had come to be known, hired Frank Earl Marsh Jr. to chair its fledgling music department, and Marsh would remain, becoming chair of the fine arts department in 1945, until his retirement in 1960. The few records that remain from the 1930s and 1940s identify Marsh as orchestra conductor from 1930 until 1948. Marsh is also credited with the organization of the Hattiesburg Choral Union and the 1948 establishment of the Opera Workshop; both endeavors were accompanied by the symphony orchestra and have continued without interruption to the present time.

2.

MISSISSIPPI NORMAL COLLEGE
AUDITORIUM

STUDENT RECITAL

WEDNESDAY, MAY 21, 1919, 8:00 P. M.

March—"On To Plattsburg" .... Lowe
Orchestra

Piano—"Mazurka D' Amour" .... Cone
Ceola Merkle

Violin Duet—"Serenade" .... Pache
Gertie Cato and Bertha Baxter

Piano—"Polka Semplice No. 4" .... Cone
Charlie Mae Sheffeed

Violin—"Souvenir" .... Drdla
Forrest Neal Pack

Voice—"Japanese Love Song" .... Thomas
Bernice Henderson

March—"Mississippi" .... Mrs. A. J. Crowe
Orchestra

Piano—"Valse Caprice" .... Newland
Edith Fife

Violin Duet—
(a) "Menuet" .... Beethoven
(b) "Marche Militaire" .... Shubert

Piano—"Melodie" .... Paderewski
Theresa Cook

Violin—"America"
Randolph Smith, Paul Tally, O. C. Grigsby, Helen Williams, Francis Osteen, Dorothy Daughdrill

Reading—"Spanish Gypsy Flower Girl"
Lucile Resler

Piano—"Scarf Dance" .... Chaminade
Serena Speed

Chorus—"Estudiantina" .... Lacome
Glee Club

March—"Officer of the Day" .... Hall
Orchestra

3.

1. ORCHESTRA CONDUCTOR LORENA TOMSON, 1920 | 2.ORCHESTRA, 1924 | 3. PAGE FROM THE *NEKA CAMON*, THE UNIVERSITY'S YEARBOOK, FEATURING MUSIC FACULTY FROM 1922 | 4. MISSISSIPPI SOUTHERN COLLEGE ORCHESTRA, 1948

SOCIETY · SCENERY

Sadly, aside from the occasional program saved by a student or faculty musician, a handful of photographs is the only proof that the orchestra existed during these two decades. The disappointing absence of orchestra records is perhaps understandable, however, due to the diminutive size of the music faculty and the college's focus, until 1940 when the institution's name was changed to Mississippi Southern College, on training public school teachers.

FROM 1950 THROUGH 1963, ELEVEN FACULTY MEMBERS CONDUCTED OCCASIONAL CONCERTS WITH THE ORCHESTRA:

Noah Knepper	1948-49
Samuel H. Scott	1950-51
Joshua Missal	1951-52
Lawrence Fisher	1953-55
Roger Phelps	1953-59
William Presser	1956-61
Rey Longyear	1960-61
Felix Ponziani	1960-61
James Hanshumaker	1960-61
Angelo Frascarelli	1961-62
Harold Avery	1962-63

The highlight of the orchestral season during these years occurred each spring when, under Marsh's baton, the orchestra embarked on a two-week tour of South Mississippi performing a shortened version of Handel's *Messiah*. All music classes were canceled for two weeks, and those students who were not in the orchestra sang in the chorus. Music faculty acted as chaperones for the two-performances-a-day tour.

1.

2.

1. LITTLE SYMPHONY ORCHESTRA, 1949 | 2. LITTLE SYMPHONY ORCHESTRA, 1950 | 3. FRANK EARL MARSH CONDUCTING A PERFORMANCE OF HANDEL'S *MESSIAH*, 1942 | 4. THIS NATIONALLY DISTRIBUTED INSTRUCTIONAL BOOKLET WAS CREATED AT MISSISSIPPI SOUTHERN COLLEGE AND PUBLISHED BY THE AMERICAN STRING TEACHERS ASSOCIATION AND AMERICAN MUSIC CONFERENCE IN 1957.

3.

The Hattiesburg Choral Union

Assisted by

The Hattesburg Little Symphony

FRANK EARL MARSH, Jr., Conductor
MARY THERESA POE BAYLIS, Pianist

PRESENTS

"The Messiah"

By GEORGE FREDERICK HANDEL

Soloists

LILLIAN COOPER, Soprano
ELIZABETH RISCHER, Contralto
EDGAR W. WRIGHT, Tenor
HASKELL BOYTER, Baritone

THE MISSISSIPPI SOUTHERN COLLEGE AUDITORIUM
HATTIESBURG, MISSISSIPPI

SUNDAY EVENING, DECEMBER 13, 1942
EIGHT O'CLOCK

4.

In 1953, Marsh created a chamber orchestra which was conducted by Dr. William Presser for two years and then disbanded. By this time, Marsh was too ill to continue as oratorio or opera director (although he would not miss directing a performance of *Messiah* until 1958). Robert Waterstripe conducted the Brahms *Requiem* in 1954, and Presser conducted Mendelssohn's *Elijah* in 1955, the last spring oratorio concert presented for a number of years.

The Hattiesburg Choral Union wishes to dedicate its Twelfth Annual presentation of Handel's "The Messiah" to the following former members of the Choral Union who are known to be in the armed forces of the United States:

Jessel Betlyon
John N. Betlyon
Wilmer Bond
David Brumley
Wilbur Bullock
Charles Burleson
Leo Burns
George Bushong
Harold Bryant
Emily D'Olive
John Frazier
Howard Gilliam
George Grace
Charles Granger
Franklin Green

Cecil Grisham
Winburn Gurney
Joseph Haddad
A. E. Harvey
Nolie W. Hickman
Trulen Hill
Pope Huff
Roy Huff
Phillip Joseph
William Leggett
Robin S. Longre
Ferrel Lowery
J. B. McDevitt
John McKewen
Martin Roy McLendon

Charles Newton
Mary Beth Oden
Joe Potter
Shelby Rogers
J. T. Selby
George Shivers
Bennie Simmons
Bill Smith
J. T. Smith
Linsey Stickney
C. E. Strahan
S. W. Swinney
Fred Walker
Frank West
Walton West

Handel commenced the composition of The Messiah August 22, 1741, and completed it twenty-four days later. It was first performed in the Music Hall, Dublin, for the benefit of charity, April 13, 1742. The text is taken from the Old and New Testaments, and arranged by Charles Jennens.

The Messiah tells the story of man's redemption, in its complete form which requires some four hours for presentation. The story is divided into three parts: the first sets forth the promise of the Redeemer, the birth of Christ, and His mission of healing and comfort; the second is devoted to His passion, resurrection and ascension, the discomfiture of the heathen, and the establishment of the Kingdom of God upon the earth; the third part deals with the triumph of the redeemed and the glory of heaven. The abridged Christmas presentation traditionally offers most of Part the First as originally arranged but combines selections from the second and third parts as Part the Second.

It is requested that there be no applause during the performance.

Sponsored by
THE MISSISSIPPI SOUTHERN COLLEGE AND
MUSIC LOVERS OF SOUTH MISSISSIPPI

WHEN I FIRST CAME, THE ORCHESTRA PLAYED ONE CONCERT A YEAR. THE TWO YEARS I WAS CO-CONDUCTOR, IT PLAYED THREE CONCERTS A YEAR. AFTER THAT, I GAVE FOUR CONCERTS A YEAR, PLUS THE REGIONAL COMPOSERS' CONCERT. FOR SEVERAL SUCCESSIVE YEARS WE HAD A SERIES OF THREE ADJACENT CONCERTS DEVOTED TO MUSIC BY REGIONAL COMPOSERS WHO WERE REQUIRED TO BE PRESENT. I WAS IN CHARGE OF THIS AND REHEARSED THE ORCHESTRA BUT DID NO CONDUCTING ON THESE PROGRAMS. WE HAD CONDUCTORS FROM THE MEMPHIS, JACKSON, MOBILE, AND BIRMINGHAM POPS ORCHESTRAS, AS WELL AS GUEST COMPOSER-CONDUCTORS. THIS, TO ME, WAS THE HIGHLIGHT OF THE FIFTIES FOR THE ORCHESTRA.

– the late William Presser
FACULTY, 1954-81

WHEN I WAS A STUDENT, WE DIDN'T GET ACTUAL CREDIT FOR BAND, ORCHESTRA, CHOIR, CHORAL UNION, OR ATTENDING RECITALS EVERY SUNDAY AFTERNOON. WE GOT ZEROES. AND WE HAD TO HAVE ENOUGH ZEROES OR WE DIDN'T GRADUATE. THERE WAS ONE DOOR INTO THE REHEARSAL HALL, AND THE BACK DOOR WAS LOCKED (A FIRE MARSHAL'S NIGHTMARE). ALL ORCHESTRA REHEARSALS WERE AT NIGHT FROM 7:00 TO 9:30 OR 10:00, AND WE HAD TO BE IN THE DORM BY 10:30. CHOIR REHEARSALS WERE AFTERNOONS AT 4:00, AND IF WE WERE TWO MINUTES LATE, THE DOOR WAS ALREADY LOCKED AND WE WERE COUNTED ABSENT. MY, HOW THINGS HAVE CHANGED!

– *Edna Rice Perkins*
VIOLA, 1950-54

In 1954, President R. C. Cook invited Frank Crockett to move Crockett's outreach program to improve the number of string programs in the state from The University of Mississippi to Mississippi Southern College. Crockett, along with Roger Di Guilian, soon established the South Mississippi Youth Orchestra, consisting of high school students from the area's public schools. Within a few years the two men had developed a first-rate youth orchestra, and Dr. Presser wrote a number of works for them, two of such works being the recipient of the National School Orchestra Association (NSOA) award. Although this string program faltered upon Crockett's departure, it served as a catalyst for the orchestra's later adoption of a dual mission: education of the university's orchestral students, of course, as well as outreach to and education of the area's kindergarten through twelfth-grade students and community citizens.

2.

3.

1. ROGER PHELPS CONDUCTING MISSISSIPPI SOUTHERN COLLEGE ORCHESTRA, 1953 | 2. VESPER CHOIR AND SINFONIETTA, 1954
3. SINFONIETTA, 1956

I TOOK OVER THE CONDUCTING OF THE MUSIC DEPARTMENT'S ORCHESTRA IN 1951. I THINK THERE WERE TWENTY-NINE IN IT THEN. I IMMEDIATELY ASKED THE CHAIRMAN, FRANK MARSH, IF I COULD WRITE THE HATTIESBURG NEWSPAPER ASKING THEM TO PUBLISH MY REQUEST FOR ANY TOWNSPEOPLE WHO WOULD LIKE TO JOIN THE COLLEGE ORCHESTRA. WE ENDED UP WITH SOME FORTY-SIX PERFORMERS BEFORE THE END OF THAT YEAR. I DON'T REMEMBER MUCH OF THE FOUR PROGRAMS THAT WE DID, BUT I REMEMBER THAT WE DID THE *CARMEN* SUITE, POLOVTSIAN DANCES, A HAYDN SYMPHONY, AND SOME HANSON. MY WIFE PEG PLAYED CELLO AND PIANO. IT WAS A GRATIFYING YEAR. PEOPLE IN THE REGION HAD NEVER HEARD MUCH CLASSICAL MUSIC, CERTAINLY NOT THEIR OWN CITY ORCHESTRA.

– Joshua Missal
FACULTY, 1950-53

AUDITORIUM ON THE TOP FLOOR OF COLLEGE HALL WHERE THE ORCHESTRA PLAYED ITS CONCERTS UNTIL 1930, WHEN BENNETT AUDITORIUM WAS COMPLETED.

Coming of Age
1964-1987

STEREO
SEVERINSEN
at
SOUTHERN
William T. Gower, Conductor
The University of Southern Mississippi Symphony Orchestra

DR. WILLIAM T. GOWER ARRIVED IN 1963 FROM THE UNIVERSITY OF IOWA AND WASTED NO TIME IN INCREASING BOTH SIZE AND STATURE OF THE ORCHESTRA, A FITTING FOLLOW-UP TO THE PREVIOUS YEAR'S ELEVATION OF MISSISSIPPI NORMAL COLLEGE TO THE UNIVERSITY OF SOUTHERN MISSISSIPPI. GOWER RECRUITED STUDENTS FROM IOWA AND THE MIDWEST, NORTHERN STATES, AND JAPAN. HE ALSO CONDUCTED CONCERTS WITH WELL-KNOWN ARTISTS.

In 1967, Doc Severinsen, who was known professionally in those days as Carl Severinsen and had just taken over leadership of Johnny Carson's *Tonight Show* band, made a guest appearance with the orchestra. This performance of Concerto for Trumpet and Orchestra by Floyd Werle, the principal composer-arranger for the United States Air Force band, was fondly remembered by student performers and audience alike as they watched Severinsen's enduring fame alongside Johnny Carson for the following twenty-five years.

Other significant artists who made guest appearances under Gower's leadership included Stuart Canin, concertmaster of the San Francisco Symphony, and pianist Rudolf Firkusny, who performed Schumann's Concerto in A Minor. Orchestra personnel at this time included several whose names are familiar to Southern Miss concertgoers. Nationally acclaimed composer James Sclater was principal clarinetist, and Dr. Tom Fraschillo, director of bands at Southern Miss, was a member of the percussion section.

Operas were produced in the Gower era, as well, and the orchestra ensemble was in the pit for productions including Pergolesi's *La Serva Padrona*, Rossini's *Il Barbiere di Siviglia*, and Puccini's *La Bohème*. In 1972, Gower established the university's Summer School Symphony Orchestra and traveled with the orchestra to perform at the National Association for Music Education Convention in Atlanta.

THE UNIVERSITY OF SOUTHERN MISSISSIPPI

SCHOOL OF FINE ARTS

presents

THE UNIVERSITY SYMPHONY ORCHESTRA

William T. Gower, Conductor

Carl Severinsen, Trumpet Soloist

Sunday, April Sixteenth

Nineteen Hundred and Sixty-Seven

Two-Thirty O'clock in the Afternoon

Main Auditorium

University of Southern Mississippi

PROGRAM

An American in Paris (1928) .... Gershwin

Fanfare for "Trumpeters and Doc" .... Sclater

Concerto for Trumpet and Orchestra .... Werle
Solo de Concours
Spiritual
Finale
Carl Severinsen, Trumpeter

INTERMISSION

Divertissement (1930) .... Ibert
Prelude
Cortege
Nocturne
Valse
Parade
Finale

Medley of Beautiful Songs .... Arr. Sclater
Lush Life
All The Things You Are
I Can't Get Started With You

TODAY'S SOLOIST

Carl "Doc" Severinsen was born in Arlington, Oregon in 1927. He was started on the trumpet by his father, who was an excellent musician as well as a dentist. At the age of nine he won the Oregon State contest for which one of the judges, Herbert L. Clark, took an immediate interest in young Carl, predicted a great future and later served as a source of much encouragement. At the age of 13, Mr. Severinsen won first in the National Senior Division contest.

After high school and Army service, he played and was featured with the orchestras of Charlie Barnett, Sam Donahue, Tommy Dorsey, Benny Goodman and Gene Krupa. In 1949, he settled in New York City as a free lance musician, and at the same time studied with the late Benny Baker, former first trumpet with Toscanini. He soon became staff musician at NBC, working such shows as Kate Smith, Dinah Shore, Eddie Fisher, Sid Ceasar, and was regularly featured on the original Steve Allen Show and "NBC Bandstand", both as a soloist and as a conductor.

In recent years Mr. Severinsen has been a featured artist and assistant conductor of NBC's "Tonight Show" with Johnny Carson. He serves as consultant/clinician to the Getzen Band Instrument Company of Elkhorn, Wisconsin, and is in constant demand as guest soloist/clinician in the educational music field.

1.

2.

1. WILLIAM T. GOWER CONDUCTING REHEARSAL, 1967 | 2. DOC SEVERINSEN REHEARSING WITH GOWER, 1967

SOMETIME IN 1966 OR '67, WHEN I WAS THE PRINCIPAL CLARINET AND BILL GOWER WAS THE CONDUCTOR, WE HAD A PERFORMANCE OF IBERT'S "DIVERTISSEMENT" WHICH FEATURED A PIANO SOLOIST WITH CHAMBER ORCHESTRA. DR. GOWER ASKED TOM FRASCHILLO TO PLAY THE PIANO PART, WHICH FEATURED TOM IN A SPOOF OF THE GREAT PIANO CONCERTI, INCLUDING BOOMING CHORDS WITH WRONG NOTES AND MUCH ATTITUDE. TOM ENTERED WITH A FANCY CANDELABRUM, A LA LIBERACE, AND PLAYED THE ROLE PERFECTLY. DURING THE THIRD MOVEMENT, WHICH FEATURES A LOVELY SOLO CLARINET LINE, I PLAYED THE PART WITH GREAT FEELING, ONLY TO LOOK UP TO SEE TOM LOOKING BORED AND SMOKING A CIGARETTE! IT HAD BEEN SECRETLY PLANNED BY DR. GOWER AND TOM, AND I WAS CAUGHT TOTALLY OFF GUARD! THIS WAS MY MOST MEMORABLE MOMENT WITH THE ORCHESTRA, AND I REMEMBER IT WITH GREAT FONDNESS TO THIS DAY.

– Doug Graham
CLARINET, 1965-67

SOMETIME AROUND 1983, THE ORCHESTRA WAS ON A RECRUITING TOUR THROUGH MISSISSIPPI AND STOPPED FOR THE NIGHT IN KOSCIUSKO. WE STAYED AT A SMALL MOTEL ON A TWO-LANE HIGHWAY THERE. ABOUT ONE O'CLOCK IN THE MORNING THERE WAS A TERRIFIC CRASH OUTSIDE, AND EVERYONE WENT TO LOOK. A HUGE CATTLE TRUCK HAD FLIPPED OVER ON ITS SIDE AND COME TO REST IN FRONT OF THE MOTEL. COWS WERE ROAMING IN THE PARKING LOT AND IN THE ROAD, AND THE DRIVER WAS DRUNK AND STUCK IN THE CAB OF THE TRUCK. AS A GROUP, WE WERE NOT EXACTLY THE BEST ON THE SCENE, BUT ONE OF OUR NUMBER, RANDY WILLIAMS, HAD GROWN UP RAISING CATTLE WITH HIS FAMILY IN COLUMBIA. RANDY TOOK CHARGE. HE STARTED TO SPEAK "COW" AND HERDED THE CATTLE INTO SOME KIND OF ORDER. WE ALL STOOD AROUND IN AMAZEMENT. WHEN THE POLICE FINALLY GOT THERE AND HAULED OUT THE DRUNKEN TRUCKER, RANDY HAD THINGS UNDER CONTROL.

–J.C. Barker
CLARINET, 1980-84

GOWER RESIGNED AS CONDUCTOR IN 1975, THOUGH HIS NUMEROUS ACHIEVEMENTS HAVE BEEN HONORED SINCE 2005 WITH THE ANNUAL "FUTURE STARS" CONCERT SHOWCASING THE EXCEPTIONALLY TALENTED STUDENT WINNERS OF THE WILLIAM T. GOWER AWARD COMPETITION.

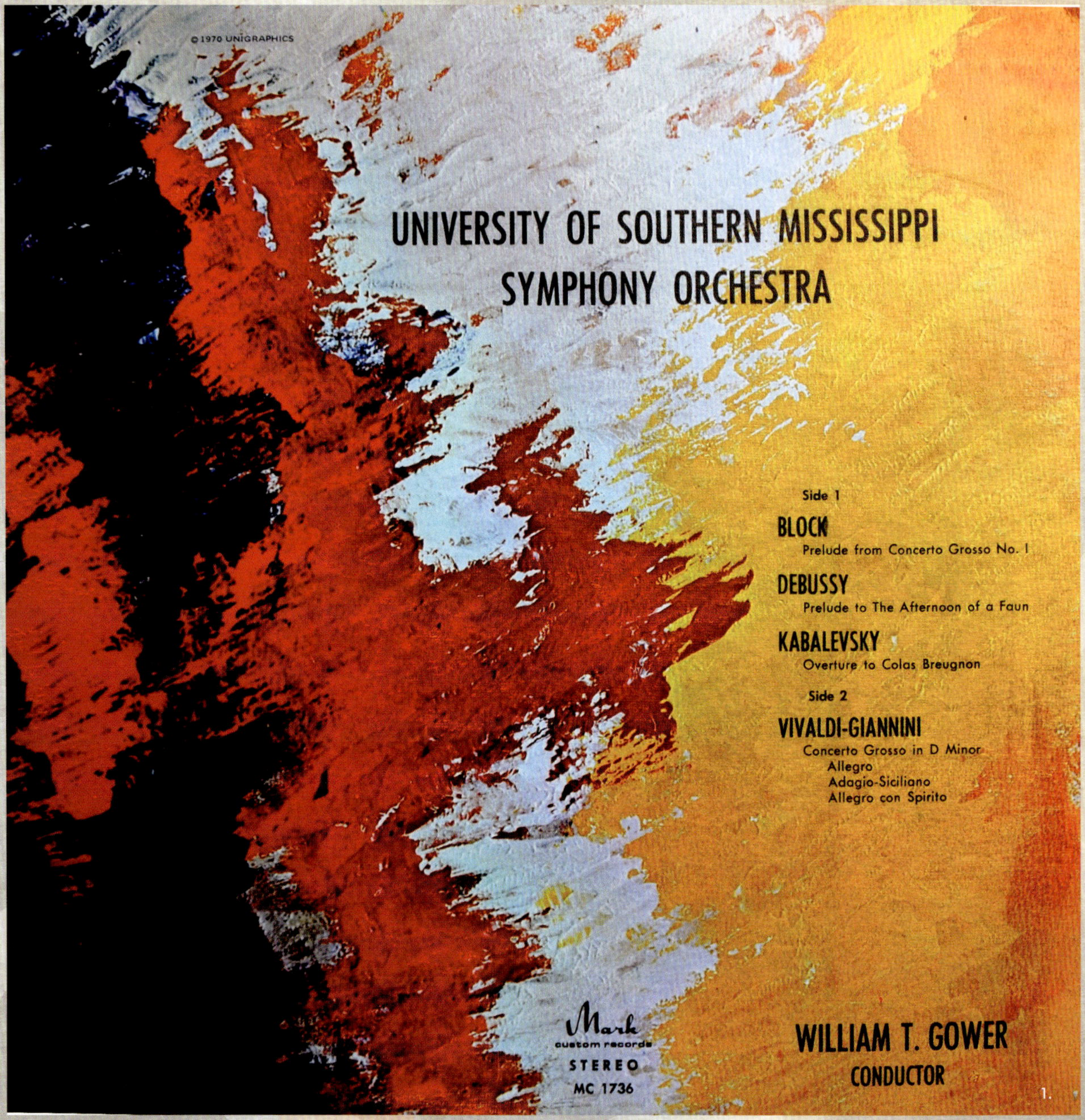

1.

2.

1. ALBUM COVERS FROM THE GOWER YEARS | 2. WILLIAM T. GOWER

With Gower's resignation, the orchestra was led by three conductors over three succeeding years: David Foltz, Director of Bands Joe Barry Mullins, and James Yestadt. They were followed by the two-year appointment of Vernon Raines, who had led the Meridian Symphony for a number of years and who brought in Alexander Toradze, silver medal winner of the 1977 Van Cliburn International Piano Competition, for an appearance with the orchestra. Raines was followed in 1978 by Ron McCreery.

1. RUDOLPH FIRKUSNY, 1971

TWO CONCERTS STAND OUT DURING MY YEARS IN THE ORCHESTRA. THE FIRST WAS THE DEDICATION CONCERT FOR THE NEW MANNONI PERFORMING ARTS CENTER IN THE SPRING OF 1972. NORMAN TREIGLE WAS BROUGHT IN TO PERFORM A COMBINATION OF THE BOITO "MEPHISTOFOLES" AND THE GOUNOD "FAUST." JAMES YESTADT CONDUCTED, AND WE PLAYED EXCERPTS FROM BOTH WORKS, JUMPING BACK AND FORTH BETWEEN THE TWO. TREIGLE WAS SPECTACULAR AND THE ORCHESTRAL PLAYING, IF MY MEMORY FROM THIRTY-EIGHT YEARS AGO CAN BE RELIED UPON, WAS INSPIRED. THE SECOND CONCERT WAS WHEN RUDOLPH FIRKUSNY PERFORMED THE SCHUMANN PIANO CONCERTO WITH THE ORCHESTRA, WILLIAM GOWER CONDUCTING. I WAS UNFAMILIAR WITH THE PIECE AT THE TIME, SO THE EXPERIENCE WAS MUSICALLY EDUCATIONAL AS WELL AS INSPIRING.

– *Mel Rogers*
CLARINET, 1968-72

THE UNIVERSITY OF SOUTHERN MISSISSIPPI
SCHOOL OF FINE ARTS
presents
THE UNIVERSITY SYMPHONY ORCHESTRA
William T. Gower, Conductor
Rudolf Firkusny, Piano

THE UNIVERSITY OF SOUTHERN MISSISSIPPI · 1910 · HATTIESBURG, MISSISSIPPI

Tuesday, January Eighteenth
Nineteen Hundred and Seventy-two
Eight Fifteen P.M.
Main Auditorium

1.

Tuesday October 10, 1972 Hattiesburg American

Stuart Canin performs tonight with USM Symphony Orchestra

Stuart Canin, violin virtuoso appearing in concert with the University of Southern Mississippi Symphony Orchestra at 8:30 tonight in the Performing Arts Cener, performed for USM Fine Arts students today during the general recital hour.

He and his former pupil, Theodore Madsen of the USM Fine Arts faculty, performed Bach's Double Violin Concerto for a large gathering of students.

Madsen first knew Canin at the University of Iowa, where he studied violin under the internationally famous recipient of the Paganini International Violin Competition and the New York City Handel Medal.

The relationship between the two violinists were reestablished when Madsen joined the Chamber Symphony in Philadelphia where Canin was concert master and violin soloist.

In recalling his long acquaintance with Canin, Madsen commented that his former teacher is considered by many to be a "violinist's violinist."

"Not only is he gracious," Madsen said, "Canin is a true artist in every sense of the word."

Tonight's concert will feature Canin as violin soloist for Brahms' "Concerto for Violin in D Major." Dr. William T. Gower will conduct the University Symphony Orchestr

Althou
season
some
balcony
$3 regul
box offi
those
mission
will op

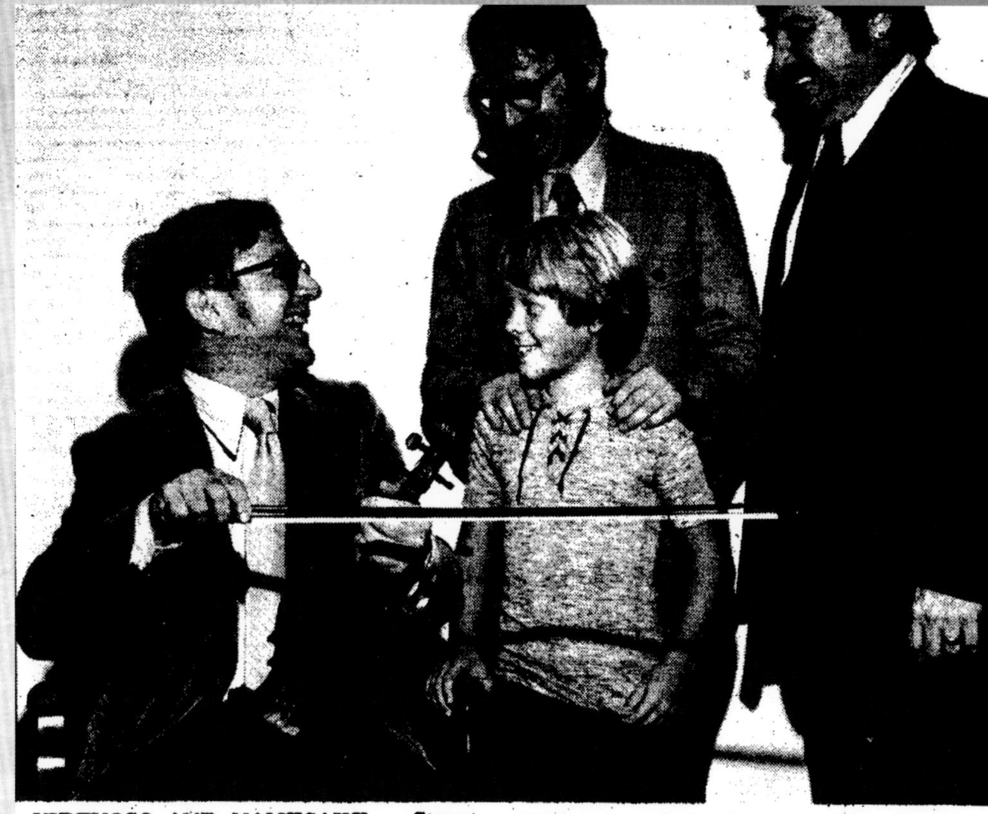

VIRTUOSO AND NAMESAKE — Stuart Canin (left), violinist appearing tonight in concert at USM, and Stuart Madsen, 9-year-old son of Theodore Madsen of the Fine Arts faculty, get acquainted in the new Performing Arts Center where the concert will begin at 8:30. Theordore Madsen's admiration for his former teacher, Canin, was expressed by naming his son for him. Madsen, concertmaster for the USM Symphony, and Dr. William T. Gower, (right) conductor, look on as the two "Stuarts" chat. (USM Photo Service)

THE UNIVERSITY OF SOUTHERN MISSISSI

DEPARTMENT OF MUSIC
OF THE
COLLEGE OF FINE ARTS

Presents
the

UNIVERSITY SYMPHONY

Ronald McCreery, Conductor

AWARDS CONCERT

PERFORMING ARTS CENTER
Thursday, March 6, 1980
8:00 P.M.

McCreery led the orchestra for the following ten years, during which time he created the University String Development Project, a two-day conference for the promotion of orchestral playing and music education in elementary and secondary schools. This conference was forerunner of the university's All-South Honor Orchestra Conference.

As it had during Gower's tenure, the opera enjoyed success under McCreery's leadership. The relationship between orchestra and opera at Southern Miss is an important one primarily because of the educational experience the opera provides for instrumentalists and vocalists alike. Additionally, the creation of the opera program in 1948 had led to substantial growth in the music department.

1.

THE ORCHESTRA, UNDER THE DIRECTION OF DR. GOWER, WAS ON TOUR IN THE NORTHERN PART OF OUR STATE. WE WERE PERFORMING AN OVERTURE THAT REQUIRED US TO STOMP OUR FEET IN A CERTAIN PLACE. OUR VIOLIN TEACHER/ CONCERTMASTER AT THE TIME WAS THEODORE MADSEN, AND HE ALWAYS FUSSED AT US ABOUT NOT STOMPING LOUD ENOUGH. SO THE TRICK, INSTIGATED BY OUR CONDUCTOR, WAS THAT ON THE FINAL STOMP, WE WERE NOT TO STOMP AND LET MR. MADSEN DO IT ALL BY HIMSELF. THE LOOK ON HIS FACE AS HIS STOMPED HIS HEART OUT AND THEN DID A HASTY DECRESCENDO (AS HE REALIZED IMMEDIATELY THAT HE WAS THE SOLOIST) WAS PRICELESS! OF COURSE, HE WAS A GOOD SPORT AND LAUGHED ABOUT IT AFTERWARDS.

–Sybil & Bob Cheesman
FLUTE, 1965-72 TRUMPET, 1967-72

ONE OF MY MOST MEMORABLE EXPERIENCES IN THE USM SYMPHONY WAS TELLING SOME HOT SHOT TRUMPET PLAYER THAT MY TYMPANI WAS NOT A TABLE FOR HIS PRECISION TRUMPET! LITTLE DID I KNOW WE WOULD LATER ROOM TOGETHER, WATCH EACH OTHER GET MARRIED AND KEEP UP OUR FRIENDSHIP FOR THIRTY-FIVE-PLUS YEARS.

– Richard Peters
PERCUSSION, 1970-73
SPEAKING OF JAY DEAN

1. SYMPHONY ORCHESTRA AND HATTIESBURG CHORAL UNION IN THE MANNONI PERFORMING ARTS CENTER, 1975

GUYS AND DOLLS, 1959

Bringing the World to

MISSISSIPPI

Opera Commences 1948-1987

OPERA AND MUSICAL THEATRE HAVE A RICH AND VARIED HISTORY AT THE UNIVERSITY OF SOUTHERN MISSISSIPPI. PRODUCTIONS HAVE RANGED FROM MUSICALS SUCH AS *L'IL ABNER* AND *THE MUSIC MAN* TO FULL-SCALE OPERAS INCLUDING *LA TRAVIATA* AND *CARMEN*. THIS DIVERSITY IS EVIDENCE OF THE FACULTY'S COMMITMENT TO EDUCATING AND CHALLENGING BOTH PERFORMERS AND LISTENERS.

1.

THE STAGE DIRECTORS WHO SPEARHEADED OPERA AND MUSICAL THEATRE PRODUCTIONS IN THESE EARLY YEARS

Lloyd Patten....................1948-49
Robert Waterstripe....................1950-52
Leonard Stocker....................1952-60
Gilbert Hartwig.................... 1958, 1960-61
Robert Treser....................1958, 1960
Robert Mesrobian.................... 1959
Ernestine Ferrel.................... 1961

THE MUSIC DIRECTORS WITH WHOM THEY WORKED

Frank Earl Marsh.................... 1950
Robert Hays....................1955, 1958
Harris Crohn....................1956-62
Raymond Mannoni.................... 1958

The opera and musical theatre program had its beginning at the end of World War II. College enrollment was dramatically increasing, and the president of what was then Mississippi Normal College, Dr. R.C. Cook, strove to capitalize on the growth. Cook wanted to see the fine arts department expand. Unlike a strictly choral music program, the opera and musical theatre program helped the music department grow by attracting both vocal and instrumental talent. Originated in 1948 by Frank Earl Marsh, the new program allowed vocal students the opportunity to perform with the orchestra. The first production was Smetana's *Bartered Bride*, directed by Lloyd Patten. Through the years, the quality performances attracted more and better students who presented marvelous performances for the community.

1. OPERA WORKSHOP, 1950 | 2. *HEY DAZE* OVERTURE SCORE, 1955 | 3. *HEY DAZE* MUSIC DIRECTOR ROBERT HAYS AND COPYIST BARY GILLMORE, 1955

2.

CAST

(In Order of Appearance)

BUD	BILL SEAY
JILL	JOY PAT PARRIS
JANE	DIBRELL COVERT
PAUL	PETE O'BRYAN
BABS	JANE AVENDANO
SID	ED McDONALD
AL	JOE BARRON
OLD GRAD	GENE CRAVEN
FRANK	BOB CADE
COKEMAN	EDDIE BELANGER
JACK	PETE O'BRYAN
COUNTER BOY	GENE CRAVEN
YELLOW JACKETS	KAPPA ALPHA ORDER
JO ANN	JANET SCHEFFLER
PAT	MARY ALICE PRICE
GIRL	RITA WALDRUP
BRIAN	EDDIE BELANGER
BOB	BOB CADE
The TEACHER	MARGARET GRANT
FRANK	MARK BLANKENSTEIN

SINGERS: Betty Farmham, Jean Freeman, Rhoda Hord, Betty King, Barbara Rhodes, Rita Waldrup, Ann Miller, Kay Crenshaw, Joyce Scimeca, Joyce Jamison, Dot May, Lady Dell Mechatto, Jo Ann Fulmer, Ann Bond, Beverly Jo McKinzie, Benny Stewart, Tom Allen, Charles Thomas, Dick Jordan, Jimmy Wilson, Russel Brandon, Bill Mason, Mal English, Harold Needham, Joe Fulmer, Pete Rogers, Ronnie Herrington.

DANCERS: Ann Miller, Joyce Dawson, Carolyn Cochran, Kay Crenshaw, Joyce Scimeca Joyce Jamison, Dot May, Lady Dell Mechatto, Jo Ann Fulmer, Ann Bond, Beverly Jo McKinzie, Betty King.

The university's talented faculty enlivened this budding tradition by composing original musicals for and about Southern Miss. *Hey Daze*, about life on campus, was produced during the 1955 season. Robert Hays, then Assistant Professor of Bands, wrote eighteen original tunes for the show, including the fight song "Southern to the Top" that remains a proud tradition at Golden Eagle football games. Another original work, a chamber opera titled *The Whistler*, was composed by William Presser and premiered at the Fourth Annual Forum of the Southeastern Composers' League in 1959 on the university's campus.

3.

HEY DAZE **WAS A HUGE UNDERTAKING PULLED TOGETHER BY A COMMITTEE OF TWELVE OR FIFTEEN OF US WORKING WITH RAYMOND MANNONI. I WAS TEACHING THEORY AT THE TIME AND HELPING DR. MANNONI WITH THE BAND. I DIDN'T HAVE TIME TO WRITE A SCORE. I'D JUST JOT DOWN NOTES TO MYSELF, A LEAD LINE, SKETCHES OF TUNES. WE DIDN'T EVEN WRITE DOWN ALL THE LYRICS. WE RAN IT A WEEK IN HATTIESBURG AND THEN TOOK IT TO THE COAST AND TO JACKSON. IT WAS GREAT FUN.**

–Robert Hays
FACULTY, 1956–69

"All-school" musicals delighted performers and audiences alike. Students from every corner of the campus were invited to audition for, perform in, and stage shows such as *Brigadoon*, *Guys and Dolls*, and *Oklahoma!* The demands of these productions eventually became too great, however, and the all-school musical was abandoned after the production of *Damn Yankees* in 1961.

1.

Fall and spring musical productions continued under the leadership of stage directors Clifford Reims (1962-63), Francis Monachino (1963-67), Clifton Ware (1967-69), and Jack Donovan (1969). The music directors during this time were Harold Avery (1962-63), Theodore C. Russell (1962), Robert Hays (1963), and William T. Gower (1963-74).

2.

3.

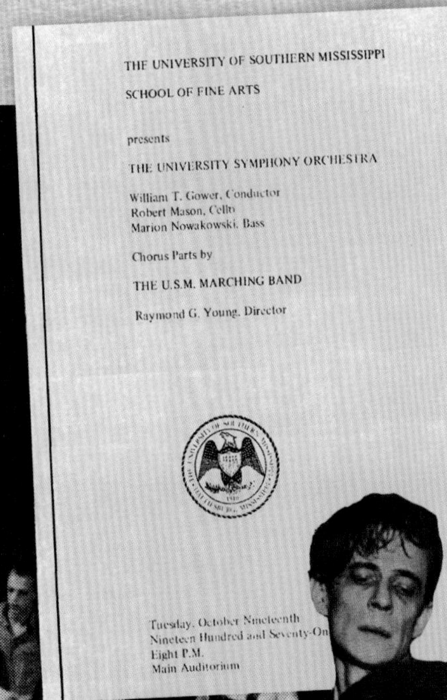

THE UNIVERSITY OF SOUTHERN MISSISSIPPI

SCHOOL OF FINE ARTS

presents

THE UNIVERSITY SYMPHONY ORCHESTRA

William T. Gower, Conductor
Robert Mason, Cello
Marion Nowakowski, Bass

Chorus Parts by

THE U.S.M. MARCHING BAND

Raymond G. Young, Director

Tuesday, October Nineteenth
Nineteen Hundred and Seventy-On
Eight P.M.
Main Auditorium

4.

Guest artists were sometimes brought in to assist with major productions and to perform. Several students had the opportunity to work with world-renowned bass Norman Treigle during the 1961 production of Carlisle Floyd's *Susannah*; Treigle had played Olin Blitch in the New York City Opera Company's performances of this well-known American opera.

1. *NAUGHTY MARIETTA*, 1953 | 2. THE CAST FROM *OKLAHOMA!*, 1960 | 3. *SUSANNAH*, 1961
4. NORMAN TREIGLE AND DIANA STEWART IN *SUSANNAH*, 1961

Polish bass **MARIAN NOWAKOWSKI** is primarily remembered for his striking voice on recordings with Sir Thomas Beecham. Brought up in Poznan, Poland, Nowakowksi studied at the Lwow Conservatory and afterwards became a member of the Polish Army during World War II. After the war he became a favorite at Covent Garden, Sadler's Wells (now the English National Opera), and the Welsh National Opera. He was also highly respected as an oratorio singer. After retiring from the stage in the mid 1960s, Nowakowski taught for many years at the Guildhall School of Music, the Royal College of Music, and The University of Southern Mississippi (1967-1973).

ROBERT MERRILL was one of the Metropolitan Opera's most enduring and acclaimed baritones. He made his operatic debut in 1944 and joined the Metropolitan Opera the following year. Merrill--known for his amazingly vigorous, yet smooth and effortless baritone voice--performed frequently on the radio, in films, in nightclubs, and on television.

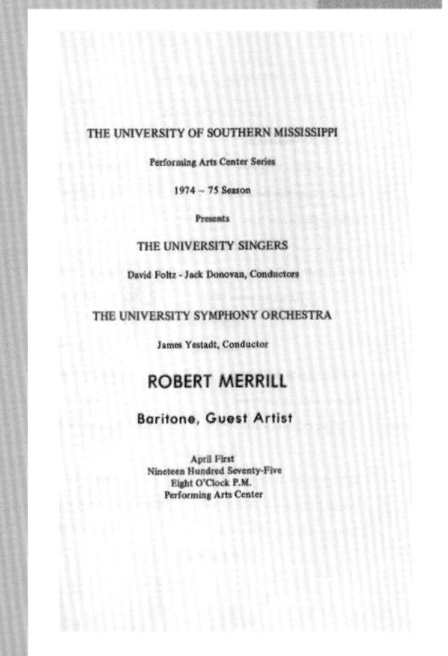

THE UNIVERSITY OF SOUTHERN MISSISSIPPI

Performing Arts Center Series

1974 – 75 Season

Presents

THE UNIVERSITY SINGERS

David Foltz - Jack Donovan, Conductors

THE UNIVERSITY SYMPHONY ORCHESTRA

James Yestadt, Conductor

ROBERT MERRILL

Baritone, Guest Artist

April First
Nineteen Hundred Seventy-Five
Eight O'Clock P.M.
Performing Arts Center

The remarkable American bass-baritone **NORMAN TREIGLE** was born in New Orleans and attended Loyola University. He made his operatic debut in 1947 with the New Orleans Opera and joined the New York City Opera in 1953, remaining with that company for twenty years. In 1958, he made his European debut at the Brussels World's Fair and in 1974 made his Covent Garden debut. Treigle became the leading bass-baritone of the Americas and was acclaimed as one of the world's greatest singing-actors, specializing in roles that evoked villainy and terror. Following Treigle's performances at Southern Miss, Raymond Mannoni encouraged Treigle to lead the university's opera program. However, in1975, at the age of forty-seven, Treigle died suddenly at his New Orleans apartment. A chronic insomniac, he was the victim of an accidental overdose of sleeping pills. His untimely death deprived American musical theatre of one of its finest talents.

In 1969, Robert Mesrobian began a seven-year tenure as artistic director of the opera program, and under his leadership productions such as *Così Fan Tutte, Faust*, *Il Barbiere di Siviglia*, and Benjamin Britten's *A Midsummer Night's Dream* were produced. The 1972 production of *A Midsummer Night's Dream* was a landmark in the musical life of Southern Miss. This was the first production staged in the new Mannoni Performing Arts Center. With a dramatic set design, wonderful costuming, and fine musical talent enhanced by guest artist Thomas Palmer, the opera was an impressive opening for the new hall. Their desire to share this great work led the faculty and students to make more than twenty visits to area schools, as well as perform two matinees on campus for middle-school-aged children.

1. *DIE FLEDERMAUS*, 1974

1.

ROBERT MESROBIAN performed professionally in opera, television, motion pictures, recitals, oratorios, and musical comedies before joining the Southern Miss faculty in 1969.

In 1974, Southern Miss students and faculty performed the first opera televised in its entirety by Mississippi Educational Television. *Die Fledermaus* had been rehearsed and performed in the Mannoni Performing Arts Center; nine days later, the cast recreated their performance to the delight of thousands watching Mississippi public television.

Between 1974 and 1980, various opera and musical theatre productions were directed by Blaine Quarnstrom, Larry D. Mullican, and Patricia Hays. Music directors during this time were James Yestadt (1973), Joe Barry Mullins (1974), Vernon Raines (1976), Robert Pressley (1978), and David Zepeda (1980). A stand-out performance during these years was the 1977 guest appearance by the great coloratura soprano and opera darling Roberta Peters who delighted her audience with "Caro Nome," Juliet's Waltz, and "Vilja." Students joined the concert with several rousing chorus numbers.

Karl Brock led the opera program from 1981 through spring of 1986, although there is little documentation of productions during that time. In fall of 1986, David Holley took the helm as artistic director. Holley stage directed and conducted his early programs including Englebert Humperdinck's *Hansel and Gretel* and Carlisle Floyd's *Susannah.*

A talented and promising young student mesmerized the audience with her moving portrayal of *Susannah*'s title role. Some years later, that former student would return as director of the Southern Miss opera program, Dr. Maryann Kyle.

1. KENNY CLAY AND MARYANN KYLE IN *SUSANNAH,* 1988

La Boheme

by Puccini

Director: Robert Mesrobian
Musical Preparation: James Yestadt
English Translation: Ted and Deena Puffer
Conductor: William T. Gower
Set Designer: Larry King
Technical Director: Robert B. Hill

CAST OF CHARACTERS

RODOLFO, a poet . . . . . Clinton Nichols
(Friday) Allan Celoria
MARCELLO, an artist . . . . . Lloyd Mims
COLLINE, a philosopher . . . . . James Cutrell
SCHAUNARD, a musician . . . . . Lloyd Rollins
BENOIT . . . . . Wayne Stevens
MIMI . . . . . Kay Paschal
MUSETTA . . . . . Lucretia Shaw
ALCINDORO . . . . . James Donovan
PARPIGNOL . . . . . Carroll Freeman
WATER FRONT GUARD . . . . . Gordon Smith

CHORUS of VENDORS, TOURISTS, CHILDREN AND PEOPLE OF NEW ORLEANS Leon Smith, Glenda Meadows, Pat Warner, Ginger Grissom, David Hill, Dan Bender, Greg Carstens, Pat Brown, Ken Yocum, Greg Cotton, Carroll Freeman, Randy Stewart, Nancy Farnum, Dean Allen, Marla Miller, Robert Clary, Stephan Wood, Gail Ladner, Donna Hearn, Sue Mason, Tip Bishop, Kathy Wilkenson, Robert Cirlot, Larry Pierce, Paul VanZandt, Gordon Smith, Gail Beardon, Pat Schraeder, Virginia Breland, Debbie Gregory, Florence Witty, Sheila Gwin, Gigi Reeks, Marilyn Uhlen, Robert Munsell, Kenneth Gower

PARADE MARCHERS - Through the courtesy of University Bands

The action takes place in New Orleans around 1971

ACT I

Christmas eve in the garret of the four Bohemians

ACT II

A little later in the French Quarter

ACT III

In February near a waterfront tavern in New Orleans

ACT IV

During the Summer in the garrett

I WAS A TWENTY-YEAR-OLD STUDENT AT SOUTHERN MISS WHEN I HAD MY FIRST OPERA AUDITION. *SUSANNAH* WAS AN OPERA I COULD PARTICULARLY RELATE TO AS A YOUNG WOMAN FROM A SMALL SOUTHERN TOWN, BUT SINCE THIS WOULD BE MY FIRST OPERATIC EXPERIENCE, I WAS SHOCKED TO BE CAST IN THE LEAD. THANKFULLY, I DIDN'T KNOW ENOUGH AT THE TIME TO BE FRIGHTENED! AS I REFLECT NOW ON THE CHALLENGES I FACED–VERY DIFFICULT VOCALS AS WELL AS A COMPLEX STORY– I'M GLAD I DIDN'T KNOW ANY BETTER. STILL, THE EXPERIENCE HAD A PROFOUND EFFECT ON ME. I LEARNED THAT NO ROLE IS INSURMOUNTABLE, AND I LEARNED TO VIEW MYSELF NOT SIMPLY AS A SINGER BUT AS AN ACTRESS WHO SINGS. IN TEACHING VOCAL TECHNIQUE, I CAUTION MY STUDENTS NOT TO SEPARATE ACTING TECHNIQUE FROM THEIR VOICES.

–Maryann Kyle
FACULTY, 2002 - PRESENT

TWO IN THE AFTERNOON, AN ORIGINAL PAINTING BY AMY GIUST, WAS COMMISSIONED TO CELEBRATE THE PUBLICATION OF *BRINGING THE WORLD TO MISSISSIPPI*. THE PAINTING'S TITLE REFERENCES THE ORCHESTRA'S LONGSTANDING PRACTICE OF REHEARSING AT 2:00 P.M.

Bringing the World to MISSISSIPPI

A New Direction 1988-1995

Conductor wants music in schools

By LYNNE WILBANKS
Special to the AMERICAN

When Jay Dean grew up in a small town in Georgia, there was no school class to teach him how to play the violin, cello, viola or bass — instruments he now conducts as head of University of Southern Mississippi's orchestra.

The schools he attended did not offer orchestral courses. Private lessons were unavailable.

So he took band courses and learned to play the trumpet instead, which he said, wrought "long periods of boredom interrupted by moments of sheer terror."

But he didn't give up on his passion for the rich sounds produced by string instruments. And he hasn't abandoned his desire to see public schools implement orchestral programs.

"Many things would be different in my life if my school had offered an orchestral program," Dean said. "I have a daughter at Woodley (elementary school) now, and I would like to see her pursue an interest if she wishes. I'd like to see all children have that opportunity." Dean's wife, Debby, a music teacher, and their children (Michelle, age 7, Alexandra, age 2) share his enthusiasm for music.

Dean's interest in string music peaked while he was studying for his bachelor's and master's degrees at USM. "I realized I was more interested in conducting rather than playing because I like being involved in all aspects of the program."

Dean taught school at all levels in Atlanta for seven years before obtaining a doctoral degree from the University of Texas in Austin. He left the Lone Star State because of the poor economic conditions affecting funding for musical events.

"I was eager to return to Hattiesburg when the job (of director of orchestral activities at USM) became available," Dean said. "I love this work. It's like getting paid for a hobby."

Dean will be conducting the April 7 benefit concert by the orchestra in USM's Bennett Auditorium. Among the features of the show will be guest performances by Dr. Stanley Waldoff, pianist, and Dr. Joe Barry Mullins, guest conductor. Tickets are $16 for god section seating and $8 for silver section seating, with all proceeds going to support foreign students at USM.

Dean

1.

2.

In 1988, having almost completed his doctoral degree at The University of Texas at Austin, Jay Dean applied for the position of orchestra conductor at The University of Southern Mississippi, his alma mater. During the interview, Dr. James Sims, whose son happened to be a professional opera singer in Germany at the time, encouraged Dean to accept the position, but the ambitious young conductor was skeptical.

"A high-quality orchestral program is an expensive thing to develop," he said. "Is this a place that will both philosophically and financially support such an orchestra program?"

Assured by Sims that this was something the university would support, Jay Dean returned to Hattiesburg.

It would not be long before Dean realized he had a lot of work to do. Peering from between the panels of the curtains to see only about sixty people in the audience at his first concert, he wondered, "Why is no one here? What did we do wrong?"

About that time, one of the violinists approached and asked, "Mr. Dean, how did we get so many people here?"

The orchestra gave six concerts that season, a significant increase in number from the year before. Highlights included Beethoven's *Symphony No. 7*, Ravel's *Boléro*, Silvestre Revueltas's incredibly difficult *Sensemayá*, and Saint-Saëns' Concerto No. 2 for Piano, with Professor Stanley Waldoff as soloist. The opera program presented Mozart's *Die Zauberflöte* that spring, directed by David Holley with Dean as music director.

Over the course of the year, Dean labored to increase the musical quality of performances as well as the morale and self-image of the orchestra. He produced the first orchestral benefit concert in the history of the organization, gave the second orchestral performance in the thirty-three

3.

year history of the Southern Instrumental Conductor's Conference, increased community awareness of the symphony while tripling the average size of the concert audience, and began an intense national and international recruiting campaign. The groundwork had been laid.

Dr. Harold Luce, dean of the College of the Arts, was an immediate and tremendous source of support, increasing the orchestra scholarship allotment and out-of-state waivers and enabling the orchestra to benefit from its first support staff: nine student orchestra members who served as orchestra manager, public relations coordinator, education coordinator, librarian, administrative assistant, production manager, personnel manager, and two graduate assistants.

With Dean's guidance, this energetic group began statewide efforts to implement string programs in the public schools, organized the first Mississippi Conference on String Education, wrote grant applications, created the first symphony orchestra recruiting brochures, and instituted advertising partnerships with local businesses.

1. *HATTIESBURG AMERICAN* ARTICLE, 1988 | 2. JOE BARRY MULLINS, DIRECTOR OF BANDS, 1970-83. DRAWING BY PAUL TURNER. | 3. SIXTEEN-YEAR-OLD ORCHESTRA CELLIST CARA PATRICK, 1990 | 4. PROGRAM FOR *THE NUTCRACKER* DESIGNED BY STUDENT WORKER AND ORCHESTRA BASSOONIST MICHAEL LOPINTO, 1989

4.

WHEN I WAS A STUDENT MUSICIAN HERE, THE ORCHESTRA WAS GOOD, BUT THERE WERE TEN TIMES MORE PEOPLE ON STAGE THAN IN THE AUDIENCE! AN EXPECTANT, ENGAGED AUDIENCE RAISES THE PERFORMANCE LEVEL, TRANSFORMING THE EXPERIENCE INTO ONE FULLY CHARGED FOR AUDIENCE AND MUSICIAN ALIKE. THERE'S NOTHING LIKE THE ENERGY OF A FULL HOUSE. JAY DEAN KNOWS THIS, HE KNOWS HOW TO FILL A HALL, AND HE WANTS IT AS MUCH FOR HIS COMMUNITY AS HE DOES FOR HIS MUSICIANS.

–Michael Lopinto
BASSOON, 1987-92, 2002-03
ORCHESTRA STAFF, 2002-09

JAY DEAN LISTENS. HE GIVES THE COMMUNITY WHAT IT WANTS, BUT HE ALWAYS DOES IT IN GOOD TASTE. HE CAN ALSO TALK YOU INTO ANYTHING! IT'S HARD TO TELL HIM NO BECAUSE HE DOESN'T ASK YOU TO DO ANYTHING HE WOULDN'T DO. THANK GOODNESS WE HAVE HIM IN OUR AREA.

–Charles M. Thomas
SYMPHONY PATRON

JAY BELIEVED THAT OUR UNIVERSITY ORCHESTRA COULD INFLUENCE THE QUALITY OF STRING EDUCATION IN MISSISSIPPI'S SCHOOLS. HE VISITED WITH PARENTS AND ADMINISTRATORS, ENCOURAGING THEM TO INITIATE AND MAINTAIN STRING CURRICULA IN THEIR SCHOOLS, AND UNDER HIS DIRECTION THE ORCHESTRA OFTEN PERFORMED FOR MISSISSIPPI'S K-12 YOUNGSTERS. IT WAS HEART-WARMING TO SEE DOZENS OF YELLOW SCHOOL BUSSES PARKED BY THE MANNONI PERFORMING ARTS CENTER, KNOWING THAT HUNDREDS OF SCHOOL KIDS WERE HEARING AN ORCHESTRA CONCERT OR SEEING AN OPERA FOR THE FIRST TIME.

–Peter L. Ciurczak
PROFESSOR EMERITUS AND DIRECTOR OF THE SCHOOL OF MUSIC, 1988-99

It was also in his first year that Dean decided to formalize in writing the symphony's dual mission. The university's music program had been born of a campus-community alliance: Frank Marsh's inclusion of local singers in the Hattiesburg Choral Union, Joshua Missal's invitation to area musicians to perform with the orchestra, Frank Crockett's creation of a youth orchestra, and Ron McCreery's conference promoting string programss for young students are but a few examples. Dean would include community outreach in the orchestra's formal mission statement, alongside the education of student musicians in preparation for their becoming professional performers and music educators. In the coming years, this dual mission would reward both symphony and community.

In 1989-90, memorable performances included Gustav Mahler's *Lieder eines fahrenden Gesellen* with mezzo-soprano Virginia Dupuy, Maurice Ravel's G Major Piano Concerto with Dr. Lois Leventhal as soloist, and Tchaikovsky's *Romeo and Juliet*.

Concert attendance increased thirty percent from the previous season, and international recruiting benefited from the establishment of annual auditions and a competition held among conservatories in and around Mexico City, Mexico. The orchestra enjoyed such tremendous growth that it was divided for operas and repertoire reading sessions. The student string chamber music program, virtually abandoned in 1955, was resurrected.

Outreach efforts took center stage as the orchestra encouraged the development of string programs in two public school districts, established the Southern Invitational High School Orchestra Conference on the Southern Miss campus, and increased the number of high school students participating in the All-South Honor Orchestra.

Dean Luce continued his enthusiastic support by securing a significant increase in outside funding for orchestra scholarships, and the assistance provided by the university president cannot be overstated. Long-time President Aubrey K. Lucas, a passionate advocate for the arts, was ever ready to encourage the new conductor's orchestral aspirations, even in difficult financial times. Needless to say, the state-funded university orchestra had maneuvered and would continue to confront many financial challenges.

The following year brought the first of many collaborative efforts Dean would present. In this instance, it was two fully staged, sold-out performances of Tchaikovsky's *Nutcracker* with Ballet Mississippi. Another highlight of the season was the performance of *Carmina Burana*, a choral-orchestral work by Carl Orff that has a special connection to Southern Miss. Bass-baritone Marion Nowakowski, a faculty member at the university from 1967 until 1973, was a personal friend of Carl Orff's during the time that *Carmina Burana* was being written. The bass-baritone solos in *Carmina Burana* were written with Nowakowski's voice in mind.

In 1990-91, the symphony produced its first digitally recorded, publicly released cassette recording and created additional performance opportunities for the orchestra and string ensembles: a Symphony Series at the Crosby Arboretum in Picayune, a scholarship concert at Hattiesburg's Cloverleaf Mall, and the expansion of a practice adopted the previous season of offering "run-out" concerts, out-of-town concerts following the ones held on campus. The spring opera production was Mozart's *Le Nozze di Figaro*, directed by David Holley.

1. CHOIR AND ORCHESTRA FOR *CARMINA BURANA* EXCEED THE STAGE'S CAPACITY, 1990

WE WERE REHEARSING *CARMINA BURANA* WITH THE ORCHESTRA AND CHORUS, AND DR. WEINERT, THE CHORAL DIRECTOR, WAS STANDING IN THE AUDIENCE. HE KEPT TALKING TO THE TROMBONE SECTION, WHICH AT THE TIME WAS TOM BRANTLEY, MIKE BROWNING, AND ME. HE TOLD US REPEATEDLY (MAINLY TOM) THAT WE WERE PLAYING TOO LOUD, THAT HE KNEW TOM COULD COVER UP THE ENTIRE ORCHESTRA BY HIMSELF, THAT WE SHOULD BACK OFF, ETC. WE DID AS HE ASKED AND PLAYED SOFTER, BUT IT DIDN'T SEEM TO BE ENOUGH FOR HIM. FINALLY, TOM TOLD US TO JUST SHADOW THE NOTES, SO WE STOPPED PLAYING COMPLETELY AND FAKED IT. AT THAT POINT, THE CHORAL DIRECTOR SAID, "THAT'S PERFECT TROMBONES, JUST LIKE THAT!"

–Billy Bargetzi
TROMBONE, 1990

THE DEVELOPMENT OF THE ORCHESTRA PROGRAM AT THE UNIVERSITY OF SOUTHERN MISSISSIPPI REPRESENTS ONE OF THE MOST REMARKABLE TRANSFORMATIONS IN AMERICA. IN MANY WAYS, IT SERVES AS A MODEL FOR HOW PROVIDING ACCESS TO STRING INSTRUCTION AND ORCHESTRAL EXPERIENCES CAN ENRICH A COMMUNITY AND STATE.

–Kirk D. Moss
PRESIDENT, AMERICAN STRING TEACHERS ASSOCIATION

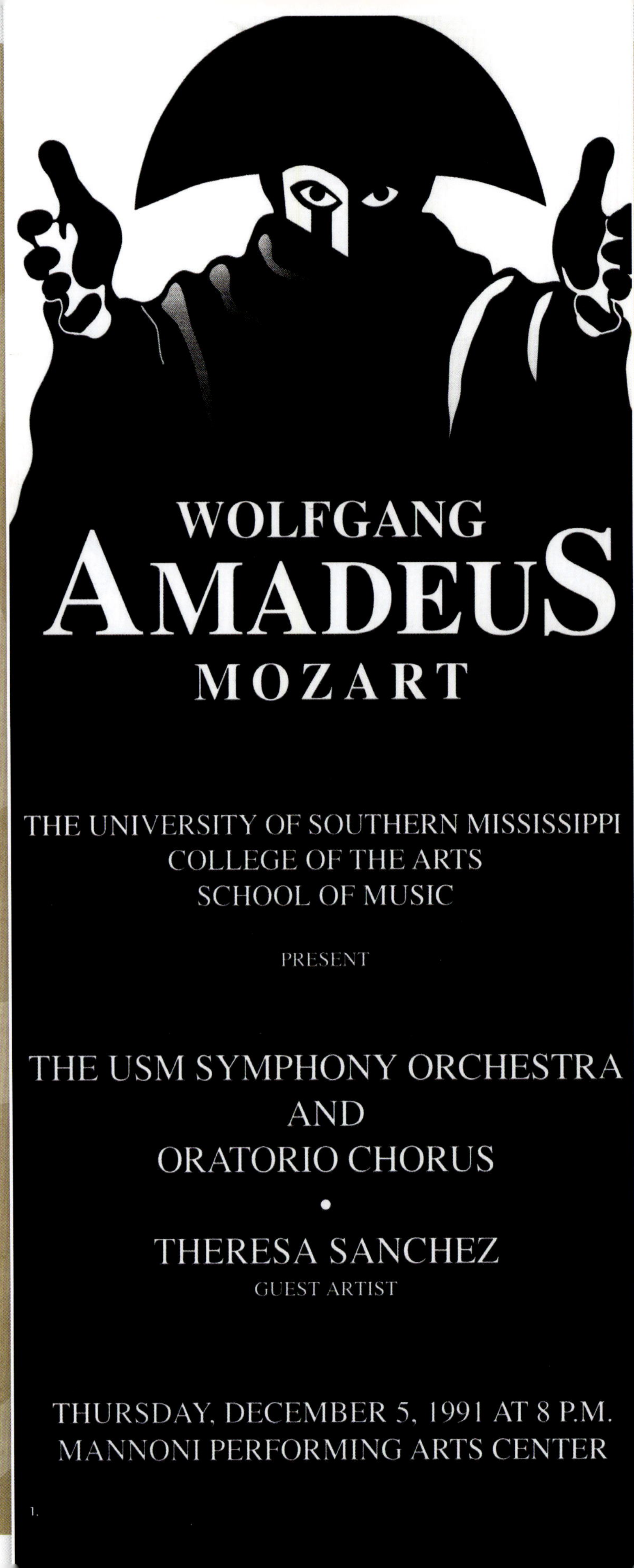

1.

2.

Outreach continued with the significant expansion of the orchestra's All-South Honor Orchestra Conference; the birth of a second orchestra, the All-South String Orchestra; and the creation of an annual Southern Invitational High School Orchestra Festival. A private school string program was started at St. John's Day School in Laurel, Mississippi.

The orchestra extended its reach in other ways, as well, establishing a collaborative relationship with the Mississippi Symphony Orchestra to develop *Premier!*, a summer string institute; hosting a regionally advertised chamber music workshop; embarking on its first String Chamber Ensemble Tour of South Mississippi; and welcoming a wider audience with the performance of the first "USM Symphony Pops" concert. Seeking to capitalize on the symphony's broadening appeal, Dean initiated the orchestra's first endowment fund drive.

On December 5, 1991, an event occurred that would have been unimaginable just three years earlier: a sold-out performance for the Mozart 200th Anniversary Celebration. The program included Mozart's *Requiem* in D Minor and featured Dr. Theresa Sanchez in the D Minor Piano Concerto.

The audience was not the only entity blossoming that year; the orchestra, string chamber ensembles, and All-South Honor Orchestra Conference all enjoyed continued growth. This was also the year that Alexandre Brussilovsky performed with the orchestra for the first time, playing the Brahms Violin Concerto. Brussilovsky would become a great friend of the university and perform with the orchestra on a number of occasions.

1. PROGRAM DESIGNED BY STUDENT WORKER AND ORCHESTRA PERCUSSIONIST RON HANCOCK, 1991 | 2. ALEXANDRE BRUSSILOVSKY, 1991

I DISCOVERED SOUTHERN MISS TWENTY YEARS AGO DURING ONE OF MY FIRST VISITS TO THE UNITED STATES. I LECTURED ABOUT MY YEARS IN THE SOVIET UNION AND MY MOVE TO WESTERN EUROPE, AND I GAVE MASTER CLASSES AND PLAYED WITH THE ORCHESTRA. AT THIS TIME THE LEVEL OF MUSICIANSHIP WAS NOT VERY STRONG, BUT THE PEOPLE WERE KIND, AND WE ESTABLISHED A FRIENDSHIP THAT HAS LASTED FOR MANY YEARS. I HAVE SINCE BEEN INVITED QUITE REGULARLY TO GIVE MASTER CLASSES, TO PARTICIPATE AS A SOLOIST AND CHAMBER MUSICIAN, AND TO PLAY WITH THE ORCHESTRA. EVERY TIME I COME, I NOTICE A CONSIDERABLE IMPROVEMENT IN QUALITY, MOTIVATION, AND LOVE FOR MUSIC.

—Alexandre Brussilovsky
VIOLINIST AND CONDUCTOR, RICERCATA DE PARIS

OPERA PATRONS MIGHT NOT HAVE NOTICED THAT THERE IS A RECURRING ROLE IN MOST OF OUR PRODUCTIONS. IT'S OUR OPERA CHICKEN! THE TRADITION STARTED IN 1991 DURING A SYMPHONY PERFORMANCE OF *PETER AND THE WOLF* WHEN, UNBEKNOWNST TO THE HIGH SCHOOL DANCERS APPEARING IN THE PROGRAM, JAY HAD SOMEONE THROW A RUBBER CHICKEN ONTO THE STAGE DURING A HUNTING SCENE. IT WAS SO FUNNY THAT JAY REPRISED THE ROLE FOR LATER PRODUCTIONS. OPERA CHICKEN HAS EMERGED FROM CLOSETS AND CLOTHES BASKETS, HAS HIDDEN IN VARIOUS PLACES ON STAGE DURING OPERATIC COMEDIES, AND EVEN PLAYED THE ROLE OF WATER FOUNTAIN IN *THE MARRIAGE OF FIGARO*. I'LL LEAVE IT TO OPERA-GOERS TO RECALL HIS OTHER APPEARANCES AND LOOK FOR HIM IN PRODUCTIONS TO COME.

—Maryann Kyle
FACULTY, 2002–PRESENT

WHEN I WAS BROUGHT ON BOARD AS RESIDENT STAGE DIRECTOR IN 1994, MY MISSION WAS TO BRING MY PROFESSIONAL THEATRE BACKGROUND TO BEAR ON THE OPERA PROGRAM. FOR MY FIRST PRODUCTION, *DON GIOVANNI*, I TOLD THE MAESTRO I WANTED TO DO A FILM NOIR VERSION IN BLACK AND WHITE WITH TOUCHES OF RED AND A TENOR ON ROLLER BLADES. HE SAID, "GO FOR IT." THAT'S WHEN I KNEW I WOULD LIKE IT HERE. THE AVAILABLE TALENT FOR THAT AND THE MANY PRODUCTIONS I'VE DONE SINCE IS STILL ASTOUNDING TO ME. WE HAVE CONTINUED TO DO DISTINCTIVE PRODUCTIONS THAT HONOR THE OPERATIC TRADITIONS. FOR EXAMPLE, OUR COMIC OPERA *COSÌ FAN TUTTE* INCLUDED A MAN FISHING FOR CHICKENS OFF A PIER, HEROINES IN BATHING SUITS, A PIZZA DELIVERY GUY, AN UNDERSTUDY FOLLOWING A LEAD AROUND AND MIMICKING HER, AND A CONFUSED STAGE MANAGER WHO OCCASIONALLY STUMBLED INTO THE ACTION ON STAGE. THE CONDUCTOR HAD TROUBLE HEARING IN THE ORCHESTRA PIT BECAUSE THE AUDIENCE WAS LAUGHING SO HARD, AND AN OPERA AFICIONADO AND SCHOLAR TOLD US, "MOZART WOULD HAVE LOVED IT. THAT'S ONE OF THE RARE TIMES A COMIC OPERA HAS ACTUALLY BEEN FUNNY."

–Rob Mulholland
STAGE DIRECTOR FOR MOST SOUTHERN MISS OPERA PRODUCTIONS, 1994-PRESENT

Other highlights of the 1991-92 season were the performances of the beautiful *Requiem* by Maurice Duruflé and Ottorino Respighi's orchestral showpiece, *I Pini di Roma*. The orchestra's first season brochure was created this year, and educational offerings were enhanced as all string players participated in regularly coached chamber music ensembles. The spring opera was David Holley's final production, *Die lustigen Weiber von Windsor*.

1992-93 brought the first performance by The University of Southern Mississippi Symphony and Chorus in Jackson and the first performance of these groups at the annual Mississippi Music Educators Association and American Choral Directors Association Conferences. Collaborative endeavors continued as the orchestra joined the university's Department of Dance for departmental and Hattiesburg Arts Council events.

Highlights of the orchestral season included Carlos Chávez's difficult and unusual *Sinfonía di Antígona*, Aaron Copland's *El Salon México*, and Giuseppe Verdi's great *Requiem*, which was performed with a choir of three hundred. The orchestra also presented the world premiere of *Fanfare and Alleluia* by the university's composer-in-residence, Luigi Zaninelli.

During this academic year, the orchestra commenced recruiting activities in Honduras and expanded its programming on the Mississippi Gulf Coast. The endowment fund drive continued with fundraising activities undertaken to address the growing orchestra's immediate scholarship needs, and a much-needed renovation was commenced of Bennett Auditorium, the symphony's main performance hall.

The next couple of years continued the flurry of activity as in-house efforts focused on significantly increasing the number of graduate students in string performance and string education. Community outreach carried on as the orchestra developed new teaching and support materials for use by string teachers in public schools, seeking to improve the quality of existing string programs throughout the state. New school programs were also established. The Gulfport Public Schools String Program, a program that today is one of the largest and best string programs in the state, was among them.

Other successful outreach efforts on the coast included the orchestra's work with The University of Southern Mississippi Gulf Park on its recital series and a partnership with the Gulf Coast Arts Council to set up children's programs led by Southern Miss organizations, students, and faculty.

Although Dean's energies during his early years were primarily directed at the growth and betterment of the orchestra and the development of string programs in the region, his focus expanded in 1993. Following David Holley's departure, Dean became artistic director of the opera program. As he had done in his collaborative work for the orchestra, Dean began establishing working relationships with regional opera companies in New Orleans, Mobile, Jackson, and the Gulf Coast. His first fully staged production was *The Mikado*, presented in February 1994.

There were several highlights of the 1994-95 symphony season. One was the orchestra's performance of Beethoven's Symphony No. 5 in C Minor, a work that every young orchestral musician aspires to play. The same can be said of Igor Stravinsky's *Firebird Suite* which the orchestra performed on the same evening it performed the Dvorák Cello Concerto with internationally known cellist Leslie Parnas, winner of the 1961 Tchaikovsky Competition. In March 1995, a special event occurred. Mozart's *Don Giovanni*, the first of many stage productions to be directed by Rob Mulholland, was performed entirely in Italian, marking the first time a fully staged opera was sung in a foreign language at The University of Southern Mississippi.

The orchestra was thriving, with more than seventy members, an appreciative audience, and a special occasion approaching. Dean now turned his attention to planning the symphony's seventy-fifth anniversary season (1995-96), commissioning two new pieces to be premiered and dreaming of the appearance of a truly exceptional guest artist.

IN 1995, IN PARIS, SOUTHERN MISS ART PROFESSOR WILLIAM BAGGETT EXECUTED A COMMEMORATIVE LITHOGRAPH TO CELEBRATE THE SYMPHONY'S SEVENTY-FIFTH ANNIVERSARY AND ITZHAK PERLMAN'S FIRST MISSISSIPPI PERFORMANCE. IN THIS DETAIL, BAGGETT INCORPORATES THE PORTE SAINT-MARTIN (RIGHT OUTSIDE OF HIS PARISIAN ATELIER) AND THE VIOLIN TO REPRESENT MAN'S ARTISTIC CONTRIBUTIONS AND THE INVERTED TREES TO REPRESENT THE DIVINE INSPIRATION FROM WHICH SUCH ART IS CREATED. HIS WORK BEAUTIFULLY CAPTURES THIS MONUMENTAL MOMENT IN THE ORCHESTRA'S HISTORY.

Bringing the World to MISSISSIPPI 1996-2010

HISTORY IS MADE BY THOSE WHO MAKE THE WAKE. NOT BY THOSE WHO RIDE ON IT, NOR BY THOSE WHO WATCH SAFELY FROM THE SHORE.

–Ronald Davis Balser

In 1996, Jay Dean began "bringing the world to Mississippi," a feat that would not have been accomplished but for the inspiration provided by two individuals. New York harmonica virtuoso Robert Bonfiglio issued the challenge, and then President Aubrey Lucas accepted the baton.

In 1993, Dean had attended a Conductors Guild convention in New York City. Robert Bonfiglio, while serving on a discussion panel, had infuriated a room full of professional orchestral conductors by telling them that they were all dinosaurs, that their orchestras were museums, and that their work was no longer relevant. He suggested that they start programming music that the general public wanted to hear, and then he made a statement that stuck with Dean. "There are only five classical music celebrities in the world today," he said, "Itzhak Perlman, Yo-Yo Ma, Luciano Pavarotti, Plácido Domingo, and James Galway."

Dean had Bonfiglio's remarks in mind when he went to his appointment with President Lucas to discuss the orchestra's approaching seventy-fifth anniversary season. He began the meeting—and one can be sure this did not come as a shock to Dr. Lucas—by asking the president for extraordinary financial assistance so that Dean might invite a well-known guest musician to celebrate such an important anniversary. Dean did not think that the meeting went very well.

1. SIR JAMES GALWAY | 2. PLÁCIDO DOMINGO | 3. YO-YO MA
4. ITZHAK PERLMAN

4.

WHEN I FIRST CONTACTED MR. PERLMAN'S REPRESENTATIVE ABOUT PLAYING WITH US, I WAS TOLD "MR. PERLMAN DOES NOT PLAY WITH UNIVERSITY ORCHESTRAS." LATER I WAS TOLD THAT HE WAS "VERY EXPENSIVE." THAT PART WAS TRUE. FINALLY I SENT SOME RECORDINGS AND ASSORTED ARTICLES ABOUT OUR ORCHESTRA. ABOUT TWO MONTHS AFTER THAT, I RECEIVED THE CALL. I DON'T KNOW WHETHER IT WAS THE ITEMS I SENT OR HIS MANAGEMENT'S WAY OF GETTING ME TO STOP CALLING, BUT ITZHAK PERLMAN AGREED TO COME AND PLAY WITH US.

– Jay Dean

THE LEVEL OF ACCOMPLISHMENT AND INTERNATIONAL ACCLAIM ACHIEVED BY DR. JAY DEAN AND THE SOUTHERN MISS SYMPHONY ORCHESTRA IS ABSOLUTELY TREMENDOUS. THERE ARE ONLY SO MANY WAYS AN INSTITUTION OF HIGHER LEARNING CAN DISTINGUISH ITSELF, AND OUR SYMPHONY HAS BECOME ONE OF THE DISTINGUISHED HIGHLIGHTS FOR SOUTHERN MISS.

–Bob Pierce
VICE PRESIDENT FOR ADVANCEMENT
THE UNIVERSITY OF SOUTHERN MISSISSIPPI

The following week, however, Dean received a note from Dr. Lucas. "Maybe we should bring Itzhak Perlman here for the orchestra's seventy-fifth anniversary," it read.

The conductor could hardly believe his eyes. He immediately scheduled another meeting with Dr. Lucas. After several presidential inquiries along the lines of "How much would he cost?" and "Do you think you could get him?" Dean received a presidential promise: If he could raise half the money, the university would cover the rest.

That task did not take long.

Convincing the world's most sought after soloist to come to Hattiesburg, Mississippi, was another matter.

On February 13, 1996, Itzhak Perlman played his debut concert in Mississippi, performing Beethoven's Violin Concerto in D Major with The University of Southern Mississippi Symphony Orchestra. The concert was the first that the orchestra had ever promoted outside the state of Mississippi, and it undoubtedly was responsible for another first, that being the first sold-out season in the seventy-five year history of the orchestra.

ITZHAK PERLMAN

March 13, 1996

c/o IMG Artists
22 East 71 Street
New York, NY 10021

Mr. Jay Dean
University of Southern Mississippi
Box 5081
Hattiesburg, MS 39406

Dear Jay,

I feel that I have to write and tell you how impressed I was with the University of Southern Mississippi Orchestra. It was such a pleasure to play with an orchestra full of enthusiastic musicians who are serious about their work. The orchestra's sound and playing was on an extremely high level and I loved making music in such an inspired atmosphere.

I congratulate you for your excellent work. Keep it up.

Sincerely,

Itzhak Perlman

IP:kp

1. ITZHAK PERLMAN, 1996 | 2. ITZHAK PERLMAN ON STAGE WITH CONDUCTOR JAY DEAN, 1996

I BEGAN A PRACTICE WITH ITZHAK PERLMAN OF TRAVELING TO HEAR AN ARTIST PLAY BEFORE BRINGING HIM OR HER TO HATTIESBURG. ABOUT A MONTH BEFORE OUR CONCERT, MR. PERLMAN WAS PLAYING AT THE UNIVERSITY OF TEXAS, SO I WENT THERE TO HEAR A REHEARSAL AND MEET HIM. WHEN I INTRODUCED MYSELF TO HIM AS THE CONDUCTOR FROM MISSISSIPPI WITH WHOM HE WOULD BE WORKING, HIS FIRST WORDS WERE "GOD, WHY DID I AGREE TO DO THAT?" I RESPONDED BY SAYING, "I HOPE THAT YOUR EXPERIENCE IN MISSISSIPPI WILL CHANGE YOUR OPINION." WHEN HE ARRIVED IN MISSISSIPPI, HE WAS POLITE AND GRACIOUS. I PICKED HIM UP AT THE AIRPORT, AND WE BEGAN TO TALK ABOUT THE CONCERT. I WANTED TO TALK ABOUT THE MUSIC, BUT HE WAS MORE INTERESTED IN TALKING ABOUT SOUTHERN FOOD AND WHERE WE WERE GOING TO HAVE LUNCH. HE WANTED TO GO TO A SOUTHERN HOME-COOKING TYPE OF RESTAURANT, SO I TOOK HIM TO A LOCAL ALL-YOU-CAN-EAT BUFFET. HE LOVED IT. HE MUST HAVE LEFT HATTIESBURG AS IMPRESSED WITH THE ORCHESTRA AS HE WAS WITH THE LOCAL CUISINE BECAUSE HE DEPARTED SAYING HE'D LIKE TO RETURN, AND HE DID SO A FEW YEARS LATER.

– *Jay Dean*

2.

1.

The University of Southern Mississippi
WIND ENSEMBLE, SOUTHERN CHORALE and SYMPHONY ORCHESTRA
salute the Palaces of St. Petersburg Exhibition with a special edition recording of

RUSSIAN MASTERPIECES

PALACES OF ST. PETERSBURG
RUSSIAN IMPERIAL STYLE

DIMITRI SHOSTAKOVICH

The USM Wind Ensemble
Dr. Thomas V. Fraschillo, Director

1 *Galop* from the musical comedy *Moscow, Cheremushky*

SERGEI PROKOFIEV

2 *March, Opus 99*

GIUSEPPI SARTI

The USM Southern Chorale
Dr. Timothy Koch, Director

3 *Nine sili nebesniya*

NIKOLAI GOLOVANOV

4 *Otche nash*

NIKOLAI TOLSTIAKOV

5 *Blagoslovi, dushe moya, Ghospoda*

MODEST MUSSORGSKY

The USM Symphomy Orchestra
Dr. Jay Dean, Director

6 *Pictures at an Exhibition*
Promenade
Gnomu
Il Vecchio Castello
Promenade
Tuileries
Bydlo
Promenade
Ballet of the Unhatched Chicks
Samuel Goldenberg and Schmuyle
Limoges: The Marketplace
The Catacombs: Sepulcrum Romanum; Con mortuis in lingua mortua
The Hut on Fowl's Legs (Baba Yaga)
The Great Gate at Kiev

Perlman certainly lived up to his billing, delighting both audience and orchestra. He also lectured to and performed for five hundred Mississippi students in a special afternoon educational performance. His appearance was a triumph for the orchestra and for the School of Music.

The seventy-fifth anniversary season premiered two new commissioned works, *Witness to Matters Human and Divine* by Southern Miss alumnus James Sclater (narrated by the distinguished American baritone William Warfield) and *Jubilate* by Luigi Zaninelli. The opera produced the world premiere production of Zaninelli's *Snow White, The Opera.*

During that spring, with the help of Drs. Tim Hudson and Stanley Hauer, the Southern Miss orchestra became the United States liaison for Das Treffen International Youth Music Festival in Bayreuth, Germany, the youth music festival affiliated with the Richard Wagner Festival.

Opportunities arose in the spring and summer of 1996 for university students and faculty to perform in a series of chamber concerts held in conjunction with the *Palaces of St. Petersburg* International Art Exhibition presented in Jackson. The chamber music series, called "Sundays at the Palaces," led to the production of *A Salute to the Palaces of St. Petersburg*, the orchestra's first CD. The orchestra's participation in this Mississippi Commission for International Cultural Exchange exhibit was at the invitation of its executive director, Jack Kyle, who would go on to develop, with the assistance of First Lady of Mississippi Pat Fordice, four major international art exhibitions. These exhibitions attracted enormous international attention for the state, and The University of Southern Mississippi Symphony Orchestra would benefit from its participation in the exhibitions.

For the 1996-97 season, aware of the public expectation following Itzhak Perlman's appearance, Dean sought an artist of equal name recognition but completely different style. Doc Severinsen is not only a superb trumpet player; he is also an experienced conductor and fabulous entertainer. *The Tonight Show* bandleader had been a resident pops conductor with the Milwaukee Symphony and the Buffalo Philharmonic, and he was happy to make a second trip to Hattiesburg.

A popular performance that summer was July's "Mississippi Holiday Spectacular," a patriotic event featuring orchestra, soloists, and fireworks, performed in celebration of Independence Day. The event would be produced twice more before being discontinued due to a change in university administration.

1. WILLIAM WARFIELD, 1996

I BELIEVE IT IS SAFE TO SAY THAT THE SYMPHONY ORCHESTRA ATTRACTS THOUSANDS OF PATRONS TO CAMPUS ANNUALLY. THIS ORCHESTRA, WHICH IS PART OF A VERY FINE SCHOOL OF MUSIC, HAS BUILT A REPUTATION FOR QUALITY PERFORMANCES AND ATTRACTING WORLD-RENOWNED GUEST ARTISTS.

–Garland Sullivan
SYMPHONY PATRON

DO YOU REMEMBER THE MANY EMOTIONS THAT WERE EVOKED THE FIRST TIME YOU HEARD A SINGER WITH AN UNBELIEVABLY RICH VOICE OR A CELLIST RENDER A MUSICAL WORK WITH SUCH EMOTION THAT IT BROUGHT TEARS OF JOY TO YOUR EYES? THESE RARE MOMENTS LIFT OUR SPIRITS, BRINGING MEANING TO OUR LIVES. AN OUTSTANDING GIVER OF SUCH MOMENTS IS THE UNIVERSITY OF SOUTHERN MISSISSIPPI SYMPHONY ORCHESTRA, LED BY ITS INSPIRING CONDUCTOR JAY DEAN. I AM DELIGHTED TO JOIN THE CHORUS OF THOSE WHO WISH TO THANK THIS OUTSTANDING MUSICAL ORGANIZATION AND ITS LEADER FOR PROVIDING MANY MOMENTS OF MUSICAL SPLENDOR.

–Jack Kyle
CHAIRMAN, MISSISSIPPI COMMISSION
FOR INTERNATIONAL CULTURAL EXCHANGE

A community arts advocacy organization, Partners for the Arts, was created in 1997. Its founding president was local physician and symphony supporter Benjamin Carmichael, and its mission was to support the university's College of the Arts both financially and with volunteer service. Dean assisted the group in its organization, and Garland Sullivan, as development officer for the College of the Arts, was instrumental in ensuring its early success. Within a few years of its inception, Partners for the Arts would grow to be of significant assistance to the orchestra, as well as other arts programs in the college.

The 1997-98 season presented musical performances ranging from the Brahms *Ein deutsches Requiem*, performed in celebration of the Brahms centennial, to Tchaikovsky's First Piano Concerto with world-renowned American pianist John Browning, and the orchestra's participation in the *Splendors of Versailles* International Art Exhibition.

For the opening ceremony of the Versailles exhibit, the orchestra performed the world premiere of *Fanfare for Versailles,* written by the French composer, organist, and conductor Christian Gouinguené. Since the work incorporated twelve herald trumpets, the orchestra was joined by the United States Army Herald Trumpets from Washington, D.C. The orchestra also had the honor of producing the world premiere recording of Gouinguené's *Splendors of Versailles* and recorded Hector Berlioz's *Symphonie Fantastique.*

In support of the exhibition, the orchestra produced a *Splendors of Versailles* CD and developed the *Splendors of Versailles International Baroque Music Festival.* A special eighteenth-century-style ensemble, The King's Violins, was formed from within the orchestra for this festival. The group, led by Dr. Stephen Redfield, professor of violin, consisted of eighteen student members who performed beautifully in full Baroque attire, complete with white, powdered wigs.

Another special festival associated with the exhibition produced a weekend of televised performances and master classes with French flutist Jean-Pierre Rampal, a legendary figure in the world of classical music.

The Opera at USM contributed the final Versaille-inspired event with a performance of Georges Bizet's *Carmen* at Thalia Mara Hall in Jackson. The sold-out production featured mezzo-soprano Denyce Graves performing the title role that has become synonymous with her name. Graves was joined by a special appearance of the Paris Opera Boys Choir as well as students, faculty, and Southern Miss alumni.

On October 13, 1998, Ray Charles performed with the orchestra as part of the Partners for the Arts Connoisseur Series. This concert drew over 4,000 people from three states. It was a memorable performance that encompassed some unusual challenges.

Ray Charles had a standing practice of refusing to allow his music to arrive ahead of his band. Some of these pieces would be challenging for any orchestra, so the student orchestra, needless to say, was anxious. The band arrived in time to give the orchestra just three hours of practice time, and the student musicians rose to the challenge. Meanwhile, Mr. Charles was awaiting the contracted limousine pick-up at the New Orleans airport when he exited the airport by a door other than the agreed upon exit. Since he was unable to find the limousine, and the limousine driver was unable to find him, he had to take a taxi all the way from New Orleans to Hattiesburg. That wrong turn cost Ray Charles several hundred dollars in cab fare!

1. RAY CHARLES PERFORMING WITH THE SOUTHERN MISS SYMPHONY ORCHESTRA IN REED GREEN COLISEUM, 1998

THERE WAS ONE DISAPPOINTMENT FOR ME IN RAY CHARLES'S APPEARANCE. BECAUSE HE WAS BLIND, HE HAD TO HAVE A CONDUCTOR WITH WHOM HE WAS FAMILIAR. I CONDUCTED THE FIRST HALF OF THE CONCERT, AND HIS CONDUCTOR CONDUCTED THE SECOND HALF, DURING WHICH HE PLAYED. WE PASSED EACH OTHER IN THE HALLWAY DURING INTERMISSION BUT DID NOT HAVE A CHANCE TO SPEAK. MR. CHARLES LEFT IMMEDIATELY AFTER THE CONCERT, SO HE HAS THE DISTINCTION OF BEING THE ONLY WORLD-CLASS PERFORMER THAT I BROUGHT TO SOUTHERN MISS AND DIDN'T EVEN GET TO MEET!

– *Jay Dean*

1.

ONCE, PERHAPS BECAUSE I HAD PLAYED A SMALL PART IN HELPING MAESTRO DEAN RECRUIT STUDENT MUSICIANS FROM AROUND THE WORLD, MY WIFE DEE DEE AND I WERE INVITED TO A DINNER HONORING LEONTYNE PRICE. TOWARD THE END OF THE MEAL, MS. PRICE SPONTANEOUSLY SANG "SUMMERTIME" A CAPPELLA. TO SAY IT WAS BREATHTAKING DOES NOT BEGIN TO CAPTURE THE ALMOST BRITTLE, EXPECTANT ATMOSPHERE IN THE SILENT, OXYGEN-LESS ROOM AS SHE SOARED AND BELIEVED AND SANG AND SANG. I'VE TRAVELED FAR AND WIDE AND HEARD CONCERTS AND PERFORMANCES OF ALL SORTS AROUND THE WORLD, BUT THANKS TO THE MAGIC OF THE USM ORCHESTRA, THAT IS A MOMENT IN TIME I WILL NEVER FORGET.

–Tim Hudson
PRESIDENT, THE UNIVERSITY OF HOUSTON AT VICTORIA

THE SOUTHERN MISS SYMPHONY IS A JEWEL IN HATTIESBURG. IT HAS BEEN AN HONOR TO BE A PART OF THE EVOLVING JOURNEY ON WHICH JAY DEAN HAS TAKEN THIS SYMPHONY. IT IS BECAUSE OF HIM AND THE HARD WORK OF HIS STUDENTS THAT WE HAVE ONE OF THE BEST SYMPHONIES IN THE REGION.

– Johnny L. DuPree
MAYOR, CITY OF HATTIESBURG

The Opera at USM was renamed Southern Opera and Musical Theatre Company that season, and the first production under the new name was Clark Gesner's *You're a Good Man, Charlie Brown*, which brought loveable comic strip characters to life for thousands of children who saw the performance at the Mannoni Performing Arts Center. This production topped all attendance records for productions held at the PAC. Aaron Copland's *Tender Land* was produced in February, and the year closed with a summer production of Harvey Schmidt's *The Fantastiks*.

Yo-Yo Ma, the premier cellist in the world, performed for the first time in Mississippi with the symphony orchestra on September 28, 1999. Mr. Ma's performance of Dmitri Shostakovich's Concerto No. 1 for Cello and Orchestra was a moving experience for all in attendance. In addition to being an impeccable musician, Mr. Ma is an extremely friendly individual. He had been contracted to play the Shostakovich Cello Concerto No. 1, but moments before the performance began, he walked into Jay Dean's dressing room and asked if Dean would mind if he played in the back of the cello section on the Brahms Symphony No. 2. The looks on the students' faces were priceless as Mr. Ma took a seat at the back of the section and played. Patrons seated in the balcony of Bennett Auditorium could see him, as well.

Opera legend teaches master class

SPECIAL TO THE PRINTZ

A diverse group of voice students from USM and William Carey College perform for one of the 20th century's most renowned operatic legends, Leontyne Price, in a master class at 2 p.m. Saturday in Bennett Auditorium.

These students will spend "An Afternoon with Leontyne Price," sponsored by BancorpSouth, in a master class offered through the Southern Opera and Music Theater series.

"This experience will change these students' lives," said Jay Dean, director of the USM Symphony orchestra and coordinator of the event.

Although she will not perform during the class, the purpose is educational in nature.

Price will critique each student's performance and will share her vast knowledge of operatic style and technique.

"She is going to work with them, and the audience, hopefully, will see an improvement immediately just from her comments on the student's performance," Dean said.

Voice professors, through their studios at USM and WCC, submitted nominations of their best students. Of the 12 vocalists invited to audition, four were chosen to perform, with two alternates.

From the studio of USM voice professor Larry Smith are finalists Cassandra Dean, a senior from New Albany, and Iwao Asakura, a doctoral student from Japan.

From the studio of USM voice professor Kimberly Davis are finalist Ulina Llieva, a DMA student from Bulgaria, and alternate Tania Leal, a sophomore from Pueblo, Mexico.

Two students from WCC join the elite group: finalist Bevin McRoberts, a senior from Plymouth, Mass., and a student of Josephine D'Arpa; and alternate Carrie Hayes, a senior from Ellisville, and a students of Dr. Connie Roberts.

The six students will join Price for a special reception at the home of USM President Horace Fleming following the master class. The reception is open to the public. Tickets are $20 per person

Tickets to be a member of the audience for the master class are $20 per person. Call the Southern Miss Ticket Office at 266-5418 for tickets.

Submitted Photo

Leontyne Price, opera legend and native of Mississippi.

1. *STUDENT PRINTZ* ARTICLE, 2000 | 2. YO-YO MA JOINS THE CELLO SECTION WEARING A BORROWED BOW TIE, 1999

ONE MEMORY DURING MY TIME IN THE ORCHESTRA STANDS OUT ABOVE THE REST. AS THE CONCERT BEGAN, SOMEONE ASKED IF I HAD AN EXTRA COPY OF THE BRAHMS SYMPHONY NO. 2, WHICH I DID. HE SAID HE NEEDED IT FOR A PLAYER IN THE BACK OF THE SECTION. I GAVE IT TO HIM, ONLY TO FIND OUT LATER THAT THE PLAYER IN THE BACK OF THE SECTION WAS NONE OTHER THAN YO-YO MA. TO HAVE AN OPPORTUNITY TO PLAY WITH THIS GREAT CELLIST WAS AMAZING AND INSPIRATIONAL, BUT TO HAVE HIM JOIN THE SECTION AND PLAY AS ONE OF US WAS AN EXPERIENCE I WILL NEVER FORGET.

–Jose Sunderland
CELLO, 1991-2000

2.

Yo-Yo E. Ma

December 6, 1999

Jay Dean, Conductor
University Symphony Orchestra
The University of Southern Mississippi
Box 5081
Hattiesburg, Mississippi 39406-5081

Dear Jay,

It has been almost two months since my visit to Hattiesburg. The memory of working with you and hearing the University of Southern Mississippi Orchestra is still very vivid.

I think you are a visionary. To be able to have an orchestra of undergraduates play a difficult Brahms Symphony early in the school year with such precision, commitment and energy, followed by a superlative rendition of the Shostakovich Cello Concerto No. 1, was absolutely remarkable. The students from Mexico and Honduras with whom I spoke with have a great passion for music coupled with a strong desire to excel. I was deeply inspired by their hunger for the orchestral experience, and I know that, along with various members of the faculty such as my wonderful cello colleague Paul York, you were the catalyst for the successful development of this orchestral program. As President Fleming so aptly stated at the beginning of the concert, he can be justly proud of the achievements of this orchestra and of your key work in its formation.

Congratulations to you, to the orchestra, and to the institution. I know that many of my colleagues will be surprised and elated when they come to Hattiesburg, as I have been.

Sincerely,

Yo-Yo Ma

Dean also learned that evening that Mr. Ma can be forgetful. As he was about to go on stage, he inquired as to whether the conductor had an extra bow tie he could borrow. Of course, the most famous example of his forgetfulness occurred two weeks after his Hattiesburg appearance when he mistakenly left his cello—a 1733 Domenico Montagnana made in Venice and valued at $2.5 million—in the trunk of a New York taxi! Thankfully, it was soon retrieved, unharmed.

Although university-wide financial woes reduced opera funding for the 1999-2000 season,the program presented a beautiful production of Mozart's *Le Nozze di Figaro* with grand sets, colorful costuming, and delightful delivery. The following year just one opera was presented, Rossini's *Il Barbiere di Siviglia*, directed by Rob Mulholland, and guest conducted by Fiora Contino, an internationally known opera conductor with a long history of affiliations with prestigious institutions such as Indiana University, The Peabody Conservatory, and The University of Texas.

In 2000-01, the orchestra presented a concert celebrating the musical heritage of Mississippi. "Mississippi Sounds" included blues, gospel, jazz, rock and roll, and patriotic music with performers including gospel choirs, dancers, the complete "Pride of Mississippi" marching band, and an Elvis Presley tribute artist who entered the coliseum on a motorcycle. Another popular program that season was "Bravo Broadway III," which featured original members from the casts of *Cats*, *Phantom of the Opera*, and *Les Misérables*. The highlight of the season was Itzhak Perlman's return to Hattiesburg for his second Mississippi appearance, performing Tchaikovsky's Violin Concerto in D Major.

1.

2.

The following season, Dean created and produced a concert for Mississippi Educational Television. "Night of A Thousand Trumpets" featured world-renowned trumpeter Doc Severinsen in his third appearance with the orchestra and included nearly 1,000 trumpet players from thirty-two states and three foreign countries. The orchestra also presented the world premiere of *The Shoe Bird* by Samuel Jones, performing it for over 10,000 people in four Mississippi cities. In addition to the orchestra's recruiting efforts in Mexico and Honduras, relationships were developed this year in Spain, Italy, France, Bulgaria, and Russia.

1. YO-YO MA ADDRESSES STUDENTS, 1999 | 2. SOUTHERN MISS PRESIDENT AUBREY LUCAS WITH DOC SEVERINSEN, 2001

THOSE FOURTH OF JULY CONCERTS WERE JINXED! ONCE, WE WERE IN VICKSBURG'S AMPHITHEATRE PLAYING THE 1812 OVERTURE, COMPLETE WITH CANNON FIRE, WHEN THE NOISE SET OFF SEVERAL CAR ALARMS. WE MANAGED TO PLAY THROUGH THEM, BUT THE COMBINATION OF NOISES AWAKENED A STORM OF MOTHS, AND WHEN THE FIREWORKS STARTED A FEW MINUTES LATER, THE MOTHS CONVERGED ON THE ONLY BRIGHTLY LIT AREA—OUR STAGE. IT WAS LIKE THE PLAGUE! THERE WERE SO MANY THAT WE COULDN'T SEE JAY CONDUCTING, AND WE ALL FOUND MOTHS IN OUR CASES FOR MONTHS AFTER THAT. IF WE WEREN'T COMPETING WITH CAR ALARMS AND MOTHS, IT WAS POURING RAIN. THAT YEAR, THE NEWSPAPER RAN A FRONT PAGE ARTICLE STATING THAT THE CONCERT WOULD GO ON RAIN OR SHINE. BUT WE HADN'T ANTICIPATED A MONSOON! IT RAINED SO MUCH THAT THE STAGE WAS SINKING, AND WE HAD TO MOVE AT THE LAST MINUTE TO BENNETT AUDITORIUM. JAY DEAN IS A "NEVER SAY NEVER" KIND OF GUY, BUT I THINK IT WOULD TAKE A LOT OF PERSUADING TO TALK HIM INTO ANOTHER OUTDOOR CONCERT.

–Michael Lopinto
BASSOON, 1987-92, 2002-03
ORCHESTRA STAFF, 2002-09

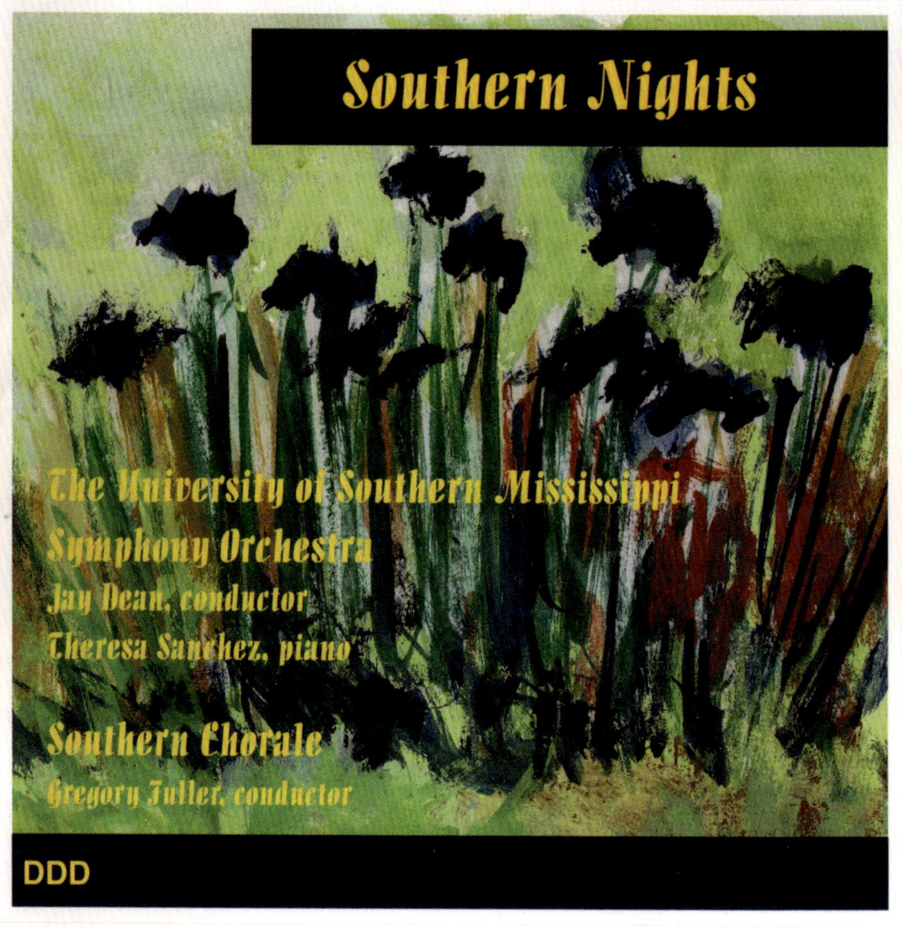

The orchestra's contribution to the 2001 *Majesty of Spain* International Art Exhibition was a stirring performance of Manuel De Falla's *Noches en los Jardines de España (Nights in the Gardens of Spain)* with Dr. Theresa Sanchez, which was recorded for inclusion on the *Southern Nights* CD.

In July 2002, the orchestra traveled to Vicksburg to present the first of three annual Independence Day pops concerts called *Vicksburg Celebrates America.* Slightly exaggerated rumor has it that, due to the city's surrender on July 4, 1862, in the American Civil War, Vicksburg had not celebrated the Fourth of July in 140 years! Whether or not this is strictly true, Jay Dean and the orchestra were proud to be a part of the new patriotic celebration which was annually attended by more than 15,000 people.

Between 1998 and 2001, the opera had gradually lost all of its state-allocated funding due to university budget cuts and had been forced to operate solely from ticket sales. In 2002, however, President Shelby Thames implemented a tuition-generated Cultural Arts Fee. This fee, requested of the president by Jay Dean along with College of the Arts Dean Mary Ann Stringer, is a source of arts funding which is still in effect today, and it would keep the opera afloat until 2008 when the program's state-allocated budget was restored.

In 2002 Maryann Kyle joined the faculty and became the artistic director of Southern Opera and Musical Theatre Company. Although there was no budget to produce opera or musicals, Kyle was committed to providing students with the stage experiences they needed in order to become professional singers. She began with a small, narrated version of *Carmen* which was presented in the round with a small orchestra. The performances were part of a Downtown with the Arts series presented in the Hattiesburg Cultural Center.

The enormously popular "Mississippi Sounds" concert had demanded a sequel performance, so in April 2003 the orchestra produced a program for Mississippi Public Television. "Mississippi, The Birthplace of America's Music" showcased 1,500 performers–the largest number the orchestra has ever included in a single event–and attracted an audience of 4,000 people at Reed Green Coliseum. Hosted by Mississippi actor Gary Grubbs, the program featured the Mississippi Mass Choir and McComb native Vasti Jackson.

1. NIKKI MELVIN JOHNSON AS CINDERELLA IN *INTO THE WOODS*, 2003

In terms of orchestral performances, highlights of the 2002-03 season included Beethoven's Sixth Symphony in F Major ("The Pastorale") and Prokofiev's suite from the ballet *Romeo and Juliet*. Roberta Peters returned for a second performance, and Kevin Kenner joined the orchestra in March for Rachmaninoff's Piano Concerto No. 2. However, the most exciting soloist this season was bass virtuoso Edgar Meyer, who performed two concertos, including his own Concerto for Bass. Many people regard Meyer, who regularly performs with Yo-Yo Ma and Bela Fleck, as the finest classical bassist in the world today. His performances were extraordinary.

Maryann Kyle's second opera production, in November 2003, was Stephen Sondheim's *Into the Woods*, in collaboration with William Carey College. Obra Quave and Constance Roberts, both faculty members at William Carey College, were stage director and music director, respectively, and Kyle was producer.

A FEW OF MY FAVORITE MEMORIES INCLUDE PLAYING WITH THE ORCHESTRA AND CHORUS AT AVERY FISHER HALL IN LINCOLN CENTER. WE PERFORMED THE MUSIC OF SAMUEL ADLER WITH HIM PRESENT, AND IT WAS GREAT TO HEAR HIS COMPLIMENTS AND SUGGESTIONS AT THE REHEARSAL. I ALSO RECALL LEONARD SLATKIN GUEST CONDUCTING A REHEARSAL OF THE BRAHMS 4TH SYMPHONY. I WAS NEVER MORE NERVOUS TO PLAY THE TROMBONE CHORALE IN THE FOURTH MOVEMENT, AND WHEN HE CONGRATULATED US AFTER THE CHORALE, IT WAS AN AMAZING VALIDATION OF PRACTICE TIME SPENT. PERFORMING THE SHOSTAKOVICH CELLO CONCERTO WITH YO-YO MA AND THEN HAVING HIM RETURN TO STAGE AND SIT IN THE BACK OF THE CELLO SECTION FOR THE SECOND HALF OF THE CONCERT WAS AN AMAZING EXPERIENCE, AND PERFORMING WITH RAY CHARLES IN REED GREEN COLISEUM WAS A NIGHT I'LL NEVER FORGET. WITH GUEST TRUMPETER ROGER INGRAM (FROM THE HARRY CONNICK JR. BAND), IT JUST COULDN'T HAVE BEEN BETTER.

–Bret Barrow
TROMBONE, 1997-2001

I WAS IN A MEETING IN MY PUBLISHER'S OFFICE ON THE UPPER WEST SIDE OF MANHATTAN, DISCUSSING MY HOMETOWN, WHEN A NATIVE NEW YORKER SEATED ACROSS THE TABLE SNIDELY ASKED, "WHAT IS THERE TO DO IN HATTIESBURG, MISSISSIPPI?" I TOLD HIM, "WELL, A FEW WEEKS AGO, I WALKED TWO BLOCKS FROM MY HOME AND SAW YO-YO MA PERFORM WITH OUR SYMPHONY." EYEBROWS RAISED. "A COUPLE OF YEARS BACK, THEY PERFORMED WITH ITZHAK PERLMAN," I CONTINUED, "AND SOON PLÁCIDO DOMINGO WILL DELIVER HIS FIRST-EVER PERFORMANCE WITH A UNIVERSITY ORCHESTRA." JAWS DROPPED. THIS ORCHESTRA MAKES ME PROUD TO LIVE IN HATTIESBURG AND REMINDS ME HOW LUCKY I AM TO LIVE IN THIS PART OF THE COUNTRY.

– Robert St. John
SYMPHONY PATRON

I DON'T THINK THAT I'VE EVER PLAYED IT THAT FAST!

– *Sir James Galway*

In spring 2004, the Mississippi Commission for International Cultural Exchange presented its fourth and final exhibition, *The Glory of Baroque Dresden*. The orchestra opened the exhibition with a sold-out performance in Thalia Mara Hall of Beethoven's Ninth Symphony. Because of the exhibition, much of the music that was programmed that year was German, including works by Beethoven, Mozart, and Handel, as well as Johann Albrechtsberger's Trombone Concerto with Jorgen van Rhyen, principal trombone of the Concertgebow Orchestra of Amsterdam. The orchestra's final exhibition-related performance was "Scenes from the Ring," a two-hour program of excerpts from Richard Wagner's *Der Ring des Nibelungen*, which included several professional Wagnerian singers from around the country, an orchestra of 103 musicians, and stunning visual images.

The opening concert in 2004-05 was a performance by the premier flutist in the world today, Sir James Galway, and his wife, Lady Jeanne Galway. Not only is Galway a truly superb musician, he is also an excellent entertainer who kept the audience either spellbound with his playing or laughing at his jokes. He dazzled with an encore performance of the badinerie from Bach's Suite in B Minor. Galway played the piece twice, first at a professionally fast tempo, and then at a tempo virtually unplayable by even the most accomplished of flutists.

James Galway

Dr. Jay Dean,
Music Director
The University of Southern Mississippi
118 College Dr. Box 5081
Hattiesburg, Mississippi, 39406-5081

Dear Jay,

I really don't know where to begin a letter like this. The concert with your orchestra was so outstanding the memory of it is still fresh in my mind. Nobody had prepared me to expect something of this standard. As you well know agents don't know about these things and when I arrived to play the first rehearsal I could not believe my ears.

This rehearsal as you will remember started off with the Dvorak "Carnival" Overture. I had not expected to hear anything like this. This is an overture with a lot of notes and they were all played brilliantly by this orchestra of young musicians. I really could not believe my ears. What enthusiasm and what brilliance. I think many of the major cities in the USA would be very happy to hear an orchestra play so inspired. The one thing lacking in classical music is the dedication and enthusiasm both of which were so obvious in your young orchestra.

In my Mozart concerto I could not have wished for a better accompaniment. This was something well rehearsed and again beautifully played. Extraordinary really. After this concert I was wondering where to go from here. You have set a standard in my mind for doing things with care and diligence that is lacking in many classical music performances.

I look forward to playing under your baton with this wonderful orchestra. Please convey my best regards to them at the next rehearsal and tell them I am hoping to see and hear them all again in the near future.

Sincerely,

1. SIR JAMES AND LADY JEANNE GALWAY PERFORM WITH THE ORCHESTRA, 2004

1.

1.

February 2005 marked the fiftieth anniversary of the premiere of Carlisle Floyd's well-known American opera *Susannah*, and Southern Opera and Musical Theatre Company honored the occasion with the university's third production of the opera and its moving portrayal of life in the rural South. Floyd had planned to attend and deliver a lecture, but a family illness prevented his attendance.

2.

A DAY DOESN'T GO BY THAT I AM NOT THANKFUL FOR THE ORCHESTRA PROGRAM AT SOUTHERN MISS. THANKS TO MY SYMPHONY SCHOLARSHIP, I HAVE HAD THE PRIVILEGE OF FINISHING MY MUSIC DEGREE, LEARNING TO SPEAK ENGLISH, GETTING A JOB IN MUSIC, AND EARNING AMERICAN CITIZENSHIP. PERHAPS IN THE STATES IT IS COMMON TO RECEIVE SCHOLARSHIPS, BUT FOR THOSE OF US FROM LATIN AMERICAN COUNTRIES, A SCHOLARSHIP IS ONLY A DREAM. THIS ORCHESTRA PROGRAM HAS NOT ONLY CHANGED HATTIESBURG INTO A MUSICAL METROPOLIS; IT HAS ALSO CHANGED THE LIVES OF MANY INTERNATIONAL STUDENTS WHO GO ON TO SPREAD WORD AROUND THE WORLD ABOUT THIS UNIVERSITY. I WILL BE FOREVER GRATEFUL FOR THIS AMAZING OPPORTUNITY WHICH REASSURES ME OF THE GREAT AMERICAN SPIRIT, GIVING HOPE TO THOSE LIKE ME IN THE PURSUIT OF HAPPINESS.

—Alejandro Encinas
VIOLIN/VIOLA, 2002-05

3.

1. EMILY HENDRICHS AS QUEEN OF THE NIGHT IN *THE MAGIC FLUTE*, 2004 | 2. TONY O'DELL AS MONASTATOS IN *THE MAGIC FLUTE*, 2004 | 3. FACULTY MEMBER TAYLOR HIGHTOWER AS OLIN BLITCH IN *SUSANNAH*, 2005

ON APRIL 2, 2005, THE MOST CELEBRATED OPERATIC AND CLASSICAL MUSIC ARTIST IN THE WORLD PERFORMED WITH THE UNIVERSITY OF SOUTHERN MISSISSIPPI SYMPHONY ORCHESTRA AT THE MISSISSIPPI COAST COLISEUM: PLÁCIDO DOMINGO.

The performance was a milestone event not only for the orchestra, but also for the university and the entire state. To date, The University of Southern Mississippi Symphony Orchestra is the only university orchestra with which Domingo has ever performed. The concert had been seven years in the making and would not have been accomplished without the sponsorship of Beau Rivage Casino and the support of its president at that time, Mr. Jeff Dahl.

1. PLÁCIDO DOMINGO PERFORMING, 2005 | 2. COVER OF *THE TALON*, THE UNIVERSITY OF SOUTHERN MISSISSIPPI ALUMNI MAGAZINE, 2005
3. PLÁCIDO DOMINGO CONCERT, 2005 | 4. PLÁCIDO DOMINGO ENJOYING A REHEARSAL BREAK WITH ORCHESTRA STUDENTS, 2005

The repertoire for "One Voice, One Orchestra, One Night Only" included standard orchestral showpieces, great tenor opera arias, and duets including "Già nella notte dense" from Verdi's *Otello* which Mr. Domingo performed with the beautiful soprano Ana Maria Martinez. Over 9,200 people were in attendance for the most extraordinary concert produced in the history of The University of Southern Mississippi.

Shortly before the concert began, Pope John Paul II died. There was much discussion backstage as to whether or not to address the audience concerning this. It just so happened that the first piece that Domingo was to sing that evening was the prayer from Massenet's *Le Cid*, "Ah! Tout est bien fini! … O souverain, ô juge, ô pére." Mr. Domingo publicly dedicated this prayer to the memory of the Pope.

3.

4.

IT WAS 1998, AND I WAS AT A MEETING IN NEW YORK CITY WHEN I LEARNED THAT THE 2001 INTERNATIONAL ARTS EXHIBITION BEING PLANNED FOR MISSISSIPPI WAS TO BE CALLED "THE MAJESTY OF SPAIN." IMMEDIATELY I WANTED TO INVITE THE MOST PROMINENT SPANISH MUSICAL PERFORMER IN THE WORLD, PLÁCIDO DOMINGO, AND AS IT HAPPENED, I LEARNED THAT HIS AGENT'S OFFICE WAS IN THE BUILDING RIGHT NEXT DOOR.

FOLLOWING MY MEETING, I WENT NEXT DOOR, SEARCHED THE OFFICE DIRECTORY, PROCEEDED TO THE OFFICE, AND, FOLLOWING THE INSTRUCTIONS ON THE DOOR, KNOCKED FOR ASSISTANCE. SOMEONE CAME TO THE DOOR, SLID OPEN ITS SMALL WINDOW, AND ASKED ME TO STATE THE PURPOSE OF MY BUSINESS. AFTER SOME TIME, THE DOOR FINALLY OPENED, AND I WAS ALLOWED TO ENTER A SIMPLE, UNPRETENTIOUS OFFICE. I MET WITH A GENTLEMAN WHO TOLD ME THAT MR. DOMINGO WAS COMPLETELY UNAVAILABLE AND EXTREMELY EXPENSIVE. I HAD HEARD SUCH WARNINGS BEFORE, BUT WHEN I INQUIRED ABOUT THE FEE, I WAS ASTOUNDED AT THE RESPONSE.

I COMMUNICATED WITH THIS AGENT FOR FOUR YEARS WITH NO SUCCESS, AND THE SPAIN EXHIBIT CAME AND WENT. THEN ONE DAY, I RECEIVED A CALL FROM THE AGENT WHO ASKED IF I WOULD BE INTERESTED IN PERFORMING A CONCERT WITH ANOTHER OF HIS ARTISTS. AFTER THAT SUCCESSFUL PERFORMANCE, I FINALLY GOT THE CALL OF MY DREAMS. "LET'S TALK ABOUT PLÁCIDO," HE SAID.

– Jay Dean

1.

2.

3.

1. PLÁCIDO DOMINGO AND ANA MARIA MARTINEZ , 2005 | 2. PLÁCIDO DOMINGO, 2005 | 3. EUGENE KOHN, JAY DEAN, ANA MARIA MARTINEZ, AND PLÁCIDO DOMINGO, 2005

JAY IS A DELIGHT TO WORK WITH BECAUSE HE CAN ACCOMPLISH ANYTHING! HE DREAMS AND PLANS BIG. HE DOESN'T GO INTO A PROJECT WITHOUT DOING HIS HOMEWORK, MAKING SURE IT WILL WORK. THANKS TO HIS EFFORTS, HATTIESBURG IS COMING TO BE KNOWN AS A DESTINATION FOR SERIOUS MUSIC.

–Susan Thomson Rutland
SYMPHONY PATRON

1.

I'LL NEVER FORGET JOKING WITH PLÁCIDO DOMINGO BACKSTAGE, THE PRINCIPAL CELLIST AND I URGING HIM TO SING ANOTHER ENCORE. HE HAD PREPARED "EL DIA QUE ME QUIERAS," A BEAUTIFUL ARGENTINE SONG, BUT HE TOLD US, "OH, MY CHILDREN, NO, NO, NO! THESE POOR PEOPLE HAVE HAD ENOUGH. THEY NEED TO GO GET SOME REST!" THEN HE AND ANA MARIA MARTINEZ RETURNED TO STAGE TO THE DEAFENING SOUND OF NEARLY 10,000 PEOPLE APPLAUDING, AND EACH OF THEM SELECTED AN ORCHESTRA MEMBER TO ESCORT FROM THE STAGE.

–Alejandro Drago
VIOLIN, 2004-08

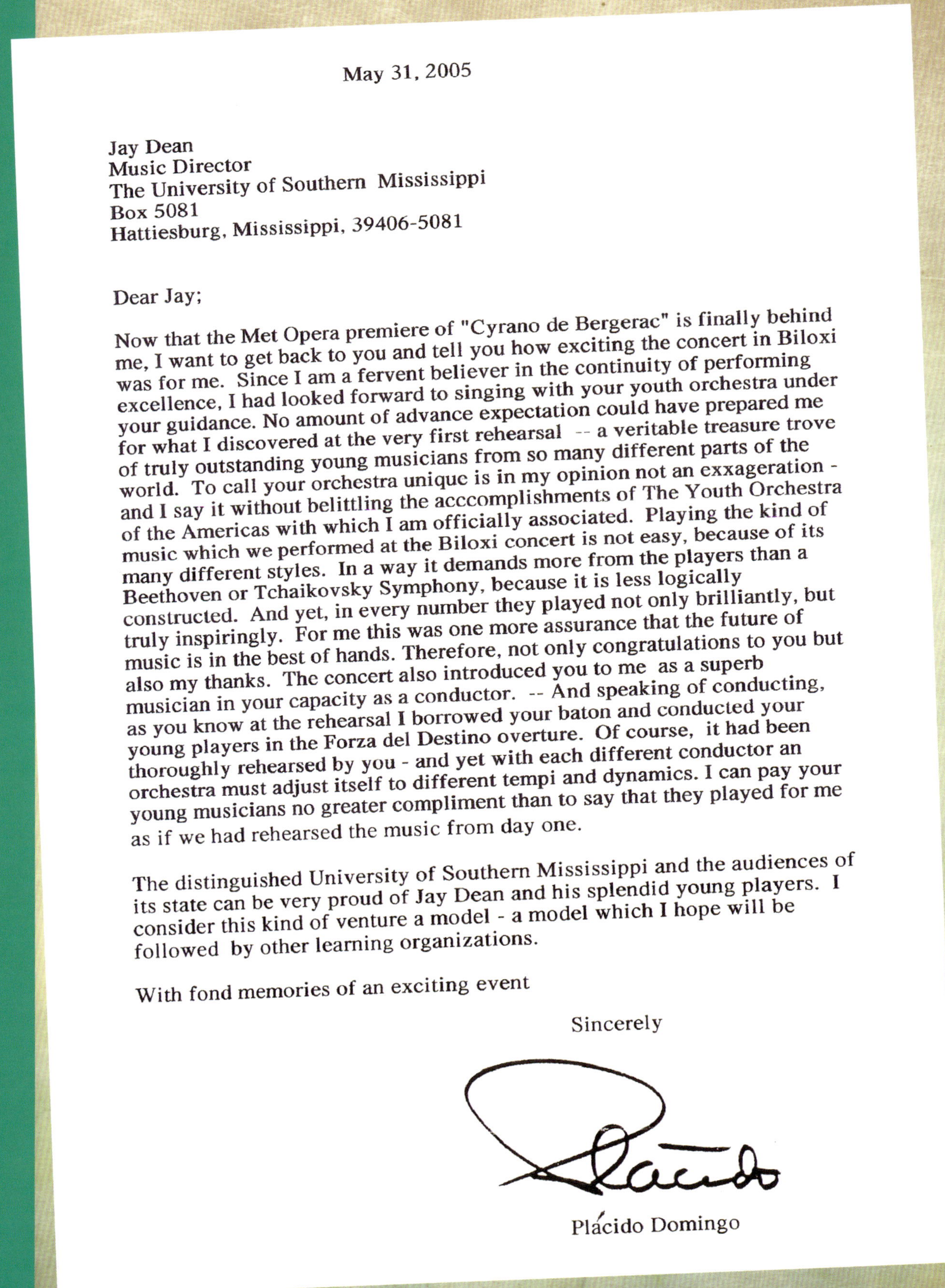
May 31, 2005

Jay Dean
Music Director
The University of Southern Mississippi
Box 5081
Hattiesburg, Mississippi, 39406-5081

Dear Jay;

Now that the Met Opera premiere of "Cyrano de Bergerac" is finally behind me, I want to get back to you and tell you how exciting the concert in Biloxi was for me. Since I am a fervent believer in the continuity of performing excellence, I had looked forward to singing with your youth orchestra under your guidance. No amount of advance expectation could have prepared me for what I discovered at the very first rehearsal -- a veritable treasure trove of truly outstanding young musicians from so many different parts of the world. To call your orchestra unique is in my opinion not an exxageration - and I say it without belittling the acccomplishments of The Youth Orchestra of the Americas with which I am officially associated. Playing the kind of music which we performed at the Biloxi concert is not easy, because of its many different styles. In a way it demands more from the players than a Beethoven or Tchaikovsky Symphony, because it is less logically constructed. And yet, in every number they played not only brilliantly, but truly inspiringly. For me this was one more assurance that the future of music is in the best of hands. Therefore, not only congratulations to you but also my thanks. The concert also introduced you to me as a superb musician in your capacity as a conductor. -- And speaking of conducting, as you know at the rehearsal I borrowed your baton and conducted your young players in the Forza del Destino overture. Of course, it had been thoroughly rehearsed by you - and yet with each different conductor an orchestra must adjust itself to different tempi and dynamics. I can pay your young musicians no greater compliment than to say that they played for me as if we had rehearsed the music from day one.

The distinguished University of Southern Mississippi and the audiences of its state can be very proud of Jay Dean and his splendid young players. I consider this kind of venture a model - a model which I hope will be followed by other learning organizations.

With fond memories of an exciting event

Sincerely

Plácido

Plácido Domingo

In July, 2005, still elated from the success of April's Plácido Domingo concert, Jay Dean attended a meeting about budgets and was told, "The orchestra is too expensive. We do not need an orchestra of this size or quality to meet our strategic mission or accreditation requirements."

After a decade of bringing the leading artists in the world to Mississippi, Jay Dean would have to (1) cut the orchestra back to an insignificant program, (2) go to work in another state, or (3) assume responsibility for privately raising the money needed for a sufficient scholarship endowment. For personal reasons, option two was not an option, and Dean couldn't bear to choose option one. He chose option three.

One month later brought even more devastation: Hurricane Katrina.

A few days after the university opened its doors for fall classes, Hurricane Katrina came ashore and closed those doors for two weeks. Jay Dean could not account for all of his students. Some had not been able to make it into the country yet, and most of the students who had been in Hattiesburg prior to Katrina had left for safer locations. It took nearly a month to determine what sort of season the orchestra could salvage.

Internationally acclaimed violinist Joshua Bell had been scheduled to perform with the orchestra in October, a concert which had to be postponed until April. Instead, the October concert was a free performance called "Spirit of Mississippi: A Concert of Hope." Held at Main Street Baptist Church, the concert drew an audience of approximately 1,200 people who heard music

2.

appropriate for the difficult time, including Samuel Barber's *Adagio for Strings* as well as inspirational works of gospel, jazz, and patriotism in a welcome reprieve from the devastation all around.

In November, the opera program managed to present its first joint project with Mississippi Opera, presenting a fully staged version of Verdi's *La Traviata.* However, the orchestra was not so fortunate with its planned production of Tchaikovsky's *Nutcracker.* The program was to be produced with La Studio, a local dance studio, but hurricane damage prevented the studio's participation.

Determined to save the program, Jay Dean spoke with four other ballet companies before finding one willing to come to Mississippi for the performance. Three weeks later, that company backed out, as well.

Dejected, Dean had no choice but to tell his staff the program would be canceled. To his surprise, marketing coordinator Michael Lopinto laughed and said, "Well, we could do something called the *Notcracker*!" Dean agreed.

1. PLÁCIDO DOMINGO ESCORTS PRINCIPAL CELLIST TAYLIS FERNANDEZ FROM THE STAGE, 2005 | 2. GUEST ARTIST MARSHA THOMPSON AS VIOLETTA ALONGSIDE STUDENT CAST MEMBERS IN *LA TRAVIATA*, 2005

1.

IN 2007, HELENE GOLDSTEIN MATHENY, THEN AN ADJUNCT HISTORY INSTRUCTOR AT SOUTHERN MISS, MADE A SPECIAL GIFT TO THE "FIVE IN FIVE" CAMPAIGN. MATHENY DONATED HER MOTHER'S PRIZED EIGHTEENTH-CENTURY GERMAN VIOLIN SO THAT IT COULD BE PLAYED IN HER MOTHER'S MEMORY BY A DESERVING STUDENT. BEULAH ROSLYN KUKLIN GOLDSTEIN, THE DAUGHTER OF RUSSIAN-JEWISH IMMIGRANTS WHO FLED TO THE UNITED STATES TO ESCAPE PERSECUTION IN THE FINAL DAYS OF THE CZARIST REGIME, HAD PLAYED THE VIOLIN UNTIL SHE WAS STRICKEN WITH MUSCULAR DYSTROPHY. SHE PASSED AWAY FROM THE DISEASE IN 1983.

The Notcracker turned out to be a stage production consisting of popular holiday music, sacred holiday music, comedy holiday music, and, as Dean says, "all the sections from Tchaikovsky's *Nutcracker* that anybody really wants to see, anyway." La Studio salvaged enough costumes to participate, and Ballet Mississippi helped with a few numbers. Mississippi composer and arranger Joseph Britain contributed a number of original holiday comedy pieces, Michael Lopinto wrote the script, and the program was held together by two guys dressed as old women who kept the audience in stitches.

The laughs were therapeutic, serving as momentary distractions from a pressing concern. How does one raise money for an already struggling arts organization after the worst hurricane in the history of the Gulf South region? It seemed impossible. Those who are professional fundraisers understand the different phases of major campaigns: the feasibility study, the silent phase, the public announcement and campaign. The orchestra did not enjoy that luxury. An immediate public effort was needed if Dean was going to continue developing a quality program. Because of this financial crisis, the "Five in Five" Scholarship Endowment Campaign was born.

The campaign had begun in Bennett Auditorium with a small group of supporters on October 29, 2005, just two months to the day after Katrina. Led by local arts patron Susan Thomson Rutland, the "Five in Five" Scholarship Committee would attempt to raise $5,000,000 over the following five years in order to protect and preserve the orchestra's future.

At the time of publication of this book, more than $2.5 million has been raised toward that goal, a figure far exceeding any arts fundraising initiative in the history of the university.

Despite the devastation of Katrina and distractions of his new fundraising responsibilities, Dean continued to improve the variety and quality of performances and strove to provide students with the best that he could offer in terms of literature, quality soloists, and performance opportunities. He created a class in orchestra administration in order to give students exposure to every aspect of orchestra management.

That spring's musical was Leonard Bernstein's *West Side Story*, directed by Rob Mulholland and presented with an all-student cast. Many in attendance described it as one of the best stage productions in the history of the university.

1. BEULAH ROSLYN KUKLIN GOLDSTEIN | 2. *WEST SIDE STORY*, 2006

2.

JAY, WHAT A GREAT TIME WE HAD WITH YOU AND THE SYMPHONY. THE LEVEL OF MUSICIANSHIP WAS AWESOME. EVERYONE WANTED TO PLAY MUSIC–THAT'S WHAT YOU DON'T SEE WITH SOME SYMPHONIES. WE'D LOVE TO COME BACK AND PLAY ANYTIME YOU'LL HAVE US.

-Ricky Skaggs

WHEN YOU TELL CLASSICALLY TRAINED ORCHESTRAL MUSICIANS THEY ARE ABOUT TO PLAY A BLUEGRASS CONCERT, THE REACTIONS ARE NOT ALWAYS POSITIVE. BUT WHEN THOSE CLASSICALLY TRAINED ORCHESTRAL MUSICIANS SIT DOWN TO REHEARSE AND PERFORM WITH ANY WORLD-CLASS ARTIST, IT NO LONGER MATTERS WHAT THE GENRE IS. THE RESPECT FOR TECHNIQUE, ABILITY, AND MUSICAL SKILL IS IMMEDIATE. THIS WAS THE CASE WHEN THE ORCHESTRA MUSICIANS PLAYED WITH RICKY SKAGGS AND KENTUCKY THUNDER.

-Jay Dean

In March, well-known bluegrass artist Ricky Skaggs performed with the Southern Mississippi Symphony Pops Orchestra in downtown Hattiesburg's Saenger Theater. Presented in cooperation with the Area Development Partnership (ADP), the concert was part of the first Arts Heritage Festival of South Mississippi.

In April, violinist Joshua Bell joined The University of Southern Mississippi Symphony for his premier orchestral performance in Mississippi, playing the Tchaikovsky Violin Concerto in D Major. Bell gave a stunning performance and left the audience and orchestra spellbound with his encore from the movie *The Red Violin*.

In May, the orchestra performed two "Link Up!" concerts for 1,500 elementary school students, part of a project that Dean developed with Carnegie Hall and the Mississippi Arts Commission.

1. RICKY SKAGGS | 2. JOSHUA BELL PERFORMS, 2006 | 3. "LINK UP!" CONCERT IN BENNETT AUDITORIUM, 2006

THE CARNEGIE HALL LINK UP! PROGRAM IS A NATIONAL EDUCATIONAL OUTREACH PROGRAM HOSTED ANNUALLY IN A NUMBER OF SELECTED STATES. IN 2005 THE MISSISSIPPI ARTS COMMISSION INVITED THE SOUTHERN MISSISSIPPI SYMPHONY TO REPRESENT OUR STATE IN THIS ENDEAVOR, WHICH ANNUALLY REACHES THOUSANDS OF MISSISSIPPI STUDENTS.

–Jay Dean

In October 2006, moved by the destruction inflicted by Hurricane Katrina and sympathetic to the orchestra's financial woes, Sir James and Lady Jeanne Galway returned to perform a benefit concert with the orchestra as part of the "Five in Five" campaign. The orchestra reciprocated with a small gesture of appreciation. In May 2000, at The Chelsea Flower Show in England, grower David Austin had presented and dedicated the "James Galway Rose." The orchestra purchased three of these roses and planted them in front of the university's impressive new Thad Cochran Center prior to the Galways' performance.

In November, the orchestra performed a concert featuring two of the most difficult and significant pieces in the orchestral repertoire. *The Planets* by Gustav Holst and the Brahms Second Piano Concerto were featured in a concert called "Out of This World," with pianist Kevin Kenner once again making a guest appearance.

In March 2007 the orchestra performed the Mississippi premiere of Stravinsky's *Le Sacre du Printemps (The Rite of Spring)*, perhaps the most significant piece of orchestral music of the twentieth century. It is a monumental work, the influence of which serious music cannot escape, and its 1913 premiere in Paris as a ballet resulted in the most infamous uproar in musical history. *Le Sacre du Printemps* is one of those rare and intimidating pieces that orchestral musicians universally aspire to perform at some point in their careers. Of the approximately 2,000 symphony orchestras in the United States, most do not program *Le Sacre du Printemps* because of its difficulty. For this performance, most of the applied instrumental faculty joined their students for a special side-by-side performance. It was an historic occasion.

Weeks later, Mississippi native and country music icon Charley Pride performed with the Southern Mississippi Symphony Pops Orchestra to conclude the ADP's second annual Arts Heritage Festival of South Mississippi.

There were two opera productions that year. In September the university celebrated the grand opening of the Thad Cochran Center with Rob Mulholland's production of Stephen Schwartz's *Godspell*, co-conducted by Kim Cargile and Darryl Harris. The two sold-out performances and two children's shows entertained more than 3,000 people. Bizet's *Carmen*, with Alan Mann as stage director and Jay Dean as music director, was the spring production, a second collaboration with Mississippi Opera. This combination of resources with Mississippi Opera proved valuable for Southern Miss students who benefited from the opportunity to perform beside and learn from professional singers, work with a professional director, and put professional credits on their résumés.

1.

1. THE ORCHESTRA PERFORMS GUSTAV HOLST'S *THE PLANETS*, 2006 | 2. *CARMEN*'S HILARY GINTHER AND CAST, INCLUDING NICHOLAS WEBB AS ZUNIGA, 2007

OPERA AMERICA, IN ITS SUMMER 2009 ISSUE, FEATURED SOUTHERN OPERA AND MUSICAL THEATRE, PRAISING THE PROGRAM FOR ITS SUCCESSFUL COLLABORATIONS WITH MISSISSIPPI OPERA.

2.

1.

The 2006-07 season concluded with an extravaganza at Reed Green Coliseum attended by 5,000 people. "United in Song" was a tribute to Southern Miss alumna Tena Clark, a Los Angeles songwriter and record producer who has composed songs for commercials, television shows, and major motion pictures in addition to writing songs for a number of popular artists. Five major recording artists and their entourages descended on Hattiesburg for an evening devoted to Tena Clark's music. Patti LaBelle, Dionne Warwick, Patty Austin, Ann Nesby, and Vesta Williams joined faculty member Maryann Kyle, student soloists Kayla Boyte, Kesia McSwain, and Tony O'Dell, the university choirs, and the symphony orchestra for one of the most electrifying evenings that Reed Green Coliseum has ever experienced.

2.

1. PATTI LABELLE PERFORMS AT "UNITED IN SONG," 2007 | 2. "UNITED IN SONG" PERFORMERS WITH TENA CLARK, 2007

THESE LIVELY LADIES BLAZED A TRAIL THROUGHOUT HATTIESBURG. DIONNE WARWICK HAD TO BE COAXED OUT OF HUDSON'S, ALMOST MISSING OUR REHEARSAL.

– Michael Lopinto
BASSOON, 1987-92, 2002-03
ORCHESTRA STAFF, 2002-09

EACH TIME THAT I REFLECT ON MY YEARS AT USM, I REALIZE THAT SOME OF THE MOST MEMORABLE MOMENTS OF MY ENTIRE CAREER TOOK PLACE THERE. TO BE ABLE TO HEAR, AND INTERACT WITH, SUCH WORLD-CLASS MUSICIANS AS YO-YO MA, ITZHAK PERLMAN, JAMES GALWAY, AND PLÁCIDO DOMINGO, TO NAME BUT A FEW, IS SOMETHING I WILL REMEMBER AND CHERISH FOR THE REST OF MY LIFE. WHEN I THINK ABOUT THE SIGNIFICANT EVENTS AT USM THAT REALLY STAND OUT IN MY MIND, THIS ORCHESTRA WAS ALWAYS PRESENT.

– Charles Elliott
DIRECTOR OF THE SCHOOL OF MUSIC, 1998-2008

THIS ORCHESTRA IS A BASTION OF MUSICAL TALENT, IS ACCLAIMED NATIONALLY, AND IS A TREASURE IN OUR FINE STATE OF MISSISSIPPI.

– Edward J. Langton
SYMPHONY PATRON

THE QUALITY OF THE ORCHESTRA AT SOUTHERN MISS ALLOWS THE CHORAL ACTIVITIES PROGRAM TO CONSIDER ANY CHORAL/ORCHESTRAL MAJOR WORK IT WANTS. THERE ARE ALMOST NO LIMITATIONS ON REPERTOIRE. THIS IS AN UNUSUAL AND ENVIABLE CIRCUMSTANCE.

–Gregory Fuller
DIRECTOR OF CHORAL ACTIVITIES
2000 - PRESENT

VISITHATTIESBURG ENJOYS A SPECIAL PARTNERSHIP WITH THE SOUTHERN MISS SYMPHONY BY SUPPORTING ITS EFFORTS TO BRING NOTABLE PERFORMERS FROM THE WORLD OF CLASSICAL MUSIC TO HATTIESBURG. THESE PERFORMANCES NOT ONLY THRILL RESIDENTS OF THE HATTIESBURG AREA, THEY ATTRACT VISITORS FROM THROUGHOUT THE SOUTHEAST. JAY DEAN HAS CREATED A TRULY UNIQUE ENTERTAINMENT PRODUCT WITH THESE COLLABORATIONS.

-Rick Taylor
EXECUTIVE DIRECTOR, HATTIESBURG TOURISM & CONVENTION COMMISSIONS

FALL 2007 OPENED WITH A TRULY UNIQUE EVENT AT HATTIESBURG'S LAKE TERRACE CONVENTION CENTER. DEAN HAD WANTED TO CREATE A SPECIAL AND FUN EVENT THAT WOULD BE MORE "FRIEND RAISER" THAN FUNDRAISER. LUCKILY FOR HIM, HE HAD THE GOOD FORTUNE OF HAVING AN EXTRAORDINARY EVENT DESIGNER ON THE ORCHESTRA STAFF.

Michael Lopinto, the symphony's marketing and educational outreach coordinator, was the creative genius who developed the concept for and design of the "Atlantis" Gala. Combining orchestral music with stunning aerial acrobats and an enchanting under-the-sea décor, "Atlantis" was named Event of the Year by *Convention South* magazine.

2.

WHEN I AGREED TO CHAIR THE "ATLANTIS" GALA, I HAD NO IDEA OF THE TALENTS OF MIKE LOPINTO AND WAS AFRAID I WOULD HAVE TO IMAGINE IT ALL. MY VISION, HOWEVER, WAS MINISCULE COMPARED TO WHAT MIKE CAME UP WITH! IT WAS A CHALLENGE PUTTING EVERYTHING TOGETHER DURING THE SUMMER WITH NO STUDENTS IN TOWN TO HELP, BUT WE HAD A FANTASTIC GROUP OF FRIENDS AT WORK. IN TWO DAYS WE TOTALLY TRANSFORMED THE CONVENTION CENTER. THREE HUNDRED GUESTS HAD A MARVELOUS TIME, AND WE RAISED ABOUT $17,000 FOR THE ORCHESTRA.

–Lynn McMullan
SYMPHONY PATRON

3.

I WAS INSPIRED TO DESIGN A SYMPHONY BROCHURE, AND LATER A CALENDAR, AFTER SEEING A PUBLICITY SHOT OF JOSHUA BELL. THE IMAGE WAS ACTIVE, WITH BELL SWEATING—NOT YOUR TYPICAL HEADSHOT. I CREATED OUR CALENDAR TO MATCH THE FEEL OF HIS PHOTO. I USED ALL STUDENT MODELS AND HOPED FOR A MARKETING PIECE THAT WOULD BE BOTH BEAUTIFUL AND FUNCTIONAL. I GUESS THE CALENDARS HAVE GOTTEN POPULAR OVER THE YEARS BECAUSE PATRONS START ASKING FOR THEM EACH SUMMER.

– Michael Lopinto
BASSOON, 1987-92, 2002-03
ORCHESTRA STAFF, 2002-09

1. "ATLANTIS" GALA, 2007 | 2. CIRQUE DE LA SYMPHONIE ACROBAT AT THE "ATLANTIS" GALA, 2007 | 3. COVER OF THE FIRST SYMPHONY ORCHESTRA CALENDAR, 2007

THE UNIVERSITY OF SOUTHERN MISSISSIPPI

presents

RENAISSANCE NEW ORLEANS

March 2, 2008 · 4 p.m.
St. Louis Cathedral

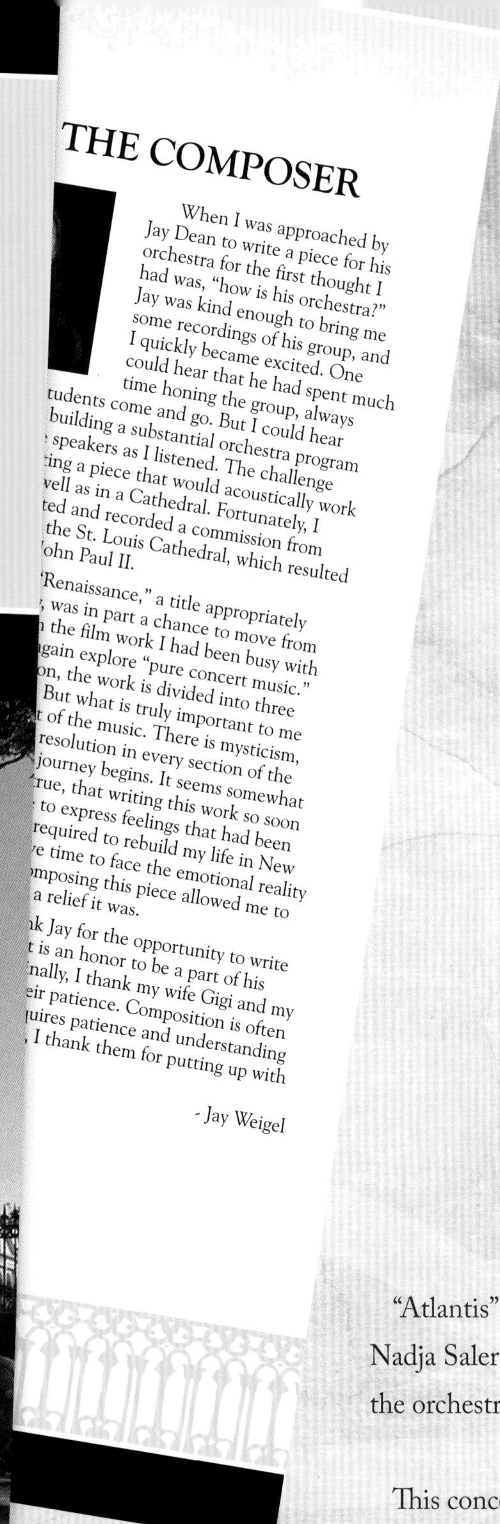

THE COMPOSER

When I was approached by Jay Dean to write a piece for his orchestra for the first thought I had was, "how is his orchestra?" Jay was kind enough to bring me some recordings of his group, and I quickly became excited. One could hear that he had spent much time honing the group, always ...tudents come and go. But I could hear ...building a substantial orchestra program ...speakers as I listened. The challenge ...ing a piece that would acoustically work ...vell as in a Cathedral. Fortunately, I ...ted and recorded a commission from ...the St. Louis Cathedral, which resulted ...ohn Paul II.

...'Renaissance," a title appropriately ..., was in part a chance to move from ...the film work I had been busy with ...gain explore "pure concert music." ...on, the work is divided into three ... But what is truly important to me ...t of the music. There is mysticism, ...resolution in every section of the ...journey begins. It seems somewhat ...rue, that writing this work so soon ...to express feelings that had been ...required to rebuild my life in New ...e time to face the emotional reality ...mposing this piece allowed me to ...a relief it was.

...k Jay for the opportunity to write ...t is an honor to be a part of his ...nally, I thank my wife Gigi and my ...eir patience. Composition is often ...uires patience and understanding ..., I thank them for putting up with

- Jay Weigel

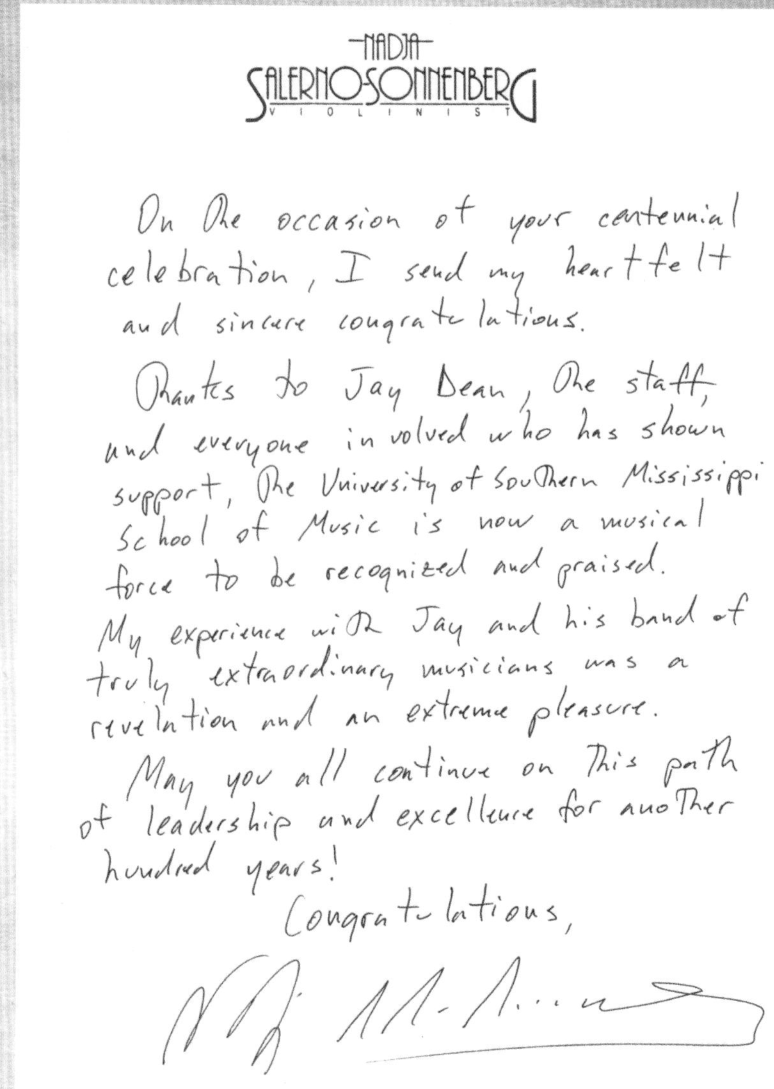

NADJA SALERNO-SONNENBERG
VIOLINIST

On the occasion of your centennial celebration, I send my heartfelt and sincere congratulations.

Thanks to Jay Dean, the staff, and everyone involved who has shown support, the University of Southern Mississippi School of Music is now a musical force to be recognized and praised.

My experience with Jay and his band of truly extraordinary musicians was a revelation and an extreme pleasure.

May you all continue on this path of leadership and excellence for another hundred years!

Congratulations,

1. SYMPHONY ORCHESTRA DURING *RENAISSANCE FOR NEW ORLEANS*, 2008

"Atlantis" was followed by the guest appearance of internationally renowned violinist Nadja Salerno Sonnenberg who performed with the orchestra in October, and in March, the orchestra traveled to New Orleans for a performance in the St. Louis Cathedral.

This concert had been suggested by Southern Miss alumnus and New Orleans attorney Ira Middleberg, a long-time friend of the orchestra, and Monsignor Crosby W. Kern, Rector of the Cathedral of St. Louis King of France. Feeling that such an occasion was worthy of a new piece being commissioned, Monsignor Kern recommended New Orleans composer Jay Weigel. Jay Dean and Mr. Weigel wanted to commemorate the rebuilding of New Orleans after Hurricane Katrina, so they decided to call the event *Renaissance for New Orleans*.

1.

IN DECIDING WHAT WORKS NEEDED TO BE ON THE PROGRAM, I FELT THAT WE SHOULD OPEN THE CONCERT WITH A REQUIEM IN MEMORY OF THOSE WHO LOST THEIR LIVES IN THE HURRICANE. I ALSO FELT THAT THE MUSIC SHOULD BE FRENCH OR SOMEHOW CONNECTED TO NEW ORLEANS, SO I CHOSE A RARELY PERFORMED REQUIEM BY NINETEENTH-CENTURY FRENCH COMPOSER CAMILLE SAINT-SAËNS. I ALSO WANTED A PIECE THAT REFLECTED THE CITY'S FESTIVE REPUTATION. THE OBVIOUS FESTIVE CHOICE WAS CLAUDE DEBUSSY'S *NOCTURNES*, THE MIDDLE MOVEMENT OF WHICH IS ENTITLED *FÈTE* OR *FESTIVAL*. THE FINAL WORK ON THE PROGRAM WAS, OF COURSE, THE WORLD PREMIERE OF THE COMMISSIONED WORK BY JAY WEIGEL, *RENAISSANCE FOR NEW ORLEANS*. COINCIDENTALLY, THERE WAS A CONNECTION WITH ALL THREE OF THE COMPOSERS TO THE CATHEDRAL ITSELF. JAY WEIGEL'S CONNECTION IS THROUGH HIS OTHER MUSICAL WORKS THAT HAVE PREMIERED THERE, AND THE CONNECTION TO DEBUSSY AND SAINT-SAËNS WAS THROUGH THEIR FORMER COMPOSITION TEACHER AT THE CONSERVATOIRE DE PARIS, ERNEST GIRAUD. MR. GIRAUD WAS BORN IN NEW ORLEANS AND BAPTIZED AT THE ST. LOUIS CATHEDRAL. IN LIGHT OF THAT, WE PROBABLY SHOULD HAVE CALLED THE CONCERT "THE FRENCH CONNECTION."

– Jay Dean

ONE OF MY GREATEST EXPERIENCES AS A PERFORMER WAS THE ORCHESTRA'S CONCERT IN NEW ORLEANS. AS CONCERTMASTER, I PLAYED A LONG AND SLOW SOLO WITH NO ACCOMPANIMENT. THE SAINT LOUIS CATHEDRAL WAS PACKED, AND FOR A FEW MOMENTS MY VIOLIN CREATED THE ONLY SOUND HEARD IN THE BUILDING. IT WAS AN EXCITING AND FRIGHTENING EXPERIENCE. I PLAYED FAIRLY WELL, SO AT THE END OF THE PIECE I STOOD PROUDLY, WAITING IN FRONT OF THE ORCHESTRA FOR THE ULTIMATE REWARD, THE CONDUCTOR'S ACKNOWLEDGMENT. AND DR. DEAN FORGOT TO SHAKE MY HAND! I THINK PERHAPS I'VE GOTTEN MORE ENJOYMENT FROM REMINDING HIM OF THIS THAN I WOULD HAVE FROM THE ACTUAL HANDSHAKE.

–Sasha Ferreira
VIOLIN, 2007-09

1.

March closed with the Grammy Award-winning Pointer Sisters performing with the Southern Mississippi Symphony Pops Orchestra at the ADP's Arts Heritage Festival of South Mississippi. The concert was a string of instantly recognizable hit songs including "I'm so Excited," "Jump (for my Love)," and "Neutron Dance."

In 2007, Jay Dean once again became artistic director of Southern Opera and Musical Theatre Company and produced Frank Loesser's *Guys and Dolls*, directed by Rob Mulholland and conducted by Kim Cargile, and Mozart's *Le Nozze di Figaro*, directed by Wendy Taucher in the program's third collaboration with Mississippi Opera.

2.

1. SCENE FROM *GUYS AND DOLLS*, 2007 | 2. KAYLA BOYTE AS ADELAIDE AND BRET LUNSFORD AS NATHAN IN *GUYS AND DOLLS*, 2007 | 3. THE POINTER SISTERS PERFORM, 2008

IT HAS ALWAYS BEEN MY GOAL TO PLAY A WIDE VARIETY OF MUSIC SO THAT THE STUDENTS LEARN TO PLAY IN ALL STYLES. THE SONGS THAT HAVE BEEN RECORDED BY THE POINTER SISTERS ARE AN IMPORTANT PART OF AMERICA'S MUSICAL FABRIC. THE STUDENTS IN THE ORCHESTRA COULDN'T BELIEVE THAT THEY WERE PERFORMING WITH THE ARTISTS THAT HAD RECORDED ALL OF THESE TUNES THAT THEY KNEW. BEFORE WE STARTED WORKING ON THIS CONCERT, MANY OF THE STUDENTS DID NOT KNOW WHO THE POINTER SISTERS WERE, BUT ONCE THEY HEARD THE MUSIC, IT WAS LIKE THEY HAD KNOWN THE POINTER SISTERS ALL THEIR LIVES.

– Jay Dean

3.

1.

1. FOUR SCENES FROM SOUTHERN OPERA AND MUSICAL THEATRE COMPANY'S THIRD COLLABORATION WITH MISSISSIPPI OPERA, *THE MARRIAGE OF FIGARO*, 2008

1.

JAY DEAN'S PERSISTENT INFLUENCE ON THE CULTURAL AND MUSICAL ENTERTAINMENT EVENTS IN THE STATE OF MISSISSIPPI IS THE STRONGEST I HAVE SEEN IN MY LIFETIME. WE ARE LUCKY TO HAVE HIM IN HATTIESBURG.

–Bobby Chain
FORMER MAYOR, CITY OF HATTIESBURG

2.

3.

Fall 2008 began with the "Shangri-La" Gala, brilliantly conceived, as the previous year's "Atlantis" had been, by Michael Lopinto. Combining orchestral music with the dazzling aerials of the Cirque de la Symphonie, the gala was enthusiastically enjoyed by its attendees, many of whom came dressed in kimonos for the occasion.

1. "SHANGRI-LA" GALA, 2008 | 2. "SHANGRI-LA" GALA DANCE FLOOR, 2008 | 3. CIRQUE DE LA SYMPHONIE ACROBATS PERFORM AT "SHANGRI-LA" GALA, 2008.

In October 2008, the symphony season opened with a performance by internationally renowned classical guitarist Manual Barrueco. That same month, it was announced by the Mississippi Arts Commission that The University of Southern Mississippi Symphony Orchestra would be a recipient of the 2009 Governor's Award for Excellence in the Arts.

The season's Holiday Choral Spectacular was a performance featuring Grammy-winning gospel artist Sandi Patty, the Hattiesburg Choral Union and Temple Baptist Church choirs. The concert, presented with the assistance of Forrest General Hospital, was attended by 2,600 people, many of whom had never been to an orchestra performance.

2008-09 marked the beginning of a new era for the opera program as, for the first time in eight years, a portion of the School of Music's state-allocated money was designated for the production of opera and musical theatre. This measure of support by Dean Denise Von Herrmann ensured the place of Southern Miss alongside other major schools of music. Jay Dean believes opera, of all the arts—music, theatre, dance, the visual arts, and literature—to be the ultimate art form, and is unaware of any serious school of classical music that is without an opera program.

1. JOHN GRISHAM, TANYA HAYES, CASSANDRA WILSON, ANDREW BUCCI, BEBE WOLFE, AND JAY DEAN RECEIVE 2009 GOVERNOR'S AWARDS FOR THE ARTS | 2. SANDI PATTY PERFORMS DURING THE HOLIDAY CHORAL SPECTACULAR, 2008 (PHOTO BY BRENT WALLACE)

COMMUNITY MEMBERS IN THE HATTIESBURG CHORAL UNION AND THE MEISTERSINGERS ENJOY OPPORTUNITIES TO SING WITH A SYMPHONY ORCHESTRA AND WITH OUTSTANDING PERFORMERS LIKE SANDI PATTY.

– Charles M. Thomas
SYMPHONY PATRON

2.

IT HAS BEEN MY PLEASURE TO SUPPORT THE SOUTHERN MISS SYMPHONY ORCHESTRA AND ITS DIRECTOR, DR. JAY DEAN. I KNOW OF NO OTHER UNIVERSITY ORCHESTRA IN THE COUNTRY THAT HAS A MORE GLOBAL MISSION AND PROVIDES A GREATER VARIETY OF ACTIVITIES FOR ITS CONSTITUENCIES. WHILE THE ORCHESTRA'S PRIMARY MISSION IS TO PROVIDE SCHOOL OF MUSIC STUDENTS A QUALITY ENSEMBLE EXPERIENCE PERFORMING STANDARD ORCHESTRAL LITERATURE, THIS ORCHESTRA ALSO PRESENTS THE HIGHEST QUALITY OF MUSICAL PERFORMANCES FOR PATRONS OF THE ARTS IN OUR REGION. UNDER DR. DEAN'S VISIONARY GUIDANCE, OUR ORCHESTRA MAINTAINS A STRONG COMMITMENT TO EDUCATIONAL OUTREACH, PERFORMING DOZENS OF EDUCATIONAL PROGRAMS IN THE PUBLIC SCHOOLS EACH YEAR. I CONGRATULATE DR. DEAN AND ALL THE FORMER SOUTHERN MISS SYMPHONY ORCHESTRA DIRECTORS FOR BUILDING THIS EXCEPTIONAL ORGANIZATION.

–Michael Miles
DIRECTOR OF THE SCHOOL OF MUSIC, 2008-PRESENT

THE UNIVERSITY OF SOUTHERN MISSISSIPPI SYMPHONY ORCHESTRA PROVIDES BOTH AN EXCELLENT TRAINING GROUND FOR TALENTED YOUNG MUSICIANS AND AN EXTRAORDINARY ARTISTIC AND CULTURAL OPPORTUNITY FOR THE LOCAL COMMUNITY AND BEYOND. WITH BLOCKBUSTER PERFORMANCES FEATURING PLÁCIDO DOMINGO AND RENÉE FLEMING AND INTIMATE, IMPACTFUL TEACHING-PERFORMANCES IN EVERY PUBLIC SCHOOL IN THE LOCAL COMMUNITY, OUR ORCHESTRA IS UNIQUE AMONG UNIVERSITY ENSEMBLES. THE OPPORTUNITIES AFFORDED OUR UNDERGRADUATE AND GRADUATE STUDENTS RIVAL THOSE FOUND IN ANY MUSIC SCHOOL, AND OUR UNIVERSITY CONSIDERS ITSELF FORTUNATE INDEED TO HAVE SUCH A TREASURE.

–Denise von Herrmann
DEAN, COLLEGE OF ARTS AND LETTERS, 2007-PRESENT

1.

The fall musical production, directed by Rob Mulholland, was Stephen Sondheim's *Company*, conducted by Tammy Mansfield, and spring's program was a workshop-style opera scenes production called *The Merry Widow (and other Stuff!)* which was directed and produced by Maryann Kyle with Jean Reis conducting.

The University of Southern Mississippi Symphony Orchestra and Jay Dean were presented the Governor's Award for Leadership in the Arts on the afternoon of February 26, 2009, in a Jackson ceremony. After receiving the prestigious award, Dean hurried home to Hattiesburg for "Operissimo," the evening's orchestra concert featuring operatic tenor David Lomelí. The season finale presented Carl Orff's secular cantata *Carmina Burana*, directed by Dr. Gregory Fuller, Director of Choral Activities, and featuring Fuller's Hattiesburg Choral Union.

The fall 2009 opera production was a double bill of Leoncavallo's tragic opera *I Pagliacci* and Puccini's "divine" comedy *Gianni Schicchi*. As this book goes to print, Southern Opera and Musical Theatre Company is preparing for its November 2010 production of Puccini's *La Bohème*, the company's contribution to the university's Centennial Celebration.

The 2009-10 orchestra season included memorable performances of Johannes Brahms's Symphony No. 1, Nicolai Rimsky-Korsakov's *Scheherazade*, and Robert Schumann's Cello Concerto with Joshua Roman, a talented young cellist from Seattle, though the pinnacle performance was delivered by the leading operatic soprano in the world today.

1. ALEX MINTON PLAYS PERCUSSION, 2009

RENÉE FLEMING'S INCREDIBLE ARTISTRY CAPTIVATED HER SPELLBOUND AUDIENCE. WITH A DIVERSE PROGRAM OF OPERA ARIAS WELL-KNOWN AND NOT WIDELY KNOWN, AS WELL AS SOME TOUCHING AMERICAN SONGS, MS. FLEMING DAZZLED. THE SPECIAL SOLD-OUT EVENING WAS MS. FLEMING'S DEBUT PERFORMANCE IN MISSISSIPPI AND A SPECIAL OCCASION FOR ALL IN ATTENDANCE, THE UNIVERSITY OF SOUTHERN MISSISSIPPI, AND THE STATE AS A WHOLE.

The final note from "Renée Fleming—Voice of the Century" still lingers beautifully and hauntingly as this publication goes to press. Beautifully, of course, because of the tone of that exquisitely trained voice, but hauntingly because of these troubling economic times.

1.

1. ORCHESTRA ON STAGE DURING THE RENÉE FLEMING CONCERT, 2010 | 2. RENÉE FLEMING PERFORMING ONSTAGE AT THALIA MARA HALL, 2010

ANY WORDS I MIGHT USE TO DESCRIBE THIS SOUTHERN MISS SYMPHONY PERFORMANCE WOULD SURELY FAIL TO DESCRIBE THE BRILLIANCE OF THE EVENING. ACCORDING TO ONE OF OUR FACULTY MEMBERS IN ATTENDANCE, THE EVENT WAS "INCANDESCENT." KUDOS TO DIRECTOR JAY DEAN AND HIS TALENTED STAFF FOR A MAGICAL NIGHT THAT WILL NOT BE SOON FORGOTTEN.

–Martha D. Saunders
PRESIDENT, THE UNIVERSITY OF SOUTHERN MISSISSIPPI

2.

DURING THIS CENTENNIAL YEAR AS WE HAVE OPPORTUNITY TO REVIEW AND ENJOY OUR RICH HISTORY, WE NOTE WITH PRIDE THAT SOUTHERN MISS HAS BEEN FORTUNATE TO HAVE HAD AN ORCHESTRA FOR ALMOST ALL OF ITS EXISTENCE. JAY DEAN TOOK THIS HERITAGE AND BUILT AN ORCHESTRA WHICH ITZHAK PERLMAN DESCRIBED AS "THE FINEST UNIVERSITY ORCHESTRA WITH WHICH I HAVE PLAYED." JAY'S VISION AND PERSISTENCE HAVE PRODUCED ORCHESTRAS WHICH HAVE MADE IT POSSIBLE FOR US TO HEAR VOCAL AND INSTRUMENTAL MUSIC AT ITS VERY BEST. HE HAS PERPLEXED HIS UNIVERSITY PRESIDENTS WITH AN INSATIABLE NEED FOR FUNDING, WHILE HE HAS ALSO PROVIDED THEM INDESCRIBABLE PRIDE AND JOY WITH THE SUPERB MUSIC HE HAS PRODUCED.

–Aubrey Lucas
PRESIDENT EMERITUS
THE UNIVERSITY OF SOUTHERN MISSISSIPPI

2.

3.

4.

1. RENÉE FLEMING TOASTS WITH STUDENT PERFORMERS, 2010 | 2. VIEW OF THE ORCHESTRA FROM THE BALCONY, 2010
3. ORCHESTRA, 2010 | 4. RENÉE FLEMING, 2010

This much loved orchestral program has—thanks to the extraordinary efforts of dedicated faculty, administration, students, and supporters—excelled against seemingly insurmountable odds. Under Jay Dean's leadership, it has achieved the unachievable. Dean jokes that in his twenty-two-year tenure, he has never been told by an administrator to expect a good year! His perseverance is amazing.

This chapter in the orchestra's history closes with Renée Fleming, the last musical superstar in a long line of artists to grace the stage with this extraordinary university orchestra. A new chapter, as yet unnamed, begins. But of one fact we may be certain: Jay Dean and The University of Southern Mississippi Symphony Orchestra will continue to present meaningful programs that change the lives of orchestra members and audiences alike. This orchestra not only *brings* the world to Mississippi, it *means* the world to Mississippi.

1. RENÉE FLEMING AND JAY DEAN, 2010 | 2. RENÉE FLEMING AND ORCHESTRA PERFORM IN THALIA MARA HALL, 2010

RENÉE FLEMING

June 10, 2010

Dr. Jay Dean
Director of Orchestral Activities
Southern Mississippi Symphony Orchestra
The University of Southern Mississippi
118 College Drive #5081
Hattiesburg, MS 39406-0001

Dear Jay,

What a joy it was to perform with the Southern Mississippi Symphony Orchestra in January 2010. Your orchestra and entire team serve as a model arts organization.

From the moment my father and I arrived, you, along with Dr. Mike Lopinto, showed us what Southern hospitality was all about. This warmth and professionalism from you and others continued throughout our stay.

Going back a full year, I marvel at your thoughtfulness in traveling to meet me to collaborate on the musical program which would make the experience a rich one for me, for the students, and for the audience. It was clear from the start that you were committed to providing the best possible experience for everyone.

And your orchestra – what a joy! The level of playing and dedication of the students clearly spoke to the great preparation and care that went into making it a memorable event. I must also mention that it's always very gratifying to perform to a sold-out house, and to that end, the marketing efforts were superb.

Thank you for inspiring these young people and for allowing me to experience your art and the care with which you prepared this event. I will always think fondly on my time with all of you. While you are "Bringing the World to Mississippi," you are also enriching those of us who visit.

With warmest regards,

Renée Fleming

2.

Major artists that have performed with The University of Southern Mississippi Symphony Orchestra since 1996

1.

2.

3.

4.

5.

6.

7.

8.

9.

10.

11.

12.

1. ITZHAK PERLMAN | 2. DENYCE GRAVES | 3. WILLIAM WARFIELD | 4. JOSHUA BELL | 5. YO-YO MA | 6 NADJA SALERNO-SONNENBERG | 7. PATTI LABELLE | 8. RICKY SKAGGS | 9. THE POINTER SISTERS | 10. CHARLEY PRIDE | 11. MANUEL BARRUECO 12. EDGAR MEYER | 13. RENÉE FLEMING | 14. JEAN-PIERRE RAMPAL | 15. ROBERTA PETERS | 16. SIR JAMES GALWAY 17. SANDI PATTY | 18. DOC SEVERINSEN | 19. PLÁCIDO DOMINGO | 20. RAY CHARLES | 21. DIONNE WARWICK 22. JOHN BROWNING | 23. CHRISTOPHER PARKENING | 24. ANA MARIA MARTINEZ

13.

14.

15.

16.

19.

17.

18.

20.

21.

22.

23.

24.

Bringing the World to
MISSISSIPPI

JAY DEAN
MUSIC DIRECTOR
Biography

Dr. Jay Dean has been the music director of The University of Southern Mississippi Symphony Orchestra since 1988. During his tenure, the orchestra has risen to enjoy an international reputation that enhances not only the university, but also the state and region. The symphony regularly performs to sold-out houses with audience members representing a diverse cross-section of the southeastern United States.

His recruiting efforts have turned the organization into a multinational conglomerate. Dean's vision literally has brought the world to Mississippi, including performances across the state with internationally known classical icons such as Plácido Domingo, Renée Fleming, Itzhak Perlman, Yo-Yo Ma, Sir James Galway, Joshua Bell, Denyce Graves, Nadja Salerno-Sonnenberg, Roberta Peters, John Browning, Manuel Barrueco, Christopher Parkening, and Edgar Meyer. He has also conducted concerts with major popular artists such as Doc Severinsen, The Pointer Sisters, Patti La Belle, Dionne Warwick, Patti Austin, Ricky Skaggs, and Sandi Patty. Dean has also guest conducted many orchestras in the United States, Latin America, and Europe.

The symphony is a study in international relations as students from over fifteen countries come together for one purpose – music. Dean's orchestra strives for professional excellence in performance and first-rate musical opportunities for its audience as well as its members. The musicians have opportunities to showcase their talents through various musical activities as well as interaction with businesses and organizations in the region. Members of the orchestra play with virtually every other orchestra within a 100-mile radius, serving not only the Hattiesburg community but also other communities in the state and beyond. Dean's skilled leadership has created unique partnerships that allow members of the orchestra to provide musical performances in every school and senior center in Hattiesburg.

In 2009, Jay Dean and The University of Southern Mississippi Symphony Orchestra received the Governor's Award for Leadership in the Arts. He is a musical ambassador for Mississippi. He does this for the community and state he loves, without thought of accolade or reward. His central mission is to provide life-changing experiences for his students and to improve the quality of life in the community and state of which he is a part.

PHOTO BY *THE HATTIESBURG AMERICAN*

THE ORCHESTRA HAS BEEN LED BY SEVERAL GUEST CONDUCTORS SINCE 1988:

Joe Barry Mullins 1989

Gunther Schuller .... 1989 (Seminar Workshop)

Cornelius Eberhardt 1990

Claire Fox Hillard 1992

Guillermo Salvador 1993

Christian Gouinguene 1994

Javier Garcia Vigil 1995

Doc Severinsen 1996

Leonard Slatkin .... 1998 (Seminar Workshop)

Louis Lane 1999

Fiora Contino 2001

Doc Severinsen 2001

Samuel Jones 2002

Plácido Domingo .... 2005 (Rehearsal)

Eugene Kohn 2005

Jean Reis 2007

Michael Miles 2008

Stefano Trasimeni 2008

SINCE 1988, THE FOLLOWING CHORAL DIRECTORS HAVE GUEST CONDUCTED CHORAL WORKS:

Gregory Fuller

Timothy Koch

William Weinert

Christopher White

CIRQUE DE LA SYMPHONIE ACROBATS BID THE AUDIENCE FAREWELL AT THE "ATLANTIS" GALA, 2007

Appendices

SCHOOL OF MUSIC FACULTY AND STAFF FROM 1912 TO PRESENT

DR. GARY WAYNE ADAM
ASSISTANT PROFESSOR OF MUSIC EDUCATION

DR. EDWIN ALEXANDER
PROFESSOR OF BASSOON AND THEORY

DR. PETER ALEXANDER
DEAN, COLLEGE OF THE ARTS

MR. CHRISTOPHER DALE ALFORD
ADJUNCT PROFESSOR OF JAZZ GUITAR

MR. CHARLES ALLEN
DIRECTOR OF BAGPIPE ENSEMBLE

MS. JOY ANN ALLEN
PROFESSOR OF VOICE AND PIANO

DR. PAUL DAVID ANDERSEN
PROFESSOR OF ORGAN AND MUSICOLOGY

MR. ALFRED ANDERSON
PROFESSOR OF VOICE AND OPERA

MS. TERRY ANDERSON
INSTRUCTOR OF PUBLIC SCHOOL MUSIC, GLEE CLUBS

MS. ELIZABETH M. ANGLIN
INSTRUCTOR OF FRENCH DICTION (DEPARTMENT OF FOREIGN LANGUAGES)

MS. MADELEEN ARMSTRONG
PROFESSOR OF VIOLIN, DIRECTOR OF ORCHESTRA

MR. HAROLD AVERY
DIRECTOR OF OPERA WORKSHOP AND ORCHESTRA CONDUCTOR

MR. GEORGE A. BAKER
DIRECTOR OF BANDS, PROFESSOR OF TRUMPET

DR. STEVEN SCOTT BAKER
ASSISTANT PROFESSOR OF THEORY

MS. JANE MCGUIRE BALLARD
INSTRUCTOR OF MUSIC

MR. JOHN BURRELL BASS III
RECORDING AGENT

MS. KATHERINE DONALD BATES
INSTRUCTOR OF MUSIC

MS. MARY THERESA POE BAYLISS
PROFESSOR OF PIANO

DR. R. DANIEL BEARD
ASSISTANT PROFESSOR OF THEORY

DR. CHRISTOPHER BECHTLER
ASSISTANT PROFESSOR OF MUSIC EDUCATION

MR. IRVING BECKER
PROFESSOR OF VIOLIN

MR. DENNIS EUGENE BEHM
PROFESSOR OF HORN

MS. FRANCES BENNER
PROFESSOR OF VOICE

MR. JOE BERRYMAN
DIRECTOR OF SUMMER CAMP, PERCUSSION

MR. HUGH BIRMINGHAM
PROFESSOR OF PIANO

DR. JOHN A. BIVINS
ASSOCIATE PROFESSOR OF BASSOON AND THEORY

MR. MARTIN L. BLACKWELDER
PROFESSOR OF VOICE

MR. AVON LEE BLAKELY
INSTRUCTOR OF MUSIC

MS. EDNA GENE BLETHEN
MUSIC EDUCATION

MS. MARY HELEN BLOSSOM
PROFESSOR OF CELLO

MS. MELISSA BOHL
OBOE INSTRUCTOR

MS. THELMA BOLIN
INSTRUCTOR OF MUSIC

MS. MARY JULIA BOLINGER
ASSISTANT PROFESSOR OF MUSIC

MR. RANDELL HOWARD BOSARGE
ADJUNCT PROFESSOR OF PERCUSSION

MS. RUTH IRENE BOXBERGER
MUSIC THEORY AND MUSIC THERAPY

MS. JANE E. BRADLEY
SCHOOL OF MUSIC SECRETARY

MS. POLLY BRADY
PROFESSOR OF PIANO

MS. MARGARET GRACE BRANDT
INSTRUCTOR OF MUSIC

MS. REBECCA BRITAIN
COORDINATOR OF GRADUATE AND UNDERGRADUATE STUDIES

MR. KARL BROCK
PROFESSOR OF OPERA

MR. THOMAS WALKER BROWN
ASSISTANT DIRECTOR OF CHORAL ACTIVITIES

MS. DORIS BRUCKNER-EDRINGTON DUNGAN
ASSISTANT PROFESSOR OF FLUTE

DR. JOSEPH L. BRUMBELOE
ASSOCIATE PROFESSOR OF THEORY

MR. ALEXANDRE BRUSSILOVSKY
VISITING PROFESSOR OF VIOLIN

DR. WILLIAM ALFRED BUFKIN
ORCHESTRA TICKET COORDINATOR

MS. JANICE M. BULLOCK
ORCHESTRA SECRETARY

MR. WILBUR BULLOCK
PIANO TECHNICIAN

DR. WILLIAM (BILL) BULLOCK
DIRECTOR OF CHORAL ACTIVITIES

MS. TOMI CHERYL BURNETTE
ACCOUNTS SPECIALIST

MR. DEWEY W. CAMP
INSTRUCTOR OF MUSIC

DR. AUGUST NORBERT CARNOVALE
PROFESSOR OF TRUMPET AND MUSIC INDUSTRY, CHAIR OF MUSIC EDUCATION

MS. DENISE MONICA CASEY
BAND SECRETARY

MR. THOMAS CAVENDISH
PROFESSOR OF VOICE

MR. DUCHEIN CAZEDESSUS
PROFESSOR OF PIANO

MS. KAYE S. CHAMBLESS
DIRECTOR, COMMUNITY ARTS SCHOOL

MS. MARY CHUNG
COORDINATOR OF PIANO ACCOMPANISTS

DR. NICHOLAS A. CIRALDO
ASSISTANT PROFESSOR OF GUITAR

DR. PETER LOUIS CIURCZAK
DIRECTOR, SCHOOL OF MUSIC

DR. WILLIAM GERALD CLAXTON
VISITING ASSISTANT PROFESSOR OF VOICE

MS. LINDA CLINTON
PROFESSOR OF ORGAN

MR. EARL COMPTON
PROFESSOR OF VOICE

F. LUNDLE CONBOY
INSTRUCTOR OF MUSIC

MS. EDNA CONSTABLE
INSTRUCTOR OF MUSIC

MR. GEORGE COOPER
PROFESSOR OF TUBA

MS. MARGARET CORBIN
INSTRUCTOR OF VOICE

MR. ALLAN EUGENE COX
PROFESSOR OF TRUMPET

MR. FRANK CROCKETT
PROFESSOR OF STRINGS

MR. HARRIS CROHN
PROFESSOR OF PIANO

MS. BONITA P'POOL CROWE
PROFESSOR OF PIANO

MS. ALISON J. CRUMPTON
MARKETING AND PUBLIC RELATIONS COORDINATOR

MS. JULIA CUDDEBACK
DIRECTOR OF MUSIC DEPARTMENT, INSTRUCTOR IN SCHOOL MUSIC,GLEE CLUB

MR. STARLING CUMBERWORTH
PROFESSOR OF THEORY, MUSIC EDUCATION AND VIOLIN

MS. MARTHA (MARTY) CUSHMAN
PROFESSOR OF VOICE

DR. ANITA P. DAVIS
ASSOCIATE PROFESSOR OF MUSIC EDUCATION

DR. KIMBERLEY MICHELE DAVIS
ASSOCIATE PROFESSOR OF VOICE

MR. MICKEY DAVIS
ADJUNCT PROFESSOR OF VIOLA

DR. JACK LEE (JAY) DEAN
DIRECTOR OF ORCHESTRAL ACTIVITIES

DR. KENNETH NORWOOD (BUDDY) DEANS
PROFESSOR OF SAXOPHONE

MR. JOHN PAUL DECHIARO
PROFESSOR OF GUITAR

MS. FORREST DELANO
VOICE AND VOCAL PEDAGOGY

DR. PERRY DENNIS
PROFESSOR OF MUSIC EDUCATION

MS. DOROTHY DEVANS
INSTRUCTOR OF VOICE

MR. SAMUEL A. DI BONAVENTURA
PROFESSOR OF THEORY AND COMPOSITION AND VIOLIN

MR. ROGER DI GUILIAN
PROFESSOR OF VIOLIN

DR. JOHN ROBERT DONOHUE
PROFESSOR OF THEORY

DR. JACK DONOVAN
CHORAL CONDUCTOR

MR. ALAN H. DRAKE
DIRECTOR OF WIND ENSEMBLE AND PROFESSOR OF CLARINET

MR. TOM DUNGAN
RECORDING ENGINEER AND DEPT. ASSISTANT

MS. JEAN EASON
PROFESSOR OF THEORY, PIANO, AND HARP

MS. KATHERINE MARIE EIDE
PROFESSOR OF CELLO, THEORY, AND MUSIC EDUCATION

DR. CHARLES A. ELLIOTT
DIRECTOR, SCHOOL OF MUSIC AND PROFESSOR OF MUSIC EDUCATION

MR. REX ENDERLIN
PROFESSOR OF TROMBONE

DR. CSABA ERDELYI
VISITING INSTRUCTOR OF VIOLA

MR. IGOR FEDOTOV
ASSISTANT PROFESSOR OF VIOLA

MS. MARGARET FIRTH
ADMINISTRATIVE ASSISTANT

MR. LAWRENCE V. FISHER
PROFESSOR OF VIOLIN, HEAD OF STRINGS, SYMPHONY ORCHESTRA

MR. HUBERT FITCH
PROFESSOR OF PIANO

MR. JOHN C. FLANERY
ASSISTANT DIRECTOR OF CHORAL ACTIVITIES

MR. GEORGE R. FLEXMAN
PROFESSOR OF CELLO

DR. DAVID FOLTZ
DIRECTOR OF CHORAL ACTIVITIES,CHAIR OF MUSIC

MS. BARBARA FORTENBERRY
ADJUNCT PIANO FACULTY

MS. LISA DENISE FORTNER
SCHOOL OF MUSIC SECRETARY

MS. LINDA P. FOSHEE
ADMINISTRATIVE SECRETARY

MR. ANGELO FRASCARELLI
PROFESSOR OF VIOLIN/ ORCHESTRA

MS. LILAJANE FRASCARELLI
STRING INSTRUCTOR

MS. CECILIA C. FRASCHILLO
ADJUNCT FACULTY MUSIC EDUCATION

DR. THOMAS VINCENT FRASCHILLO
DIRECTOR OF BANDS

MR. AUDIE F. FUGITT
INSTRUCTOR OF BAND, CORNET, FRENCH HORN, AND TROMBONE

DR. GREGORY ALAN FULLER
DIRECTOR OF CHORAL ACTIVITIES

DR. VALERIE M. FULLER
COORDINATOR OF GRADUATE STUDIES

MS. JANICE FUQUAY
PROFESSOR OF PIANO

MS. LINDA GANNETT
ADJUNCT PROFESSOR OF BASS

MS. MARY LEILA GARDNER
INSTRUCTOR OF MUSIC

MS. LINNIE M. GARNER
FINANCIAL ASSISTANT AND GRANT SPECIALIST FOR ORCHESTRA

MR. DOUGLAS RUDOLPH GATLIN
ADJUNCT VOICE FACULTY

DR. JOHN GAY
PROFESSOR OF VIOLIN

MS. ANNA E. GEORGE
INSTRUCTOR EMERITUS IN MUSIC

MR. NEWTS GILBEAU
PROFESSOR OF VIOLA

MS. MARGARET GILLARD
PROFESSOR OF VIOLIN, VIOLA, CELLO, BASS, ORCHESTRA

MS. SUE MCGEEHEE GILVIN
PROFESSOR OF VOICE

DR. CHRISTOPHER J. GOERTZEN
PROFESSOR OF MUSICOLOGY

DR. VALERIE W. GOERTZEN
ADJUNCT ASSOCIATE PROFESSOR OF MUSICOLOGY AND COORDINATOR OF GRADUATE STUDIES

MS. SANDRA GOLDBERG
PROFESSOR OF VIOLIN

MR. LEWIS GORDON
CHORAL CONDUCTOR

DR. ALBERT EDWARD GOWER
PROFESSOR OF THEORY,COMPOSITION, AND SAXOPHONE

DR. WILLIAM T. GOWER
DIRECTOR OF ORCHESTRAL ACTIVITIES, PROFESSOR OF WOODWINDS, AND CHAIR OF MUSIC EDUCATION

MS. MICHELE LEIGH GRAYBEAL
ORCHESTRA SECRETARY

MS. LINDA GREEN
PROFESSOR OF VOICE

MS. MARY GREEN
PROFESSOR OF HARP AND PIANO

MR. KARL GREENSHIELDS
PROFESSOR OF VIOLIN

MR. YENOIN GUIBBORY
PROFESSOR OF VIOLIN

DR. LAWRENCE STEPHEN GWOZDZ
PROFESSOR OF SAXOPHONE

DR. EDWARD M. HAFER
ASSISTANT PROFESSOR OF MUSICOLOGY

MS. FRANCES ALTA HALLOCK
DIRECTOR OF GLEE CLUBS AND QUARTETTE

MR. ROBERT CURTIS HAMLET
CHORAL CONDUCTOR

MR. JAMES HANSHUMAKER
PROFESSOR OF MUSIC EDUCATION AND ORCHESTRA CONDUCTOR

MR. RODERICK HARKINS
DIRECTOR OF MARCHING BAND

MS. MARY STUART HARMON
PROFESSOR OF PIANO

MS. KATHRYN HARNEY
PROFESSOR OF VOICE

DR. STANLEY HAUER
PROFESSOR OF OPERA HISTORY (DEPARTMENT OF ENGLISH)

MR. JERRIE HAYNIE
PROFESSOR OF HORN

MS. PATRICIA RUTH MCCOY HAYS
PROFESSOR OF VOICE

DR. ROBERT D. HAYS
PROFESSOR OF MUSIC THEORY, TROMBONE, AND ASSISTANT DIRECTOR OF BANDS

DR. CHARLES HEIDEN
PROFESSOR OF VIOLIN

MS. JEANNE HENDERSON
PROFESSOR OF PIANO

DR. J. TAYLOR HIGHTOWER
ASSISTANT PROFESSOR OF VOICE

MS. KERRIN D. HIGHTOWER
ADJUNCT VOICE FACULTY

MS. BETTY JEAN HILL
VOICE AND MUSICOLOGY

MR. MARSHALL HILL
DIRECTOR OF CHORAL ACTIVITIES

MR. ROGER HARVEY HILL
ASSOCIATE PROFESSOR OF PIANO

MR. WALTER HINDS
PROFESSOR OF VOICE

MS. DAISY E. HINKLE
ASSISTANT PROFESSOR OF MUSIC

DR. MARTA JEAN HOFACRE
PROFESSOR OF TROMBONE

DR. JONATHAN HOLDEN
ASSISTANT PROFESSOR OF CLARINET

MR. DAVID BLAIR HOLLEY
PROFESSOR OF VOICE AND OPERA

MS. ANNE HOLLIDAY
PROFESSOR OF PIANO

DR. SHERMAN HONG
PROFESSOR OF PERCUSSION

DR. REGINALD HOUZE
ASSISTANT TO THE DIRECTOR OF BANDS

MR. JOSEPH HUCK
CHAIR OF PIANO DIVISION

MS. JEAN HUDSON
PROFESSOR OF VIOLIN

MR. MILTON LEANDER (LEE) HUDSON
ADJUNCT FACULTY

MS. EVANGELINE HUR
PROFESSOR OF VOICE

MR. FARLEY K. HUTCHINS
PROFESSOR OF MUSICOLOGY AND ORGAN

MR. GEORGE IMBRAGULIO
PROFESSOR OF PIANO

MS. ARLENE K. INGRAFFIA
BAND AND SCHOOL OF MUSIC SECRETARY

MS. MARJORIE A. RASCHE JACKSON
PROFESSOR OF ORGAN

MS. ALTHEA L. JEROME
ASSISTANT PROFESSOR OF MUSIC EDUCATION AND VOICE

MR. RAOUL FRANK HOWARD JEROME
CHAIR OF THEORY, ASSOCIATE PROFESSOR OF JAZZ STUDIES AND TROMBONE

MR. MICHAEL JOHNSON
GUITAR AND DOUBLE BASS

MS. VICTORIA JOHNSON
ADJUNCT PROFESSOR OF PIANO

DR. LEROY JOHNSTON
PROFESSOR OF CLARINET

MR. WARREN A. JOSEPH
CHORAL CONDUCTOR

MS. MELINDA B. JUNIPER
ORCHESTRA SECRETARY

MS. FLORENCE GOODMAN KEARNS
PROFESSOR OF CELLO

MS. JEANNE KECK
PROFESSOR OF PIANO AND THEORY

MR. WILLIAM KECK
PROFESSOR OF TUBA

DR. HOWARD T. KEEVER
ADJUNCT THEORY FACULTY

MR. WILLIAM MORGAN KELLER
VIOLIN, VIOLA, WIND INSTRUMENTS, AND BAND DIRECTOR

DR. DANIEL PATRICK KELLY
ASSISTANT PROFESSOR OF TRUMPET

MS. EILEEN A. KELLY
INSTRUCTOR OF MUSIC

MS. LINDA J. KELLY
BAND SECRETARY

MS. GOOYWON EILISSA KIM
PROFESSOR OF VOICE

DR. MICHAEL W. KIMBER
PROFESSOR OF VIOLA

MS. ALICE BENITA KING
SCHOOL OF MUSIC SECRETARY

MR. NOAH KNEPPER
ORCHESTRA CONDUCTOR

DR. TIMOTHY KOCH
DIRECTOR OF CHORAL ACTIVITIES

MS. VIVIAN M. KUHL
SUPERVISOR OF MUSIC EDUCATION

MS.BETTY JANE KUHLMAN
PROFESSOR OF VIOLIN

DR. MARYANN KYLE
ASSOCIATE PROFESSOR OF VOICE

MR. W. REESE LAND
VISITING ASSISTANT PROFESSOR OF TRUMPET

MR. GERALD LANDON
PROFESSOR OF VOICE

MS. SHARON ELAINE LEBSACK
PROFESSOR OF FLUTE

DR. LYNN LEDBETTER
PROFESSOR OF VIOLIN

DR. HSIAOPEI LEE
ASSISTANT PROFESSOR OF VIOLA

MS. ELEANOR LEEK
ASSOCIATE PROFESSOR OF MUSIC AND CELLO

DR. PETER LEMONDS
PROFESSOR OF CELLO

DR. LOIS ANN LEVENTHAL
PROFESSOR OF PIANO

DR. PAUL S. LINDEN
ASSISTANT PROFESSOR OF ENTERTAINMENT INDUSTRY

MS.ROBIN SWEATT LONGRE
PROFESSOR OF VOICE

MS. KATHERINE EIDE LONGYEAR
PROFESSOR OF CELLO AND THEORY

DR. REY MORGAN LONGYEAR
PROFESSOR OF MUSICOLOGY

MS. BLANCHE LOPER
INSTRUCTOR OF PIANO

MS. MARGUERITE LOPER
PROFESSOR OF VIOLIN

DR. JOHN MICHAEL LOPINTO JR.
MARKETING AND EDUCATIONAL OUTREACH COORDINATOR FOR ORCHESTRA

MR. DALE KELLY LOVE
MARCHING BAND DIRECTOR

DR. HEIDI A. LUCAS
ASSISTANT PROFESSOR OF HORN

DR. HAROLD LUCE
DEAN, COLLEGE OF THE ARTS AND PROFESSOR OF MUSIC THEORY

DR. JERRIE CADEK LUCKTENBERG
PROFESSOR OF VIOLIN AND VIOLA

MR. JACK LAWRENCE LYALL
PROFESSOR OF MUSIC EDUCATION/CHORAL ACTIVITIES

DR. RAYMOND M. LYNCH
PROFESSOR OF WOODWINDS (OBOE), THEORY, AND MUSICOLOGY

DR. MARCOS MACHADO
ASSISTANT PROFESSOR OF BASS

MR. SCOTT MACMORRAN
PROFESSOR OF TUBA

MR. THEODORE MADSEN
PROFESSOR OF VIOLIN

DR. PATRICIA ANN MALONE
PROFESSOR OF OBOE AND THEORY

DR. RAYMOND MANNONI
DIRECTOR OF BANDS, CHAIRMAN OF MUSIC, AND FOUNDING ARTS DEAN

MS. SHIRLEY MARCELLUS
PROFESSOR OF THEORY, VOICE, AND MUSIC EDUCATION

DR. FRANK EARL MARSH
DIRECTOR, SCHOOL OF MUSIC

MR. ROBERT MASON
PROFESSOR OF CELLO

DR. BARBARA MATHIS
ADJUNCT VOICE FACULTY

DR. WILLIAM MAYSON
VISITING PROFESSOR OF TUBA

MR. RONALD MCCREERY
DIRECTOR, SCHOOL OF MUSIC, CELLO, ORCHESTRA DIRECTOR

MS. TARA P. MCCRINK-BURCHAM
ALTERNATIVE LEARNING COORDINATOR

MS. HELEN JANET MCDONALD
PROFESSOR OF VIOLIN

MR. MARK W. MCKEAN
ASSISTANT PROFESSOR OF MUSIC INDUSTRY

MS. CONSTANCE L. MCKOY
VISITING ASSISTANT PROFESSOR

MR. ROBERT MCNALLY
PROFESSOR OF VIOLIN

MS. ELIZABETH MEAD
VOICE AND MUSICOLOGY

MR. HARVEY MEIER
MUSIC EDUCATION

MRS. JANICE MESROBIAN
ADJUNCT PIANO

MR. ROBERT MESROBIAN
PROFESSOR OF VOICE AND OPERA

MS. RUTH METCALFE
PROFESSOR OF VOICE

DR. DANILO MEZZADRI
ASSISTANT PROFESSOR OF FLUTE

DR. MICHAEL ALAN MILES
DIRECTOR, SCHOOL OF MUSIC

MS. ELIZABETH DRUKEN MILLER
INSTRUCTOR OF VOICE

MR. JOSHUA MISSAL
PROFESSOR OF THEORY/ COMPOSITION, VIOLA, ORCHESTRA

MS. MARGARET MITCHELL
INSTRUCTOR OF PIANO

MS. PATRICIA ANNE MITCHELL
DIRECTOR OF AUXILIARY UNITS-BAND

DR. ELIZABETH W. MOAK
ASSOCIATE PROFESSOR OF PIANO

MR. FRANCIS L. (FRANK) MONACHINO
OPERA DIRECTOR

DR. WILLIAM J. MOODY
DIRECTOR OF BANDS

MS. JUANITA MOORE
PROFESSOR OF VOICE

MR. MARK (MICKY) MOORE
PROFESSOR OF TUBA

MR. WILBUR LAFE MORELAND
PROFESSOR OF CLARINET

MS. LEAH MORRIS
INSTRUCTOR IN PIANO AND HARMONY

MS. RUTH MORROW
PROFESSOR OF VIOLA

DR. STEVEN R. MOSER
ASSOCIATE DEAN AND PROFESSOR OF MUSIC

DR. JOE BARRY MULLINS
DIRECTOR OF BANDS

DR. DONALD T. MUNSELL
PROFESSOR OF BASSOON AND MUSICOLOGY

DR. JAMES IKE NAIL
DIRECTOR OF BANDS

DR. PETER NEUBERT
VISITING ASSISTANT PROFESSOR OF VIOLA

DR. KARL NEUMANN
PROFESSOR OF CELLO AND MUSICOLOGY

DR. CLINTON C. NICHOLS
ADJUNCT PROFESSOR OF VOICE

DR. AMBER SHAY NICHOLSON
ASSISTANT PROFESSOR OF PIANO

MR. MARION NOWAKOWSKI
PROFESSOR OF VOICE

DR. GREGORY WAYNE OAKES
ASSISTANT PROFESSOR OF CLARINET

MS. MARY ANNE ODEN
INSTRUCTOR OF PIANO

DR. WILLIAM ODOM
PROFESSOR OF GERMAN DICTION (DEPARTMENT OF FOREIGN LANGUAGES)

MS. MILDRED OGDEN
PROFESSOR OF VIOLIN

MR. KENNETH DOAN ORTLEPP
INSTRUCTOR OF HORN

DR. WALTER OSADCHUK
PROFESSOR OF CELLO AND BASS

MR. VERNON OVERMYER
PROFESSOR OF PIANO

MR. JOHN EDWARD OWEN
PROFESSOR OF TUBA

MR. JOHN W. PALENSKY
ADJUNCT INSTRUCTOR OF BASS

MR. LAWRENCE M. PANELLA
ASSOCIATE PROFESSOR OF JAZZ STUDIES

MS. SHERRY ALETA PARKER
BUDGET AND CURRICULUM COORDINATOR

MS. PATRICIA PARKER-WALKER
PROFESSOR OF PIANO AND THEORY

MR. LLOYD PATTEN
PROFESSOR AND HEAD OF VOICE

MS. NANCY PAYETTE
PROFESSOR OF CELLO

MR. JUAN CARLOS PENA
VISITING ASSISTANT PROFESSOR OF BASS

DR. ANNA PENNINGTON
ASSISTANT PROFESSOR OF OBOE AND THEORY

MR. EDISON C. PERRY
PROFESSOR OF STRINGS

DR. RICHARD H. PERRY
ASSOCIATE PROFESSOR OF TUBA

MS. MARY LILLIAN PETERS
PROFESSOR OF PIANO

MR. JAMES BYRON PETERSON
WIND INSTRUMENTS AND MUSIC EDUCATION

MS. MILDRED PHELPS
PROFESSOR OF MUSIC EDUCATION

MR. ROGER PHELPS
PROFESSOR OF MUSIC EDUCATION, ORCHESTRA CONDUCTOR

MR. FELIX A. PONZIANI
PROFESSOR OF CONDUCTING AND DIRECTOR OF YOUTH ORCHESTRA

DR. GOMER JEFFERY POUND
PROFESSOR OF INSTRUMENTAL MUSIC EDUCATION/CLARINET

DR. ERIC RICHARD PRENSHAW
PROFESSOR OF MUSIC EDUCATION

DR. WILLIAM PRESSER
PROFESSOR OF THEORY AND COMPOSITION,VIOLA, AND ORCHESTRA CONDUCTOR

MS. JESSICA L. PRUTZ
SCHOOL OF MUSIC SECRETARY

SCHOOL OF MUSIC FACULTY AND STAFF, CONTINUED

MS. KAREN QUARNSTROM
DIRECTOR OF AUXILIARY UNITS FOR BAND

DR. DANA OUGH RAGSDALE
PROFESSOR OF PIANO AND PERFORMANCE PRACTICE

MR. VERNON RAINES
DIRECTOR OF ORCHESTRAL ACTIVITIES

MR. BENNETT RANDMAN
ADJUNCT PROFESSOR OF CELLO

MS. HAZEL HORTON READ
INSTRUCTOR OF VIOLIN AND CONDUCTOR OF ORCHESTRA

DR. STEPHEN C. REDFIELD
ASSOCIATE PROFESSOR OF VIOLIN

MS. VERA D. REEVE
SUPERVISOR OF MUSIC EDUCATION

MR. CLIFFORD REIMS
PROFESSOR OF VOICE/ DIRECTOR OF OPERA WORKSHOP

MS. ALISON M. REYNOLDS
ASSOCIATE PROFESSOR OF MUSIC EDUCATION

MR. SAMUEL PATTON RICE
ASSISTANT PROFESSOR OF VOICE

MS. MARGARET MARY RICKERD
PROFESSOR OF ORGAN AND CHURCH MUSIC

MS. LISA ROBERTSON
PROFESSOR OF VIOLIN

MR. DAREN M. ROBBINS
VISITING ASSISTANT PROFESSOR OF HORN

MR. CARL (RUSTY) ROLISON
FACILITIES MANAGER

MR. GERALD (JERRY) ROSENBAUM
PROFESSOR OF VIOLIN

MR. ROBERT P. ROUBOS
PROFESSOR OF ORGAN

MS. SUSAN RUGGIERO-MEZZADRI
ADJUNCT VOICE FACULTY AND COORDINATOR OF GRADUATE STUDIES

MS. BELINDA S. RUNNELS
SECRETARY FOR CHORAL ACTIVITIES

DR. ALEXANDER RUSSAKOVSKY
ASSOCIATE PROFESSOR OF CELLO

MR. THEODORE C. RUSSELL
DIRECTOR OF OPERA WORKSHOP

DR. DOUGLAS M. RUST
ASSISTANT PROFESSOR OF THEORY

DR. GILBERT T. SAETRE
PROFESSOR OF MUSIC EDUCATION AND BAND DIRECTOR

DR. RICHARD XAVIER SANCHEZ
ASSOCIATE PROFESSOR OF MUSICOLOGY

DR. THERESA SANCHEZ
ADJUNCT PROFESSOR OF PIANO

MS. HELEN SMITH SANDLER
INSTRUCTOR OF MUSIC

MS. LYNN SCHUBERT
PROFESSOR OF FLUTE

MR. MOHAMAD S. SCHUMAN
ASSISTANT PROFESSOR AND ASSOCIATE DIRECTOR OF BANDS

MR. SAMUEL H. SCOTT
PROFESSOR OF CLARINET, INSTRUMENTAL MUSIC

DR. JENNIFER S. SHANK
ASSOCIATE PROFESSOR OF MUSIC EDUCATION AND ASSOCIATE DIRECTOR OF THE SCHOOL OF MUSIC

MR. JAMES SHANNON
INSTRUMENTAL MUSIC, VIOLINIST, FOUNDER/ CONDUCTOR OF GULF COAST SYMPHONY

MS. LUCRETIA SHAW
PROFESSOR OF VOICE

DR. ROLLAND SHAW
DIRECTOR OF CHORAL ACTIVITIES

MR. IVAN SHOW
PROFESSOR OF EUPHONIUM

MS. LUCILE SKINNER
INSTRUCTOR OF PIANO AND HARMONY, HEAD OF MUSIC DEPARTMENT

MS. THELMA WRIGHT SKIPWORTH
INSTRUCTOR OF MUSIC AND PIANO

MS. KATIE ARNOLD SMITH
PROFESSOR OF VIOLIN

DR. LARRY DEARMAN SMITH
PROFESSOR OF VOICE

MS. MARIA LYNN SMITH
SECRETARY FOR ORCHESTRAL ACTIVITIES

MS. TRACY MICHELLE OTT SMITH
DIRECTOR OF AUXILIARY UNITS FOR BANDS

MR. BURDETTE W. SMYTHE
PROFESSOR OF HORN

MS. ETHEL LYNDA SNODGRASS
PROFESSOR OF PIANO AND MUSIC HISTORY

DR. DONALD BRADLEY SNOW
POST-DOCTORAL MARCHING BAND DIRECTOR

MR. KLAUSS SPEER
PROFESSOR OF ORGAN AND HARPSICHORD

MS. EVA SPELLBRING
INSTRUCTOR OF MUSIC

MS.BERNICE SPRATLER
VOICE AND MUSIC APPRECIATION

DR. JAMES ERNEST STANDLAND
INSTRUCTOR OF MUSIC/BANDS

MS. REBEKAH STARK-JOHNSON
PROFESSOR OF CELLO

MR. RALPH MARTIN STEFFEN
VISITING ASSISTANT PROFESSOR

MR. THOMAS G. STEIN
ASSOCIATE PROFESSOR OF TUBA

DR. LEONARD STOCKER
ASSOCIATE CONDUCTOR OPERA WORKSHOP/HEAD OF VOICE

MS. SUSAN STRALEY
PROFESSOR OF VOICE

DR. MARY ANN STRINGER
ASSOCIATE PROFESSOR OF PIANO/ INTERIM DEAN

MS. NELLIE STUART
PROFESSOR OF VOICE

MS. STEPHANIE BARBARA SULINSKI
PROFESSOR OF CELLO AND THEORY

MS. VELMA TALMADGE
PROFESSOR OF VOICE

MS. MATTIE SUE TARRY
INSTRUCTOR OF MUSIC

MS. LORENE THAMES
PROFESSOR OF PIANO

MS. ELIZABETH CAROL THOMAS
ORGAN AND MUSIC LITERATURE

DR. NAYMOND BOICE THOMAS
PROFESSOR OF VOICE

DR. MARTHA R. TISDALE
ASSISTANT PROFESSOR OF PIANO AND THEORY

MS. KATHRYN TOBEY
MUSIC EDUCATION/VOICE

MS. LORENA TOMSON
SCHOOL MUSIC, ORCHESTRA CONDUCTOR, PIANO

DR. CAROLYN MARIE TREYBIG
COORDINATOR OF GRADUATE STUDIES

DR. JOEL A. TREYBIG
ASSISTANT PROFESSOR OF TRUMPET

DR. ROBERT JOSEPH TULEY
PROFESSOR AND COORDINATOR OF MUSIC EDUCATION

MS. MEME TUNNELL
INSTRUCTOR OF CLASS PIANO

DR. MICHAEL TUNNELL
INTERIM PROFESSOR OF TRUMPET

DR. BRUCE D. TYCHINSKI
ASSISTANT PROFESSOR OF TROMBONE

MR. THEODORE ULLMANN
PROFESSOR OF PIANO

MS. LIBBY M. VANATTA
ADJUNCT PIANO FACULTY AND COORDINATOR OF GRADUATE STUDIES

MR. DARKO VELICHKOVSKI
ASSISTANT PROFESSOR OF ENTERTAINMENT INDUSTRY

MS. LUCILE K. WACHTEL
PROFESSOR OF VOICE

DR. STANLEY WALDOFF
PROFESSOR OF PIANO

MS. MAMIE D. WALTERS-NAVARRO
ADMINISTRATIVE ASSISTANT

MR. CLIFTON WARE
CHORAL CONDUCTOR/VOICE

MR. ROBERT E. WATERSTRIPE
PROFESSOR OF VOICE AND DIRECTOR OF OPERA WORKSHOP

DR. LARRY WEED
PROFESSOR OF TROMBONE AND MARCHING BAND DIRECTOR

DR. WILLIAM WEINERT
DIRECTOR OF CHORAL ACTIVITIES

DR. CHRISTOPHER D. WHITE
INTERIM ASSOCIATE PROFESSOR OF CHORAL ACTIVITIES

MS. BARBARA WIEMAN
PROFESSOR OF PIANO

DR. MARIAN WILSON KIMBER
ASSOCIATE PROFESSOR OF MUSICOLOGY

MS. ROWLENE WOMBLE
SUPERVISOR OF MUSIC EDUCATION

DR. VIVIAN POATES WOOD
PROFESSOR OF VOICE

DR. KIMBERLY A. WOOLLY
ASSISTANT PROFESSOR OF BASSOON AND THEORY

DR. JOHN ANDREW WOOTON
PROFESSOR OF PERCUSSION

MR. DIETER WULFHORST
INTERIM ASSISTANT PROFESSOR OF CELLO

DR. JAMES F. YESTADT
PROFESSOR OF MUSIC AND ORCHESTRA CONDUCTOR

MR. PAUL A. DIEBOLD YORK
ASSISTANT PROFESSOR OF CELLO

MR.DAVID YOSS
PROFESSOR OF VOICE

MS. CELIA C. YOUNG
FINANCIAL SECRETARY FOR THE SCHOOL OF MUSIC

MR. LONNIE R. YOUNG
PIANO TECHNICIAN

MR. RAYMOND YOUNG
DIRECTOR OF BANDS/ EUPHONIUM PROFESSOR

MR. MERTON ZAHRT
PROFESSOR OF MUSIC EDUCATION/ ORGAN

MR. LUIGI JOHN ZANINELLI
PROFESSOR OF MUSIC/ COMPOSER IN RESIDENCE

DR. PAMELA JONES ZANINELLI
ADJUNCT PROFESSOR OF DICTION

MR. DAVID ZEPEDA
PROFESSOR OF VOICE

MS. PATTIE ZIEGLER
INSTRUCTOR OF MUSIC

SYMPHONY ORCHESTRA ALUMNI FROM 1919 TO PRESENT[1]

FARKHAD ABDIKADIROV
VIOLA

JUDITH (JUDY) ABENDSCHEIN
VIOLA

RONALD ABLE
TROMBONE

AMR SALAH ABOUEL-NAGA
HORN

KELLY ROBERT ABRAHAM
CLARINET

BOBBY ABRAMS
CLARINET

JOSEPH ROBERT ABRAMS
OBOE

CATHERINE (EILEEN) ACKERMAN
PERCUSSION

DONALD ACREY
BASS/TUBA

TIM ADAM
TROMBONE

CHAD ADAMS
TROMBONE

FRANKLIN J. ADAMS
PERCUSSION

JAMES ADAMS
BASS

JAMES E. ADAMS
TROMBONE

JAN M. ADAMS
VIOLIN

JANIS ADAMS
VIOLIN

JOE BILL ADAMS
TRUMPET

JOHN ALLEN ADAMS
HORN

MARCUS ADAMS
TRUMPET

MARK ADAMS
VIOLIN

PAUL (JEFF) ADAMS
TROMBONE

PEGGY ADAMS (NADALICH)
OBOE/ENGLISH HORN

ROBERT ADDISON
VIOLIN

FERNANDO AGUIRRE
VIOLIN

CHRIS AHLERS
VIOLIN

JASON ALBERT

LUIS GUSTAVO ALBERTO
VIOLIN

MAYARA ALENCAR
CELLO

EDWIN ALEXANDER
BASSOON

SUSAN MAGG ALEXANDER
FLUTE

CAROL ALLEN
HORN

JACQUELINE ALLEN (HAND)
FRENCH HORN

JAMES ALLEN
MANDOLIN

JANE ALLEN
VIOLIN

JAY ALLEN
BASS

JERRIE ALLEN
OBOE

KIM ALLEN

RIE ALLEN (LINTON)
PERCUSSION

WHITNEY ALLEN

MARCOS ALTAMIRANO
BASS

LUDWIG ALVARADO
CELLO

EURIDICE ALVAREZ
OBOE

MARCO ALVAREZ
CELLO

PAUL ANDERSEN
ORGAN

CATHERINE ANDERSON
HARP

LESLIE A. ANDERSON
FLUTE

MARK ANDERSON
PERCUSSION

REBECCA ANDERSON (MILLER)
CLARINET

WILLIAM ANDERSON

ELIZABETH ANGLIN
CELLO

ALBERT ANGSTADT

DON ANTHONY
TROMBONE

JOHN ANTHONY
PERCUSSION

BUDDY APPERSON
PERCUSSION

HENRY APPERSON
TYMPANI

CONSUELO AQUINO
VIOLIN

MARCELINO ARACENA
VIOLIN

HENRY ARAGON
VIOLA

JOSHUA ARD
PERCUSSION

ENRIQUETA ARELLANES
VIOLIN

LUZVIC NATHALI ARIAS
BASS

ANN ARMUS

JOAN ARNO (YOUNG)
FLUTE/PICCOLO

JAMES DAVID ARNOTT
VIOLA/VIOLIN

ISABEL ARRIAGA
VIOLIN

MARIA ARRUA
VIOLIN

MARJORIE (KAY) ASP (KUENN)
VIOLA/VIOLIN

DAVID B. ASPINWALL
CLARINET

LYNNE ASPNES
HARP

MARSHA ASQUITH (ANDERSON)
FRENCH HORN

BRENDA AVERA

DAWN AVERY
VIOLA

NATHAN B. AYCOCK
TROMBONE

LYLE BABCOCK
BASS

KRISTEN BABIN
CLARINET

JENNIFER BAGGETT
HARP

HOWARD BAHR
VIOLIN

KATHY BAHR
FLUTE

DONALD BAILEY
FLUTE

JAMES BAILEY

DEBBIE (DEBORAH) BAKER (CARRINGTON)
BASS

DIANE BAKER
Bb CLARINET

GEORGE BAKER
TRUMPET

KEN BAKER
TROMBONE

BRIAN ROBERT BALDWIN
PIANO

FELECIA BALL

JAMES BALL
BRASS

JENNIFER LEE BALL

PHILIP BALL
TROMBONE

MARCUS BALLARD
SAXOPHONE

J.P BANKS, JR.
PERCUSSION

SICILIA ANA CRISTINA BARBOSA ABRANTES
CELLO

WILLIAM ANDREW BARGETZI
TROMBONE

JOHN CRAIG BARKER
CLARINET

JAMES BARNETT
PERCUSSION

ERIC BARONI
CLARINET

SAMMY BARR
PERCUSSION

ARIELLE BARRIENTOS
VIOLIN

BRET DAVID BARROW
TROMBONE

ELLEN BARRY
PICCOLO

JUDITH BARTELS (SYKES)
HORN

CARRIE BARTSCH

JONATHAN DAVIS BASS
BASS

MICHAEL EDWARD BASS
TRUMPET

KAREN BATES
FLUTE

LEE ANN BATES (HONEA)
FLUTE

FERRIS BATSON
VIOLIN

ELIZABETH BATTEN

JULIE ANN BATURA (HAMILTON)
OBOE/ENGLISH HORN

BETSY BAUER
TRUMPET

JEFFERY BAUGHMAN
BASS

ERIC T. BAUMGARTNER
TROMBONE

MARY THERESA POE BAYLISS
PIANO

LINDSAY BEASLEY

TRUETT BEASLEY
HORN

IRVING BECKER
VIOLIN

LISA BECKLEY

DENNIS BEHM
HORN

LT. MAX. R. BEITMAN
VIOLA

MARK BELL
TRUMPET

CAROL BENEDICT (SIMMONS)
VIOLA

PATRICIA BENEDICT
CELLO

RODOLFO BENITEZ
VIOLIN

DAVID A. BENOIT
OBOE

ALICE R. BERRY
VIOLA

DAVID BERRY
OBOE/ENGLISH HORN

JOE BERRYMAN
PERCUSSION

DEBBIE BEYEA

BRIAN BISHOP

DARCIE BISHOP
TRUMPET

CINDY BIVINS
ENGLISH HORN

JOHN BIVINS
BASSOON

JOSEPH BLACKMON
TRUMPET

MARK BLACKWELL

MEGAN BLACKWELL
OBOE

SONYA BLAKELY (PUTMAN)

STEPHEN BLAND
VIOLA

BERNIE BLANKENSHIP
TROMBONE

EARL BLESSEY
BASS

LINDA BLOUNT (JONES)
HORN

WALTON BOBO
VIOLIN

RUSSELL BOBROWSKI
VIOLIN

MARY BOGGS (GRONDE)
FLUTE

MELISSA BOHL
OBOE

NANCY BOISTURE
BASS/CONTRABASSOON

DOUGLASS BOND
VIOLIN

MICHELLE BONECUTTER

EDDIE BONILLA
VIOLIN

GUILLERMO BONILLA MEJIA
CELLO

GENE BONNER

AMANDA BOONE

JASON BOOTH
TROMBONE

SYLVIA BOOTH (HUBBARD)
VIOLIN

CARLOS BOTELLO

J RUSSELL BOURDETTE
VIOLIN

RUSTY BOURDETTE
TRUMPET

SHERRY BOUSHELL
VIOLIN

CAROL JOYCE BOUTWELL (GEMEINHARDT)
PERCUSSION

GUY BOWERING
BASS

JOHN BOWLING
VIOLIN

JAMIE BOX

ERIN ELIZABETH BOYD
OBOE

J. THOMAS BOYD
BASS

JOHN BOYD
CLARINET

OSCAR KYLE BOZEMAN
HORN

RUTH BRADEN
FLUTE

JAMES BRADLEY
OBOE

JULIUS ALAN BRADY
CLARINET

ERIKA BRANCH (REED)
CLARINET

JOHN BRANCH
VIOLA

JOE D. BRANNON

TOM BRANTLEY
TROMBONE

BRIDGEET BRAXTON
CELLO

MARK BRAY
TROMBONE

KAREN BRAZZELL (CABRERA)

BETTY BRELAND
VIOLIN

JENNIE LOU BRELAND (MOORE)

MRS.W. M. BRELAND JR.
VIOLIN

LEAH C.BREMSETH (ADAMS)
VIOLIN

GEOFFREY ADAM BREWER

JAMES BREWER
TROMBONE

ARNOLD BRIDGES JR.

FRANCES BRIGNAC (MILDRED VAN WICK)
Bb CLARINET

WILLIAM BRINDZA
TROMBONE

JOSEPH BRITAIN
CLARINET/HARPSICHORD

DONNA BRITT
OBOE

CRYSTAL BRITTON

JULIE BROCKWAY (ARISCO)
CLARINET

RODERICK JAMES BROGAN

SHONA BROGDEN
VIOLIN

PATRICIA A. BRONTE
VIOLIN

JOHNSON BROOKE
VIOLIN

BILLY BROWN
VIOLIN

BINA RUTH BROWN
VIOLA

(DICK) CARL R. BROWN
CELLO

ELIZABETH BROWN

ERIN RUTH BROWN
VIOLA

JAMES BROWN
CELLO

JUDY BROWN (KLUG)

KELLY BROWN
FLUTE

LAWRENCE BROWN
TROMBONE

LOWELL BROWN
FRENCH HORN

MARY BROWN
TUBA

RICHARD BROWN

MICHAEL BROWNING
TROMBONE/BASS TROMBONE

DORIS BRUCKNER (EDRINGTON) (DUNGAN)
VIOLIN

ZOE BRUMFIELD (MARTY)
BASS

LUC BRUST
PERCUSSION

SAM BRUTON
PIANO

BECKY BRYAN
VIOLIN

JOSEPHINE BRYAN
PERCUSSION

REBECCA BRYAN
VIOLIN

JOEY BRYANT
BASS CLARINET

ERIN BUCHWALD

JAMES (JIMMY) BUCKALEW
VIOLIN

CELESTE BUCKHALTER
FLUTE

JOEY BUCKLEY

WILLIAM BUFKIN
CELLO

CARLA BUICE (REINLIE)
TRUMPET

MARTHA ANN BULLARD (GUICE)
VIOLIN

SHERRI BULLARD
VIOLIN

BENJAMIN BULLOCK
TRUMPET

WILBUR BULLOCK
HORN

CLAY BUNYARD
HORN

PEARL BURKE
HARP

NINA BURKEY

JAY BURNELL

BENJAMIN BURNETT
PERCUSSION

ELIZABETH BURNETT

MELODIE BURNS

SYMPHONY ORCHESTRA ALUMNI, CONTINUED

LOUISE BURROUGHS (NUCKOLS)
HORN

MIKE (JOHN) BURSON

MICHAEL W. BURT

VONNEICE BURT
VIOLIN

BRYAN BURTON
HORN/BASS

ELIZABETH BUSTON
PIANO

INEZ BUTLER

WINONA BUTLER

MILDRED BUZZELL
VIOLIN / VIOLA

BRUCE BYRD

HALEY BYRD
TROMBONE

PIETRY CABRERA
BASSOON

JERRY A. CADDEN
TUBA

CRAIG (JONATHAN) CAGLE
TRUMPET

REBEKAH (BECKY) CAGLE (BUTLER)
FLUTE

RELDA (REBECCA) CAGLE
FLUTE

BROCK ADAM CAIN

HUGH CAIN
TRUMPET

PATRICIA MERCEDE CALDERON

FRANCISCO CALDERON JAMIREZ
VIOLIN

ANN CALDWELL (PAVESIC)
BASSOON

JAMI N. CALDWELL
VIOLA

WILLIAM CALDWELL
VIOLIN

KAREN CALLENDER (MOSS)
BASS

CYNTHIA (CINDY) CAMBURN
BASSOON

DONALD CAMERON
TUBA

DAVID CAMP
PERCUSSION

HOWARD CAMP
TYMPANI

CHARLES CAMPBELL
HORN

BRANDON CANNON
TUBA

ROBERT (BOB) CANNON
TRUMPET

MARK (STEVEN) CANTRELL
TRUMPET

BARBARA CARDEN
FLUTE

DEBORAH CARINGTON

MATTHEW LEE CARL
CLARINET

DAVID CARLSON
TRUMPET

EDDIE CARNES
VIOLIN / VIOLA

NORBERT CARNOVALE
TRUMPET

EDUARDO CARPINTEYRO LARA
CELLO

GUSTAVO CARPINTEYRO LARA
CELLO

SEARLE CARSON
OBOE

CAMILLE CARTER
BASSOON

CECILIA CARTER (FRASCHILLO)
TROMBONE

JAY CARTER
BASS

JAY CARTER
TUBA

SYLVIA CARTER
VIOLIN

TRACY CARTER
OBOE/ENGLISH HORN

ROY M. CARUBBA
TRUMPET

MARIA E. CASERTA
VIOLIN

LAUREN CASEY
HORN

LEAH CASEY
HORN

BEN CASTILLE
TROMBONE

FRANCIS CASTILLO
VIOLA

JOSHUA CATHEY
CELLO

GLENDA SUE CATON (BLANKENSHIP)
BASSOON

LINDA CAULEY
VIOLA

ALEX CAUTHEN
TUBA

CASEY CAVINESS
PERCUSSION

VICTOR M. CAVOLA
PERCUSSION

CECILIA CEDILLO (PINEDA)
CLARINET

ROBERT CHABOT
PERCUSSION

HELEN CHADIMA
VIOLIN

KAREN CHAMBLISS
VIOLIN

JOSHUA CHANCE
TROMBONE

DON CHAPMAN
TRUMPET

MARK CHAPMAN
OBOE

RICK CHAPMAN
TRUMPET

STANLEY CHAPMAN
HORN

WILLIAM HOUSTON CHAPMAN
TUBA

ROBERT CHEATHAM
TRUMPET

BRIAN CHEESMAN
PERCUSSION

ROBERT DALE (BOB) CHEESMAN
TRUMPET

SYBIL CHEESMAN (MARTY)
FLUTE

CHRISTOPHER CLARK CHESTER
VIOLIN

MARIA CHISHOLM
FLUTE

FREEMAN W. CHRISTIAN JR.
VIOLA

MARY CHUNG
PIANO

LASHUNDRA SHANAY CLARK

MARY EVELYN CLARK
CLARINET

TIFFANY CLARK
FLUTE

DOUGLAS CLEM
TROMBONE

LAWRENCE (LARRY) CLEMENS
TRUMPET

CYNTHIA CLEVENSTINE (BRIGGS)

MICHAEL ANTHONY CLIFTON
PERCUSSION

STEVEN (CHRIS) CLINE
TROMBONE

CATHERINE CLODFELTER
CELLO

JEFF CLUBB
TROMBONE

WILLIAM TRAVIS COAKLEY
TROMBONE

CHARLES COCHRAN
HORN

MARCIA COCHRAN (KAUFMAN)
FLUTE

MITCHELL COCHRAN
HORN

JERRY COGDELL
HORN

HOWARD COHEN
CLARINET

JENIFFER COHEN
ALTO FLUTE

WESLEY COLE
VIOLA

BEVERLY COLLIER
VIOLIN

SUE COLLIER
VIOLIN

DAVID S. COLLINGS
TUBA

ANNABELLE COLLINS
VIOLIN

ANN COLLINS
VIOLIN

DORIS COLLINS (HOLLOWAY)
FLUTE

MARY ELIZABETH COLLINS
VIOLIN

STAN COLLINS
PIANO

VALENCIA COLLINS
VIOLIN

CHRISTOPHER COLLINSWORTH
TRUMPET

JOEL COMER
OBOE

CAROLYN COMMISKY
CELLO

HOLLY COMPTON (CUMMINGS)
CELLO

CHRISTOPHER CONDON
SAXOPHONE

GAVIN CONERLY
PERCUSSION

ROBERT CONN
CELLO

CELEST CONNER
CELESTA

MICHAEL CONROY
TROMBONE

THOMAS CONTINE
BASS

GARY COOK
TROMBONE

PAM COOK (DEDEAUX)
FLUTE/PICCOLO

VAN COOK
BASS

WHITNEY COOK
CLARINET

GINGER COOLEY
CELLO

JILL COOLEY
CONTRABASSOON

GEORGE COOPER
TUBA

LYNETTE COOPER
VIOLIN

CARRIE CORBETT
CELLO

JOHN CORNACCHIONE
TROMBONE

ANTHONY (SONNY) CORRERO
PERCUSSION

BARBARA CORRERO (WORKMAN)
HORN

LUIS EDMUNDO CORTES
VIOLIN

NICOLE D.COSTA
VIOLIN

JOHN LINWOOD COTE
PERCUSSION

CARLA COTRUVO
VIOLIN

ARMAND COULLET
VIOLIN

JOE COUNCIL
HORN

MEGAN COUNTS
TRUMPET

HAROLD TOM COURSEY
PERCUSSION

JAMES COVELLI
CLARINET

ANNE COVINGTON
VIOLIN

JENNY COVINGTON
OBOE

ALLAN COX
TRUMPET

BRUCE B. COX
TRUMPET

GEORGE DONOVAN COX

KYLE COX
PERCUSSION

RAYMOND COX
HORN

VIRGINIA COX (BOWEN)
BASS

CHERYL CRAFT (BARBER)
VIOLIN

STEPHEN CRAIG

CORY CRANE
OBOE

GILBERT O. CRAVEN
TRUMPET

CAROLYN CRAWFORD
HORN

JAMES CRAWFORD
CLARINET

JAN CRAWFORD
FLUTE

SIOBHAN L.O. CRAWFORD
VIOLIN

RANDALL PATRICK CREEL
HORN

KATHERINE CREWS
VIOLA

DAVID CRISPIN
OBOE/ENGLISH HORN

BRUCE (ROBERT) CRISWELL
TROMBONE

JAMES CROCKER
TRUMPET

FRANK CROCKETT
VIOLIN

ERNEST CROPP

DYANN R. CROSS
HORN

JAMES PATRICK CROSSLAND
TROMBONE

JOSE LUIS CUELLAR
BASS

MARIA TERESA CUELLAR
VIOLIN

STARLING CUMBERWORTH
VIOLIN

WALTER CUMMINGS
TROMBONE

DURAND CURTIS
BASS

PATRICIA A. DA SILVA
BASS

GENESES DA SILVA OLIVIERA
CELLO

DONALD DABNEY
TRUMPET

EDWARD DACUS
HORN

JEANNE DAHMER
VIOLA

SAMUEL DAHMER
BASS

JACKIE DALVIT
VIOLIN

MATTHEW DAMMES
PERCUSSION

JOSEPH DANIEL
TRUMPET

LEON DANIEL
TUBA

WILLIAM DANIEL
TROMBONE

RHONDA DANIELS
VIOLA

MICHAEL DARBY
VIOLIN

WILMA DARNAUER
CLARINET/HARP

DOROTHY DAUGHDRILL
VIOLIN

JACQUALINE DAVIDSON
HORN

HAROLD DAVIS
TROMBONE

HOPE DAVIS
VIOLA

IRENE DAVIS

JAMES TREADWELL DAVIS
TRUMPET

MARION DAVIS
VIOLIN

MICHAEL DAVIS
VIOLA

MICKEY DAVIS
VIOLA

RANDALL DAVIS
TRUMPET

ROBERT DAVIS
BASSOON

ROY DAVIS
BASS

JAMES DAWSON
PIANO/CELESTE

GREGORY DAY
BASS

LANALEE LITZ DE KANT
HARP

RICHARD DE LA FUENTE
PERCUSSION

CARINA MARCELA DE LA HOZ RODRIGUEZ
VIOLIN

MONICA PAMELA DE LA HOZ RODRIGUEZ
VIOLIN/VIOLA

DANIEL DE SOUSA
BASSOON

DAN DEALY
HORN

CHRISTOPHER DEAN
VIOLIN

JAY DEAN
TRUMPET/VIOLIN

JOHN DEAN
BASS

CONSTANCE DEARDEN (HAYNIE)
HORN

MARK DEATON
TRUMPET

GIOVANNI DECHIARO
GUITAR/ BASS

SIDNEY DEDEAUX
TRUMPET

PLIA DEES
CELLO

LORI DEHERTOGH
BASSOON

MARK DEHERTOGH
SAXOPHONE

JOANNA DELAUNE
HORN

MICHAEL DELAUNE
TRUMPET

JOSE DELGADO
VIOLA

LEONARDO DELGADO DUARTE
BASS

COLBY DEMPSEY
TUBA

DOROTHY DENMAN
VIOLIN

BEVERLY DENNIS
VIOLA

NORMAN RANDOLPH DENNIS
HORN

MARGARET (PEGGY) DENNISTON
VIOLIN

WILLIAM DENT
VIOLIN

ASHA DEPOLO
VIOLIN

ROBERT DEVINE
PERCUSSION

SAM DI BONAVENTURA
VIOLIN

ROGER DI GUILIAN
VIOLIN

AMALIA DIAZ
VIOLIN

LEDA DIAZ (GORDON) (NELSON)
FLUTE

GERALD DICKERSON
TRUMPET

RANDY DICKERSON
TRUMPET

NANCY ELIZABETH DICUS

JAQUELYN DILL

JAYSON EARL DILLON

MEGAN DISTASIO
CLARINET

JAMES DIXON
PERCUSSION

JAMES DIXON
TRUMPET

CATHERINE DOBLADO
FLUTE

PERRY DOGGRELL
OBOE

WILLIAM DOLE
BASSOON

CHRISTY DONNERSBACH
FLUTE

DENT DONOHOO
BASS

JAMES DONOVAN
OBOE

DRULINDA DORMAN
CLARINET

HELEN DORNBUSH
FLUTE

GELON DOSWELL
BASS/GUITAR

KIMBERLY MICHELE DOTSON

ROBERT DOUGLAS
PERCUSSION

LARRY DOVE
PERCUSSION

ROBERT DOWDY
TRUMPET

JOHN ALLEN DOWLER

JENNIFER DOWNEY
VIOLIN

LYNDELL DOWNEY
FLUTE

LYNDELL DOWNEY (WHITLOCK)
VIOLA

DAWN M. DOYLE

WHITNEE DOYLE
CLARINET

ALEJANDRO DRAGO
VIOLIN

JOHN DRISCOLL
HORN

SCOTT (LARRY) DRISKELL
PERCUSSION

ALICIA DUBOSE (PARKER)
PIANO

PEGGY W. DUBUISSON
BASSOON

PETER DUBUISSON
VIOLIN

JOEL DUCKWORTH
BASS

BENJAMIN TUCKER DULIN
TROMBONE

DANICE (DANY) DUNCAN
TRUMPET

DANIEL DUNCAN
PERCUSSION

RICKIE DUNCAN
TROMBONE

THOMAS WILLIAM DUNCAN
PERCUSSION

BENJAMIN PAUL DUNN
CELLO

DAVID J. DUNNING
TROMBONE

TERRY DURBIN
VIOLIN

ROBERT DURHAM
TUBA

SEAN DYKE
TROMBONE

AMON (CHARLES) EADY
TRUMPET

GERALD EASLEY
FRENCH HORN

JEAN EASON
VIOLA

ANDREW EASTERLING
BASS

MIKE (ROY) ECHOLS
PERCUSSION

SABRINA EDENS (HOWARD)
VIOLIN

BETH EDISON
VIOLIN

BILLY EDMONDSON
TROMBONE

CARLA EDMONDSON
VIOLIN

LAWRENCE EDON
BASS

GUY EDRINGTON
HORN

JAMES EDWARD

ALBERT G. EDWARDS

PAMELA EDWARDS
BASSOON

JOHN OKLEY EGGER
HORN

GUILHERME EHRAT ZILS
BASS

KATHERINE M. EIDE (LONGYEAR)
CELLO

CHARLES ELLIOTT
CLARINET

JASON ELLIOTT
TROMBONE

MARIE ELLIOTT
FLUTE

KAREN ELLIS
VIOLA

KATHRYN ELLIS
CELLO

YOLANDA ELLIS
VIOLIN

MICHAEL ELLZEY
TRUMPET

EDDIE ELSEY JR.
TROMBONE

VALLIE ELY
BASSOON

VESTER EMERSON
PERCUSSION

ALEJANDRO ENCINAS
VIOLIN/VIOLA

CLAUDIA ENCINAS
VIOLIN/VIOLA

TATIANA ENCINAS
CELLO

REX ENDERLIN
TROMBONE

SUSAN ENDERLIN
OBOE

ANTHONY ENGLERT
BASS

SYLVIA ENLOE
VIOLIN

GAYLE ENTREKIN
FLUTE

MEADE ENTREKIN
HORN

GORDON EPPERSON
CELLO

ISABEL ESCALANTE (INFANTE)
VIOLIN

RODOLFO ESCOTO
VIOLIN

LEONARDO ESPINOSA
VIOLIN

JAMES ESTES
TRUMPET

JAY ESTY
TRUMPET

DAVID ETHRIDGE
BASS

MARGIE EUBANKS
VIOLIN

TREVOR EVANS-YOUNG
VIOLIN

PAUL A. EVERETT
TRUMPET

ROBERT EVERSMAN
VIOLIN

TERESA FAINT
HORN

HOPE FAIRCHILD
PIANO

TOMAS FAJARDO
VIOLIN/VIOLA

NATHALIE FARINACCI
CELLO

WILLIAM FARMER
HORN

SARA MARION FARNSWORTH

JEREMY FARRIS

CARLOS A. FAUL JR.
BASS

ROBERT FAYARD
TRUMPET

JANE FEAMSTER
VIOLIN

KATHY FEARING (BIGLER)
FLUTE/PICCOLO

CAROL FEINBLATT
VIOLIN

CAROL FELIS
BASSOON

CARLOS H. FELLER
FLUTE

EDVARD FENDLER
CONDUCTOR

EMILY FENDLER
VIOLIN

LIGIA CARINA FEO (DRAGO)
VIOLA

TOMMY FERGUSON
BASSOON

GERARDO FERNANDEZ
PIANO

HECTOR FERNANDEZ
BASS

TAYLIS FERNANDEZ
CELLO

ALEJANDRO (SASHA) FERREIRA
VIOLIN

CARLOS OMAR FERREIRA FADUL

LAWRENCE FISHER
VIOLIN

RUSSELL FLAGG
VIOLA

BARBARA FLEISCHER
VIOLIN

ALYSON FLEMING (BOWLING)
CELLO

GIULIANA FLEMING (KERR)
FLUTE

SHIRLEY FLEMING
VIOLIN

JAMES FLETCHER-LAND
VIOLA

GEORGE FLEXMAN
VIOLA

LUCILLE FLOHR
VIOLIN

GERSON D. FLORES SALGADO
BASS

ROBERT FLURREY
BASS

CHARLES FLURRY
BASS

MUSETTE FORBES (BOONE)
VIOLIN

ROBERT GLENN FORBES
TROMBONE

AMY LYNN FORD (CARLEY)
OBOE/ENGLISH HORN

JAMES FORD
TRUMPET

RONDA FORD
FLUTE

MIKE FORESTIERI
TRUMPET

GINA FORSYTH
VIOLIN

ALDO FORTE
TROMBONE

ROBERT FORTENBERRY
TROMBONE

WILLIAM FORTENBERRY
PERCUSSION

PATRICIA FORTNER
HARPSICHORD

JAMES FOSHEE
TUBA

JORDAN FOSTER
TRUMPET

KYLE CLIFFORD FOSTER
VIOLIN

ANNA FOWLER
VIOLIN

JACK FOWLER
BASSOON

JIMMY (JAMES) FOWLER
GUITAR

ROBERT SCOTT FOWLER

CHRIS FOX
HORN

SUZANNE FOX
VIOLIN

RHONDA K. FRANKLIN (FOWLER)
CLARINET

ANGELO FRASCARELLI
VIOLIN

LILAJANE FRASCARELLI
VIOLIN

THOMAS VINCENT FRASCHILLO
PERCUSSION/PIANO/HARP

STEPHEN FRAZIER

CHRISTIAN FREEMAN
VIOLA

GAIL (ANITA) FREEMAN
HORN

ROBBIE FREEMAN
EUPHONIUM

CINDE FREIL
OBOE

LARRY FRENCH
VIOLIN

MIKE (CHARLES) FREUND
TRUMPET

RACHAEL FROHMAN
HARP

SUZANNE FRY (BUSHFIELD)
CELLO

A.F. FUGITT
HORN

DAVID FUHR
BASS CLARINET

ALLEN FULLER
VIOLIN

VALERIE FULLER
HORN

ALLEN FULTON
VIOLIN

JEFFREY FUNDERBURK
TUBA

GRANT FUTCH
TROMBONE

MIKE GALASSO
VIOLIN

EVAN T. GALLAGHER
PERCUSSION

WARREN GALLE
HORN

CREEL GALLOWAY
HORN

DISA GAMBERA
VIOLIN

SHULI GAO
CELLO

MARIO GARCIA
BASS

MAURICIO GARCIA
CELLO

DANA GAREN
VIOLA

KATY GAREN
VIOLIN

STEPHEN CRAIG GARRETT
TRUMPET

MICHAEL GATOZZI
VIOLIN

JUSTIN GAUTREAUX
BASS TROMBONE

CHARLES GAVIN
HORN

JULIANA GAVIRIA
VIOLIN

JOHN GAY
VIOLIN

WILLIAM O.GEBHART
BASS

JERRY GEE
TRUMPET

PHYLIS GEIGER
CLARINET

MARION GEISSINGER
CELLO

CHARLES GEMEINHARDT
TRUMPET

HELEN REGINA GEORGE
BASS CLARINET

CHRISTINE TATE GERALD
FLUTE

DALE GIBSON
TROMBONE

WALTER GIBSON
TRUMPET

MICHAEL GILL
PERCUSSION

MARGARET GILLARD
DIRECTOR/VIOLIN

JEROME GILMER
PIANO/KEYBOARDS

CLAY (GILBERT) GILMORE
PERCUSSION

EVELYN GILMORE
BASSOON

RICHARD GILPIN
CLARINET

DEBBIE GIPSON
HORN

MARY BESS GIRLING
VIOLIN

JOHN GLAESER
HORN

ESTA CHANEL GLASS
VIOLIN

WILLIAM GLEATON
VIOLIN

MRS. WILLIAM GLEATON
FLUTE/VIOLIN

DAVID GLENN
CELLO

LARRY GLENN
OBOE

TALIA GLENN
VIOLA

JONATHAN GLOVER
HORN

NANCY GODSEY (MANN)
VIOLA

NEIL GODWIN
HORN

PAUL GODWIN
HORN

LAWRENCE GOFF
HORN

TREY GOFF
CLARINET

ALAN GOLD
BASSOON

SANDRA GOLDBERG
VIOLIN

DONALD GOLDMAN
TROMBONE

ADONIS GONZALES
PIANO

ANDREA GONZALEZ
VIOLIN

HUMBERTO GONZALEZ
VIOLIN/VIOLA

JORGE GONZALEZ
VIOLIN

JOHANNA SLAUGHTER GORDON

KRAIG GORETH
PERCUSSION

TERRENCE GORTON
SAXOPHONE

TREY GOSSETT
VIOLIN

SYMPHONY ORCHESTRA ALUMNI, CONTINUED

JOHN GOSSMAN
HORN

JEREMY GOTT
SAXOPHONE

MARIA GOUVAS
VIOLA

PATTI GOUVAS
VIOLA

GERRY GOWER (EDWARDS)
VIOLIN

JAMIE GOWER
CELLO/PERCUSSION

JOHN GOWER
VIOLIN

WILLIAM R. GOWER
VIOLA

WILMA GOWER
HORN

BOBBYE FRANCIS GRAHAM
VIOLIN

DOUGLAS GRAHAM
CLARINET

JEFFERSON GRANT
PERCUSSION

LARRY GRANT
FLUTE

MARK GRANT
PERCUSSION

TOM GRANT
PERCUSSION

BRUCE GRANTHAM
VIOLIN

DANIEL GRANTHAM
HORN

DOUGLAS GRANTHAM
CELLO

KATHRYN GRANTHAM
VIOLIN

KATHY GRANTHAM (HELPENSTELL)
VIOLIN

LARRY GRANTHAM

CANDICE GRAVES
OBOE

PAMELA GRAVES (DANIEL)
CELLO

REUBIN GRAVES
TRUMPET

WILLIAM GRAVES
VIOLA/BASS

SUSAN GRAWE
HARPSICHORD

BERRY GRAY
TROMBONE

PATRICK D. GRAY
TRUMPET

DAVID GREATWOOD
TROMBONE

CALLIE GREEN
FLUTE

ROBERT GREENHAW
BASSOON

JAMES BRIAN GREER
TRUMPET

DAVID GREGORY
BASSOON

STEPHANIE GREGORY
PIANO

BRENDA GREMILLION
PIANO

TERESA GREY
PIANO

ROBERT WAYNE GRIFFIN
BASSOON

ROBERT GRIFFITH
PIANO

BARBARA GRIFFITHS (MASON)
CELLO

THELMA S. GRISSETT
VIOLIN

MEGHAN KILPATRICK GRIZZLE (SHEEHY)
HORN

WILBURN GRIZZLE
CLARINET

JOHN GROVES
HORN

YENOIN GUIBBORY
VIOLIN

BONNIE GUILBEAU
VIOLIN

MARGARET GUILBEAU
CELLO

MARK GUILBEAU
VIOLIN

NEWTS GUILBEAU
VIOLA

KAY (ANITA) GUILES
ORGAN

JACKSON GUILLEN ALFARO
VIOLIN

ALINE GUILLOT
VIOLIN

DAVID GUNN
TRUMPET

LARRY GUNN
VIOLIN

BRANDY NICOLE GUNTER

GAIL GUNTER

JERRY GUNTER
BASSOON

SAMUEL GUNTER
TROMBONE

VANESSA GUNTER
FLUTE

JORGE GUTIERREZ
VIOLA

STEPHEN GUTTERY

LORENA GUZMAN
VIOLIN

MYRIAM SOLEDAD GUZMAN
VIOLA

GAIL GWOZDZ
VIOLIN

STEPHEN JOSEPH GWOZDZ
VIOLIN

CHRIS HAAR
HORN

LEE HAE REE
VIOLA

STEPHEN J. HAFFLY
TRUMPET

CARL HAGAN
CONTRABASS CLARINET

KAREN HAGENSON
FLUTE

SALLY HAGENSON
VIOLIN

RAYMOND HAIR
PERCUSSION

JOSHUA HALE
VIOLIN

CHRISTINE HALL (MISENCIK)
BASSOON/ CONTRABASSOON

JONATHAN HALL
PERCUSSION

LESLIE HALL
HORN

MARA HALL
CLARINET

SCOTTYE HALL (RACKLEY)
HORN

JONATHAN HALLMAN
PERCUSSION

JOHNNY HALLMAN
PERCUSSION

MELISSA HALLOCK
CLARINET

KAREN HAMBURG
CELLO

TODD HAMIELEC
TROMBONE

CRAIG HAMILTON
TRUMPET

DEBORAH HAMILTON
CELLO

JAMES HAMILTON
PERCUSSION

LAWRENCE HAMILTON
CELLO

MELANIE HAMILTON
OBOE

GARY HAMME
OBOE

BRENT K. HAMMER
HORN

JENNIFER A. HAMMON
VIOLIN

TAYLOR HAMMONS
TROMBONE

CLAUDETTE HAMPTON (KOLOSOWSKI)
VIOLIN

REBECCA HAMPTON (WHARTON)
PERCUSSION

RONALD DAVID HANCOCK
PERCUSSION

JOSEPH HANDY
TRUMPET

CRAIG HANKENSON
HORN

JAMES HANNAH
TROMBONE

CHARLES HANSEN
BASSOON

LEONARD HANSEN
VIOLIN

CARROLL HARDIN (CADDEN)
PERCUSSION

RAY HARDIN
VIOLIN

MARY STUART HARMON
PIANO

WYNNE HARMON (MAILY)
VIOLIN

PRENTISS HARPER
CLARINET

TALMAGE HARPER
CELLO

JAMES EDWARD HARRELL
PERCUSSION

LEE HARRELSON
EUPHONIUM

JAMES HARRINGTON
TRUMPET

DARRYL HARRIS
BASSOON

GREGORY HARRIS
BASS

JEANNE HARRIS
BASS

MARTHA ANN HARRIS
CELLO

RODNEY HARRIS
PERCUSSION

SEAN HARRIS
PERCUSSION

SHELBY HARRIS
PERCUSSION

SPIKE HARRIS
HORN

MARY CLAIRE HARRISON
FLUTE

JAMES HARTZ
VIOLIN/VIOLA

KELLY HARVEY
VIOLIN

MARGARET HARVEY
FLUTE

PATRICIA HARVEY
FLUTE

PATTY HARVEY
CELLO

JUSTIN HARVISON
TROMBONE

GARY HASKINS
VIOLA

STEFFEN HASS
SAXOPHONE

ZACHARY HASSELL
CLARINET

CASSIDY HASTY (WEATHERMON)
BASSOON

MARK HATCH
TRUMPET

LARRY HATTEN
PERCUSSION

CALVIN HAUFFE
VIOLIN

MARY TOM HAUN
VIOLIN

KRISTINA HAVARD
FLUTE

MARIANNE HAYDEN
PIANO

MICHAEL HAYMAN
BASS

JERRY HAYNIE
HORN

WILLIAM HAYNIE
VIOLA

ARMINE HAYRIKYAN
VIOLIN/VIOLA

ROBERT HAYS
TROMBONE

CATHY HEAD

LAUREL HEAD

LAUREN HEAD
VIOLIN

MARY FRANCES HEAD
CLARINET

NANCY HEAD
VIOLIN

VERNON HEAD
VIOLA

WILLIAM HEARD
TROMBONE

JUDITH HEARNE
CELLO/BASS

CLIFFORD HEARON
VIOLIN

JAMES HEARON
VIOLIN

MARYANN HEBERT
CELLO

ROY W. HEDGES
VIOLIN

JOHN HEDMAN
BASS

PAUL HEDMAN
BASS

LORI HEFLIN

CHARLES HEFNER
PERCUSSION

LUCY HEIBERG
VIOLIN

SARAH HEIDELBERG
VIOLIN

CHARLES HEIDEN
VIOLIN

JEANNE HEIDEN
VIOLIN

ALEXANDER HELLMAN
OBOE

PAMELA HELTON
CLARINET

FAYE HENDERSON
VIOLIN

MERLIN HENDERSON
TROMBONE

VALERIE HENDERSON
VIOLA

DEBRA HENDRICKS
PERCUSSION

PAUL E. HENLEY, JR.
CELLO

MAIDIE HENNINGTON
VIOLIN

SHILLOY SUZANNE HENTGES (ACREY)
VIOLIN

ROBERT HERMETZ
BASS

JOYCE HERNANDEZ (BOURDETTE)
VIOLIN

PABLO HERNANDEZ
OBOE

JOHNATHAN HERNDON
TRUMPET

ALEXANDER HERNER
CLARINET

ANTONIO HERRERA
PERCUSSION

BRYAN HERRING
TROMBONE

JESSICA HERRING

CHIP HERRINGTON
TRUMPET

ISAAC (IKE) CLEVELAND HERRINGTON
CELLO

RONALD HERRINGTON
TROMBONE

JEFF HERRON
TRUMPET

KIMBERLY HICKEY
FLUTE

JOSEPH LOWERY HICKS
BASS/ELECTRIC BASS

ERIC HILGENSTIELER
BASS

CHERYL HILL
VIOLIN

EDDIE WESLEY HILLMAN
TROMBONE

EMILY MARTA HINDRICHS
PIANO

RONALD HINES
PERCUSSION

PAUL HINLEY
CELLO

HAROLD HINTON
VIOLIN

HARRIS (H.A.) HINTON
VIOLIN

DAVID HOBBS
CLARINET

RICHARD HOBSON
CLARINET

DANIEL HODGES
TROMBONE

SKYE HODGES
FLUTE

WILLIAM HODGES
TRUMPET

MIKE HOEFLICH
TUBA

JAMIN HOFFMAN
HORN/BASS

JONATHAN HOFFMAN
PERCUSSION

TED HOFFMAN
TUBA

JONATHAN HOGAN
SAXOPHONE

SARAH HOGREFE (MABARY)
VIOLIN

DONNA HOGUE

BETH HOLCOMB (FRANZEN)
VIOLIN

JOHN HOLCOMB
HORN

THOMAS HOWARD HOLDER

HERBERT HOLEMAN
BASS

JOHN HOLLAND
CELLO

KAYLAH HOLLAND
VIOLIN

NORMAN HOLLIDAY
TRUMPET

MARLAYNA HOLLINS
CLARINET

MARKITA WEAVER HOLLOWAY
FLUTE

RALPH HOLMAN
BASS

BYRON HOLT
PERCUSSION

SHERMAN HONG
PERCUSSION

VIRGINIA HOOGENAAKER
VIOLIN

VERNON HOOKER
HORN

MELISSA HOOPER (LOPEZ)
CLARINET

BRYAN HOOTEN
TROMBONE

RONALD HOOTEN
TROMBONE

KATHRYN HOPPE
VIOLIN

WILLIAM HOPPE
VIOLIN

MICHELLE HOPPER (ALSEITZ)
VIOLIN

NANCY HOPPER
VIOLIN

WILLIAM HOPPER
OBOE/ENGLISH HORN

JOHN HORNE
BASS

DAVID HORTON
HORN

JOHNATHAN HORTON
HORN

MICHAEL HOWARD
HARPSICHORD

NANCY HOWELL
VIOLIN

MIROSLAV HRISTOV
VIOLIN

ERIC HSIEH
VIOLIN

HUGH HU
VIOLIN

TOMMY HUBARD
VIOLIN

ROBERT HUBBARD
CELLO/BASS

GEORGIA HUCKABAY (FILLINGHAM)
BASS/FLUTE/OBOE

ERIC BRENT HUCKABEE

BETH HUDSON
VIOLA/VIOLIN

GENE HUDSON
VIOLA

JEAN HUDSON
VIOLIN/VIOLA

JULIE HUDSON
OBOE

LAWRENCE HUDSON
VIOLIN

TOMMY HUFFORD
VIOLIN

CAROL HUGHES
OBOE

CLIFTON HUGHES
TUBA

DAVID HUGHES
CELESTE

MARK HUGHES
VIOLA

TIFFANY HUGHES
VIOLIN

BRIAN B. HUGHLEY
PERCUSSION

EDWARDS HULETT
VIOLIN

JOSEPH HULL
TRUMPET

LYNNE HULSING
CELLO

THOMAS HUNDEMER
HORN

ANTOINETTE HUNT
VIOLIN

BARBARA HUNTER
CLARINET

IAIN HUNTER
TROMBONE

EVAN PATRICK HURLEY
VIOLIN

WENDY HUSBAND
OBOE

FARLEY K. HUTCHINS
ORGAN

MIRIAN HUTCHINS
VIOLA

ROLAND (BUDDY) HUTHMAKER
VIOLIN

KATHY HYATT
OBOE

BRYAN D. INJAIAN
VIOLIN

ANNETTE INMAN
BASSOON

EDGAR IRIAS
HORN

SAMIE ELLEN IRVING
CLARINET

ANGEL ISLAS ANGUIANO
CELLO

HOMER IVY
HORN

KAZUMA IWABUCHI
TRUMPET

LUIS A. IZAGUIRRE
CELLO

BETTY JACKSON
ORGAN

CHARLES JACKSON
TRUMPET

JACKIE JACKSON

JENNIFER JACKSON
TRUMPET

JERLANDO F.L. JACKSON
PERCUSSION

MARJORIE JACKSON
VIOLA/VIOLIN

ROBERT JACKSON
VIOLA

TIM JACKSON
TUBA

TOMMY JACKSON
PERCUSSION

TOMMY JADESON
PERCUSSION

JORGE JAENZ
BASSOON

NESTOR JAENZ
OBOE

WILLIAM JALBERT
PERCUSSION

MELANIE ROSE JAMES (HAMILTON)
OBOE/ENGLISH HORN

NATHANIEL JAMES
HORN

PATRICIA JAMES
OBOE

ZACH JAMES
TROMBONE

JOHN JANNEY
PERCUSSION

ANDREAS JANSEN
BASS TROMBONE

WILL JAYROE
TROMBONE

JULIE JEFFRIES
ENGLISH HORN

EVA (TOOTSIE) JENKINS
BASS

JAMES JENKINS
TRUMPET

JOHN JENKINS
BASS

THOMAS JENKINS
HORN

ERICA JENNINGS (SCHLICHTING)
OBOE

ASTRID JEREZ
VIOLA

RAOUL JEROME
BASS/TROMBONE

KIRK JESSMER
BASS

JULIA JETTON
BASSOON

AARON JIMENEZ
VIOLIN

BILL JOHNSON
TRUMPET

BRYAN JOHNSON
HORN

DANIEL JOHNSON
BASSOON

GREGORY JOHNSON
BASS

HILDEGARD JOHNSON
ORGAN

MEMRIE JOHNSON
VIOLIN

MICHAEL JOHNSON
BASS

RICHARD JOHNSON
CLARINET

SADIA JOHNSON
FLUTE/PICCOLO

SCOTT JOHNSON
SAXOPHONE

TERRY JOHNSON
CLARINET

THOMAS JOHNSON
BASS

ANNETTE JOHNSTON (ROLLINS)
OBOE

CECIL JOHNSTON
PERCUSSION

KEN JOLLEY
OBOE/ENGLISH HORN

CYNTHIA JONES
OBOE

DAVID JONES
VIOLIN

JANET JONES
CLARINET

LANA KAY JONES (MERTON)
FLUTE

LINDA JONES (BLOUNT)
HORN

MICHAEL JONES
BASS

MOLLY JONES
TRUMPET

RAY JONES
TUBA

SARA LOU JONES
VIOLIN

STACEY JONES
CELLO

TONY JONES
TROMBONE

MARCUS JORDAN
TYMPANI

MICHAEL JORDAN
VIOLIN

ROBIN JORDAN
CELLO

DARYL JOYCE
BASS

SVETLANA KALTCHENKO
VIOLA

LANALEE LITZ DE KANT
HARP

JOANNE KARN
CELLO

HIROKO KATO
VIOLIN

THEODORE KATZ
VIOLIN

LOIS KAUFMAN
VIOLA

BRIAN KAUTH
SAXOPHONE

KEVIN KEAL
CELLO

FRANK KEARLEY
CELLO

JEANNE KEARLY
PERCUSSION

FLORENCE KEARNS
CELLO

ALAN VAUGHAN KEATING
CLARINET

LARRY KEATING
CLARINET

ROBERT KEATING
TRUMPET

CHRISTY KEATON
BASSOON

JEFFERY KEATON
BASSOON

LINDSEY KEAY
FLUTE

WILLIAM KECK
TUBA

RACHEL KEELY-WALLACE
OBOE

KATHRYN KEENER
VIOLA

CAMILLA KEEVER
CLARINET

CYNTHIA KELLER (KING)
FLUTE/PICCOLO

WILLIAM MORGAN KELLER
VIOLIN/VIOLA

FRANKIE KELLY
CLARINET/PIANO

HARVEY KELLY
TENOR

KARLA KELLEY
FLUTE

KRISTIAN KELLY
PERCUSSION

NANCY KELLY
CLARINET

NANCY KELLY
VIOLIN

THELMA KELLY
VIOLIN

MELISSA KENDRICK
CELESTE

CYNTHIA KENNEDY
HORN

GEORGIA KENNEDY
CLARINET

LUANA LAURIE KENNEDY (BLUMER)
CELLO

DEBORAH KERN
CELLO

E.A. KEY
TRUMPET

FRANK KILGARD
VIOLA

SUNGJIN KIM
CELESTE

MICHAEL KIMBER
VIOLA

DUSTIN KING

LEANNE KING
VIOLIN/VIOLA

MICKEY KING
VIOLIN

CASEY KIRK
PERCUSSION

ERNEST KIRKPATRICK
TRUMPET

SUE KISH
VIOLA

LARRY KITCHENS
VIOLIN

CONNIE KITZMAN
BASSOON/CONTRABASSOON

KAREN KLINE
VIOLIN

WENDY KLOPFTENSTEIN
VIOLIN

NOAH KNEPPER
FLUTE

BETH KNIGHT
FLUTE/PICCOLO

BENE KNOWLES
OBOE

NONA KNOX
FLUTE

DEBBIE KOHLER
CLARINET

MELISSA KOHLER
FLUTE

STEPHEN L. KOIVISTO
CLARINET

LAWRENCE KONECKY
BASS

WALTER KOONCE
FLUTE

LOWELL KOONS
VIOLIN

CAROL KORNEGAY
CELLO

LELAND KORNEGAY
TRUMPET

SHARON KOSTELECKY
TRUMPET

PATRICIA KOWALCZYK
HORN

JAMES KRAFT
PERCUSSION

DONALD KRAMER
TRUMPET

SUSAN KRAMER
OBOE

ERIC KREBS
PERCUSSION

CHRISTOPHER GABRIEL KRELL
TROMBONE

KARI J. KRUEGER
BASSOON/CONTRABASSOON

PAULA KRUPICZEWICZ
VIOLA

JOE KRZYSIAK
BASS

TOYOTA KUDO
CLARINET

BETTY J. KUHLMAN
VIOLIN

ROBERT KULLMER
TRUMPET

JEREMY KUSHNER
PERCUSSION

PENNY KWIATKOWSKY
VIOLIN

SCOTT A. LA BORDE
BASS/PERCUSSION

JAMES C. LA FRENZ
OBOE

KELLI LAGARDE
HORN

ALEXANDER LAGOS
BASS

JOSEPH LAGRANGE
BASSOON

JORGE LAGUNA
VIOLIN

GINGER LAI
HORN/PIANO/CELESTE

BRANDON LAIRD
TRUMPET

MIKE LAIRD
TRUMPET

HANK LAMBERT
TROMBONE

NATHAN LAMBERT
VIOLIN

MARY LAMPROS (WOOD)
HORN

REESE LAND
TRUMPET

FRED LANDERS
HORN

SCOTT LANDES
CLARINET

RAIFORD LANDRETH
TRUMPET

ELIZABETH LANE
CELLO

DAVID LANGLOIS
PIANO

CHRISTOPHER LANIER
VIOLIN/VIOLA

LUIS FERNANDO LANZA
VIOLA

VIRNA LANZA
CELLO

L.N. LAPP
HORN

ALICE LASATER
VIOLA

LANE JASON LASHBROOK
CELLO

MATTHEW LAUBE
TROMBONE

DAVID ALLEN LAUDERDALE

LEE ANN LAWRENCE
PERCUSSION

TERRY MARLING LAWSON

KEVIN LAY
CELLO

JAVIER LAYA
VIOLIN

KEN LEACH
OBOE

KENNETH LEACH
ORGAN

OSCAR LEAL
CELLO

COURTNEY LEARD
BASS

VIVIAN LEBLANC
VIOLIN

SHARON LEBSACK
FLUTE/HARP

HOYT LECROY
PERCUSSION

LYNN LEDBETTER
VIOLIN

KEVIN LEDGEWOOD
CLARINET

ELLEN LEDOUX
PERCUSSION

LOWELL NELSON LEDOUX
PERCUSSION

BARBARA LEE
TRUMPET

PAUL LEE
PIANO/HARPSICHORD

SIRMON LEE
TRUMPET

KAREN LEECH (JOHNSON)
FLUTE

ELEANOR S. LEEK
CELLO

REBECCA LEITCH
BASSOON

KENDALL LEJEUNE
PERCUSSION

SYMPHONY ORCHESTRA ALUMNI, CONTINUED

PETER LEMONDS
CELLO

SHAWN LEOPARD
BASSOON

DOROTHY LERNER
VIOLA

WILLIAM LERNER
BASS

STUART LEVIN
VIOLIN

DEBORAH J. LEVINE
CLARINET

ANGELA LEWIS
HORN

CLOVICE LEWIS
CELLO

DANIEL LEWIS
BASSOON

DONALD LEWIS
TROMBONE

JOHN LEWIS
BASSOON

JUSTIN LEWIS
HORN

LAURA LEWIS
HORN

NICK LEWIS
PERCUSSION

ROBERT LEWIS
CELLO

TIEN LI
CELLO

ANTHONY LICATA
HORN

WILLIAM LIDINSKY
CELLO

LOGAN EUGENE LINDSEY
TUBA

MELANIE (MIMI) LINEHAN (DRAUT)
HORN

DANA LINES
VIOLIN

RODNEY LIPPINCONTT
TRUMPET

CHARLES LIRETTE
TRUMPET

MICHAEL LISENBY
CLARINET

GUS T. LITTLE, JR.
OBOE

JASON LITTLETON
VIOLIN

JONATHAN LITTLETON
VIOLIN

JO ELLEN BROOKS LIVINGSTON
PERCUSSION

JONATHAN LIVINGSTON
BASSOON

CHARLES LOGAN
BASS

FRED LOMENZO
VIOLIN

MIROSLAV LONCAR
GUITAR

EDWARD F. LONDON
VIOLIN

PRICILLA LONG
VIOLIN

RHONDA KAY LONG (FRANKLIN)
CLARINET

GAIL LONGBOTHOM
VIOLIN

FRANK LONGINO
TROMBONE

PRICILLA LONGYEAR

REY MORGAN LONGYEAR
PERCUSSION/CONDUCTOR

CARLOS ENRIQUE LOPEZ
HORN

VANESSA EDNA LOPEZ
VIOLIN

JOHN MICHAEL LOPINTO
BASSOON

SUZANNE (MARY JEANNE ROURE) LORD
FLUTE

MICHAEL LORMAND
TROMBONE

AMANDA LOTT
CLARINET

BRUNO LUIZ LOURENSETTO
TRUMPET

KELLY LOVE
TROMBONE

PHIL LOWE
VIOLIN

JUDITH LUBRITZ
OBOE/CLARINET

JERRIE CADEK LUCKTENBERG
VIOLIN

TED LUCKTENBERG
CELLO

TOM LUER
SAXOPHONE

JUDY LUKE
OBOE

ROBERT LUPER
VIOLIN

SUSAN LUSK
VIOLIN

MELANIE LUTTRELL
FLUTE

PAM LUTZ
OBOE

JACK LYALL
CONDUCTOR

ANTONIO C. LYMON
PERCUSSION

RAYMOND LYNCH
OBOE

SUSAN LYNCH
CELLO

ALBERT LYND
HORN

JEFFREY T. LYNN
PERCUSSION

LINDE LYNN (FREIL)
CLARINET/OBOE

KENNETH LYONS
TROMBONE

MAX MABEL
VIOLIN

MAC MACBRIDE
PERCUSSION

GLADYS MACK
VIOLIN

SHERRY STENO MACK

LAURA MAC-KNIGHT
CELLO

ANN MACNALLY
VIOLIN

JULIE MACTAGGART
TRUMPET

THOMAS MACTAGGART
TROMBONE

LEORA PEARL MADDEN

ALBA VARINIA MADRID
VIOLIN

JON MADSEN
FLUTE/PICCOLO

THEODORE MADSEN
VIOLIN

EMILY MAHLER
VIOLIN

CAREN MAHONEY
FLUTE

WYNNE (GUSTAVE) MAILY
VIOLIN

COLIN W. MAIN
BASS

JULIE MAISEL (MARTIN)
PICCOLO

RALPH TYLER MAISEL
VIOLIN/VIOLA

CARL MAJOR
PERCUSSION

MICHAEL MAKI
CELLO

PATRICIA MALONE
OBOE

CHARLES MANCHESTER
CELLO

JASON THURMOND MANN

MARTHA MANN
VIOLA

PAUL MANN
CELLO

BARBARA MANNONI
VIOLIN

KAREN MANNONI
PIANO/CELLO

MARTHA MANNONI

RAYMOND MANNONI
HORN/PIANO

SHIRLEY MARCELLUS
CELLO

COLLEEN MARCOU
CELLO

AMY SERVICE MARINO

BEN MARKWELL
VIOLIN

IKE C. MARR
VIOLA

ELIZABETH MARSDEN (WINGARD)
VIOLIN

FRANK EARL MARSH
CONDUCTOR

ALEXANDRIA MONIQUE MARSHALL

GUSTAVO MARTIN
CELLO

KIRA PAULINE MARTIN

MARY ANN MARTIN
BARITONE SAXOPHONE

PANSY MARTIN
VIOLA

STEPHANIE MARTIN
CLARINET

ALAN MARTINEZ
PIANO

CAMILO MARTINEZ
VIOLIN

CLAUDIA MARTINEZ
VIOLIN

DANIEL MARTINEZ
CELLO

GUSTAVO MARTINEZ

JENEE MARTINEZ (WRIGHT)
VIOLIN

JOEL MARTINEZ
VIOLIN

JULIE MARTINEZ

JULIO MARTINEZ
VIOLA

LOUIS MARTINEZ
GUITAR

RACHEL MARTINEZ
OBOE

RAQUEL RUTH MARTINEZ
OBOE

ROLANDO MARTINEZ
VIOLA

MARIA DEL PILAR MARTINEZ ROSAS
CELLO

ANDRE MARTINS DE OLIVEIRA
FLUTE

CHRISTINE MASIELLO (RUDACILLE)
VIOLIN

ANN MASON
VIOLA

ANNA COVINGTON MASON
VIOLIN

ANNE MASON
VIOLIN/VIOLA

CAROLYN MASON
HARPSICHORD

ROBERT MASON
CELLO

SKIPPER MASON
BASS

JAMES CHRISTOPHER MASSENGALE

VINCENT MASSIMINO

JASON MATHENA
PERCUSSION

CYNTHIA MATTHEWS (WOLVERTON)
CLARINET

ELLEN MATTHEWS
HORN

MARY BESS MATTHEWS (WOLVERTON)
VIOLIN

EMILY MATTLER
VIOLIN

RICHARD MATTSON
CELLO

BRYAN MAXWELL
PERCUSSION

JASON MAXWELL
TUBA

WILLIAM RANDALL MAY

FREDERICK MAYER
VIOLA

RONALD MAYEUX
TROMBONE

DAVID MAYFIELD
TUBA

PEGGY MAYFIELD
OBOE/ENGLISH HORN

FLOSSIE MAYNARD
VIOLIN

PVT. HENRI MAYTON
VIOLIN

JAMES MCAFEE
CELLO

JOHNNIE MCARTHUR
TROMBONE

MAC MCBRIDE
PERCUSSION

EMMA MCCAIN
VIOLIN

MARTIN MCCAIN
TROMBONE

JOYCE MCCALL
CLARINET

MAX MCCARTNEY
BASSOON

NANCY MCCLELLAND
VIOLA

J.W. (WARREN) MCCLESKEY
TROMBONE

JANE MCCLURE
CELLO

SUSAN MCCONNEL
VIOLIN

SCOTT MCCOOL
BASSOON

AMY L. MCCOUL
CELLO

TIMOTHY L. MCCOUL
TRUMPET

JAMIE MCCRAKIN
CLARINET

BONNIE MCCRARY
VIOLA

MARK MCCREERY
VIOLIN

ROBERT MCCULLAR
TROMBONE

DAVID MCCULLOUGH
HORN

LE NIL MCCULLOUGH
VIOLIN

KEITH ANTHONY MCCULLUM

JAMES MCDANIEL
HORN

GENE MCDANIELS
BASS

JAMES MCDILL
TROMBONE

LINDA MCDILL
VIOLIN

HELEN JANET MACDONALD
VIOLIN

JAMIE MCDOWELL
VIOLIN

CATHERINE MCDUFFIE (KIRK)
VIOLA

CHRIS MCEWEN
BASSOON

AMANDA KELLY MCGEE (MAGEE)
PERCUSSION

FORREST MCGEHEE
PERCUSSION

LAURA MCGINTY
CELLO

RITA MICHELLE MCGINTY

MARCIA MCGOWEN
CELLO

HARRY MCGRAW
VIOLIN

SHERRY MCGRAW
VIOLIN

DALE MCGREGOR
HORN

FRED MCINNIS
PERCUSSION

ROBERT MCKEE
BASS

JOHN MCKENDREE
BASS

ALBERT MCKENZIE
BASS

SHERRY MCKENZIE
CELLO

JOHNATHAN MCLEARN
PERCUSSION

JEFF MCLELLAND
ORGAN

MARTHA MCLELLAND
TRUMPET

MAE STEVENS MCLEMORE
VIOLIN

LINDA MCLEOD
VIOLA

JONATHAN DAYTON MCLERAN
PERCUSSION

TIMOTHY MCMILLEN
TRUMPET

BARBARA MCMILLIAN
BASS

JANE BLAIR MCMORRAN
VIOLIN

GLORIA MCMULLAN
FLUTE

MARTHA MCMULLAN
VIOLIN

NEAL MCMULLAN
BASSOON

REBECCA MCMULLAN
VIOLIN

LINDA MCMURTREY
BASS

ROBERT MCNALLY
VIOLIN

ROBERT MCNAMEE
HORN

LEISA MCNEELY
FLUTE

LYNDA L. MCNEIL
BASSOON

JAMIN ANDREW MCPHETRIGE
TUBA/TRUMPET

DANIEL MCQUAGGE
CELLO

JANE MCWILLIAMS (TANKERSLEY)
FLUTE/PICCOLO

LARRY MCWILLIAMS
TRUMPET

ALANA MEADOR
HARPSICHORD

PEGGY MEADOWS
FLUTE

BEVERLY MEDEL (FRITTELLI)
FLUTE

JUDY MEISTER
VIOLIN

SUSAN MENDEL
CLARINET

BARBARA MENTZEL
CLARINET

STEVE MERRIT
PERCUSSION

LANA KAY MERTON (JONES)
FLUTE

WILLIAM MERTON
HORN

WILLIAM MERTON
TROMBONE

JANICE MESROBIAN
PIANO

ERIN MEYLAN
VIOLIN

KIRK MIDDLETON
BASS

CONSTANZA MIER (GONZALEZ)
VIOLIN

BERNARDO MIETHE
FLUTE

URSULA MIETHE
CELLO

CARRIE MILLER
CLARINET

D.A. MILLER
TRUMPET

IRENE MILLER
VIOLIN

JEFFREY WAYNE MILLER
PERCUSSION

JOHN MILLER
TRUMPET

JUDY ROYALS MILLER
CLARINET

KRISTINA MILLER
FLUTE

MARVIN MILLER
FRENCH HORN

ROBERT MILLER
CLARINET

WAYNE MILLER
OBOE

ELISABETH (ZABETTE) MILLSAPS (DEMAREST)
FLUTE

GREG MILLSAPS
VIOLA

LLOYD MIMS
BASS

MARIA DEL PILAR MIÑARRO
CELLO

NATHANAEL MINOR
HORN

ALEXANDRA MINTON
PERCUSSION

JOSHUA MISSAL
VIOLA

PEG MISSAL
VIOLIN

AKIKO MITAMURA
VIOLIN

MARGARET MOEHLMANN (WILLS)
CELLO

SUSAN MOELLERS
CLARINET

DONALD MOEN
VIOLIN

IVA LOU MOFFETT
VIOLIN

SCOTT MOLLING

FREY MONROE
CELLO

ROMINA A. MONSANTO
CELLO

MICHAEL MONTAGUE
SAXOPHONE

MARIA ALEJANDRA MONTANO
VIOLA

JASON MONTGOMERY
CLARINET

MICHAEL MONTGOMERY
BASS

CAROL MOODY
VIOLIN

SAMUEL PATRICK MOONEY
BASS

TIMOTHY MOONEY
CELLO

BARBARA MOORE (MCDONALD)
PERCUSSION

COLLEEN MOORE (DI GUILIAN)
VIOLIN

EDYTHE MOORE (MCARTHUR)
TROMBONE

JAMES MOORE
PERCUSSION

JAMES W. MOORE
CELLO

JUANITA MOORE
BASS

KAREN MOORE
HORN

KAREN MOORE
VIOLIN

LINDA MOORE
HORN

MARK MOORE
TUBA

RONNIE MOORE
BASS

THOMAS EDWARD MOORE
HARPSICHORD/ORGAN

CHARLES MOORMAN
VIOLIN

ROBIN LOUISE MORAN
VIOLIN

WESTLEY MOREHEAD
TROMBONE

CRISTINA MORELAND
HARPSICHORD

ROBERT MORELAND
VIOLIN

WILBUR MORELAND
CLARINET

REYNALDO MORENO
BASS

BRUCE MORETON
BASS

GAYLE MORGAN
VIOLIN

JEREMY MORGAN
TRUMPET

JOY MORGAN
HORN

MELANIE MORGAN
TROMBONE

RICHARD MORGAN
TROMBONE

EIJI MORIYA
FLUTE

PAUL MORMINO
HORN

KAREN MORRE
VIOLIN

APRIL MORRIS (FUNSTON)
FLUTE

JAMES MORRIS
CELLO

RUTH MORROW
VIOLA

KATHLEEN ROSE MORSE
OBOE

MARY MOSELEY
VIOLIN

CHRISTOPHER T. MOSS
PERCUSSION

MARY MUELLER (SCHLEICHER)
CELLO

JAMES MULLEN
CELLO/CLARINET

ADAM MULLER
SAXOPHONE

EDWARD MULLER
TROMBONE

TIM MULLER
TUBA

JIMMY MULLIN
CLARINET

ASHLEY MULLINS (NOBLE)
OBOE/ENGLISH HORN

WILLIAM MULLISON
OBOE/ENGLISH HORN

VALERIE MULLISON (ANDERSON)
OBOE

JOAN MULVEY (EIGHMEY)
ORGAN/PIANO/CLARINET

RAUL MUNGUIA
VIOLIN

CHARLES MUNOZ
CELLO

DONALD MUNSELL
PIANO/BASSOON/HARPSICHORD

RICHARD MUNSELL
BASSOON

RIGOBERTO MURILLO
VIOLIN

BILL MURPHY
SAXOPHONE

EARL MURPHY
ALTO SAXAPHONE

ESTELLE MURPHY
FLUTE

NEIL MURPHY
TROMBONE

JULIA MURRAY
CLARINET

JEFF MYERS
BASS

JOHN MYRICK
VIOLA

JOHN MYRICK
VIOLIN

KENNETH MYRICK
BASSOON

REBECCA MYRICK
VIOLIN

JOHN MYRIE
VIOLIN

YOSHITO NAGASE
CLARINET

SARAH NAGY
BASS

MICHAEL NAPIERALSKI
CLARINET

ANGELA NASS
CLARINET

ENRIQUE NAVARRO
VIOLIN

LISA NEAF
CELLO

SAMANTHA NEAL
VIOLIN

GILLIAN NELSON
HORN

JACKIE NELSON
PERCUSSION

LARRY NELSON
TRUMPET

EDITH NEUMANN
VIOLIN

KARL NEUMANN
CELLO

CHARLIE NEWMAN
BRASS

JOSEPH ANTHONY NEWMAN

LOUCINDA NEWMAN (HERRINGTON)
FLUTE

DANIEL NEWTON
TROMBONE

GREGORY NEWTON
BASSOON

WILLIAM NIX
CELLO

GRANT NOOE
VIOLIN

JED ALAN NORMAND

CYNTHIA NORRIS
OBOE

STEVEN NORRIS
TROMBONE

CLYDE NORTHROP
HORN

LOUISE NUCKOLS
HORN

JIMMY O'CAIN
PERCUSSION

SAMMY ELLEN ODEN
CLARINET

MILDRED OGDEN
VIOLIN

LOUIS A. OGLETREE
BASS

LOUIS OLDS
TRUMPET

DAVID OLIVER
BASS

HUGH OLIVER
TUBA

CHESTER OLSEN
BASS

THOMAS O'NEAL
CLARINET

GERALD O'NEIL
TRUMPET

HOMER G. O'NEIL
TRUMPET

SATOKO (TOKIE) ONODA (BRIDEAUX)
VIOLIN

SIOBHAN O'QUINN
VIOLA

LAURA ORANGE
VIOLIN

FRANCY LORENA ORJUELA
VIOLIN

ROMA ORNELAS
VIOLIN

JORGE ABDIEL OROZCO ALEMAN
VIOLIN

KENNETH ORTLEPP
HORN

WALTER OSADCHUCK
CELLO

NANCY OSBORNE (RECTOR)
HORN

KRONDA OSBY
CELLO

FRANCIS OSTEEN
VIOLIN

JOSEF OSZUSCIK
CLARINET

DOUGLAS OTT
CELLO

KATHERINE ELIZABETH (KAKI) OUZTS
FLUTE

TERRI OUZTS
HORN

CHERYL LEE (SHERRY) OWENSBY
FLUTE

CARLYLE PACK
HORN

JOSEPH PACKWOOD

BRIAN PADEN
TROMBONE

BETTY PAGE
CELLO

CHARLES PAGE
TUBA

JOHN PALENSKY
BASS

RAYMOND PALMER
VIOLA

JOEY PANELLA
BASS

LARRY PANELLA
SAXOPHONE

JAMES PAPIZAN
PERCUSSION

ALAN PARKER
BASS

ALICIA PARKER
CELESTE/PIANO

CHARLES PARKER
CLARINET

DERRICK PARKER
HORN

JOHN WESLEY PARKER
TROMBONE

CHRIS PARKIN
SAXOPHONE

CHARLES PARSONS
TRUMPET

WAYNE PARSONS
HORN

RONNIE PASCAL
PERCUSSION

CARALIE MORGAN PATRICK
CELLO

BOBBY PATTERSON
TUBA

DAVID PATTERSON
BASSOON

PATTIE PATTERSON
VIOLIN

JORGE ALFREDO PAULIN ARENAS
CELLO

DENNIS LEONI PAZ
CELLO

THOMAS RAIFORD PEACOCK
TUBA

GLEN PEARSON
VIOLIN

JOHN PEARSON
CLARINET

PATRICIA PEARSON
HORN

BETTY KUHLMAN PEASE
VIOLIN

SHERRY PECKENS
FLUTE

MARGARET PEDEN (DOLLARHIDE)
PIANO

KEN PEELER
VIOLIN

REBECCA L. PEEVY
TROMBONE

MICHAEL PEKAREK
HORN

PEGGY PELLETT (WOOD)
VIOLA

RONALD PENCE
TRUMPET

ALEXANDRE PERCHOUNINE
BASS

LARISSA PEREIRA DOS SANTOS
VIOLA

JORGE PEREIRA GUTIERREZ
VIOLA

JOYCE PERKINS
CLARINET

KATIE PERKINS (GLAESER)
HORN

EDSON PERRY
VIOLA/VIOLIN

JACQUELINE PERRY
VIOLIN

ALEXANDER PERSHOUNIN
BASS

FRANCK PESCI
ELECTRIC GUITAR

RICHARD SPENCER PETERS
PERCUSSION

RUTH PETERS
HORN

ASHLEY PETERSON
CLARINET

KAREN PETTERSON
VIOLIN/VIOLA

CINDE FREIL PETTEY
OBOE

STEVEN PETTEY
OBOE

CECIL J. PETTIS
PERCUSSION

VIET PHAM
VIOLIN/VIOLA

MILDRED PHELPS
VIOLIN/VIOLA

ROGER PHELPS
OBOE/CONDUCTOR

ANN PHILLIPS
VIOLIN

BETSY PHILLIPS
OBOE

HANK PHILLIPS
BASSOON

JAMES PHILLIPS
VIOLA

ROBERT PHILLIPS
TRUMPET

GEORGE K.PIAZZA
PERCUSSION

VERONICA PIAZZA
VIOLIN

CHRISTOPHER PICKENS
HORN

SARAH PIERI
VIOLIN

WILLIAM PIERSON
PERCUSSION

DARREN G. PIFER
TROMBONE

RANDI PIGFORD
VIOLIN

ROBERTO PINEDA
BASS

VENUS C. PINEDA
VIOLIN

JERROD PINTER
TROMBONE

BONNIE PIPER
HORN

ALLAN PIRTLE
VIOLIN

BARBARA PITTMAN
FLUTE

DANNY PITTMAN
TROMBONE

DAVID PITTMAN

GARRICK PITTS
CLARINET

JAVIER PLATAS
CELLO

JOHN PLEASANT
CLARINET

JOHN PLUCKER
BASS

JESSICA POGUE
HORN

SYMPHONY ORCHESTRA ALUMNI, CONTINUED

CHARLES POLK
BASS/VIOLA

SAMMY POLK
ORGAN

PAMELA POLLARD
PIANO/CELESTE

ELVA ZANE POLSON
TROMBONE

WILLIAM POMEROY
TRUMPET

FELIZ PONZIANI
CONDUCTOR/VIOLA/VIOLIN

HENRY (HURD) POPE
FLUTE

CHARLES PORTER
TROMBONE

WARREN B. PORTER
VIOLIN

WILLIAM PORTER
VIOLA

RALPH POTTLE
VIOLA

DEBRA POULIN
BASSOON

LINDA POUNCEY (SPARKS)
OBOE

GOMER POUND
CLARINET

CHRISTOPHER PRATHER
TRUMPET

KEVIN RYAN PRATHER
BASS

BRIAN PREEN
PERCUSSION

DAVID PRESSER
VIOLA

JERE PRESSER
BASSOON

WILLIAM PRESSER
VIOLA/CONDUCTOR

ANDREW PRETZELLO
PERCUSSION

ELLEN PRICE
PIANO

JOE PRICE
HORN

CHARLES CHRISTOPHER PRITCHARD
TUBA

PETER PROSSER
CELLO

JESSICA L. PRUTZ
HORN

GREGORY PUCKETT
TRUMPET

LOUIS PULLO
CELLO

DIANNE PULVER
CLARINET

JOHN PURSER
PERCUSSION

ELOISE QUACKENBOS
VIOLIN

CHERYL QUINN
VIOLIN

HOWARD QUINN
CLARINET

ERIN RABER
VIOLIN

BENNY RACKARD
BASSOON

DANIEL RACKARD
BASSOON

GEORGE LEE RADFORD
VIOLA

ROBERT RADMER
VIOLA

DANA RAGSDALE
PIANO/HARPSICHORD

VERNON RAINES
VIOLIN

JOSUE RAMIREZ
BASS

EFRAIN RAMOS
CELLO

MARY BETH RAMOS
VIOLIN

NANCY RAMOS
VIOLIN

JOHN RANDERSON
CELLO

JUDITH RANDLE (BREWER)
FLUTE

JOE M. RANKIN
CLARINET

BRIAN RANSOM
SAXOPHONE

CHRISTOPHER RASMUSSEN
PERCUSSION

NANCY RATH
VIOLIN

RICHARD RATH
OBOE

KATHERINE RAXDALE (CARLTON)
TROMBONE

ATICO APOENA RAZERA DE AZEVEDO
VIOLIN

CHARLENE REDDING
FLUTE

MICHAEL SCOTT REDDOCH
PERCUSSION

STEPHEN REDFIELD
VIOLIN

DANIELLE REED
VIOLIN

JANEL M. REED
TRUMPET

SCOTT REED
BASS

LOORIE REEVES
FLUTE

WILLIAM REHMANN
TRUMPET

ELIZABETH LANE REID
HORN

JEAN REIS
VIOLIN

PATRICK RETTGER
TUBA

LESLEY RETZER
CELLO

JOAN RETZKE
TRUMPET

EDNA RICE (PERKINS)
VIOLA

JAMES RICE
SAXOPHONE

JASON JOHN RICE

SUSAN RICE
OBOE

RONNIE RICH
HORN

CRANDALL RICHARD
VIOLA

EDDIE RICHARD
TROMBONE

FRED RICHARDS
VIOLIN

JOEL RICHARDS
TRUMPET

PATRICK RICHARDS
HORN

GWENDOLYN RICHARDSON (PATE)
FLUTE

MARY JANE RICHARDSON
VIOLA

MARY JANE RICHMOND (MOSS)
VIOLA

RHONDA RICHMOND
VIOLIN

WIL RICHMOND
PERCUSSION

MARGARET CHERYL RICKER
HORN

VERONICA L. RICKS
HORN

JAMES RIGDON
HORN

WILBERN RIGDON
HORN

ELIZABETH DIANE RILES (PULVER)
CLARINET

CHRISTINA RILEY
PIANO

MATTHEW E. RIPPERE
BASSOON/CONTRABASSOON

TOM RISHER
PERCUSSION

MEG RISSEN (RISSER)
VIOLA

CARROLL RITCHIE
OBOE

DENISSA RIVAS
FLUTE

FREEMAN ROBBIE
EUPHONIUM

LEO W. ROBERTS
CLARINET

PAUL STANTON ROBERTS
VIOLIN

ANDREW ROBERTSON
VIOLA

LISA ROBERTSON
VIOLIN

WILLIAM ROBERTSON
BASSOON

CHERYL ROBINSON
VIOLIN

GREG ROBINSON
BASS

LEE A. ROBINSON
PERCUSSION

MARCIA ROBINSON (MARTIN)
FLUTE

CHARLES ROBITAILLE
OBOE

PAUL ROBY
VIOLIN

ANDERSON ROCHA
VIOLIN

DAVID RODRIGUEZ
TRUMPET

GISELA RODRIGUEZ
VIOLA

HECTOR JAVIER RODRIGUEZ (CARCAMO)
HORN

RAUL RODRIGUEZ
HORN

SARA RODRIGUEZ
VIOLIN

BARRY ROGERS
VIOLIN

DENISE ROGERS (ROWAN)
BASSOON

JEFF ROGERS
PERCUSSION

MELVIN ROGERS
CLARINET

PAMALA ROGERS
FLUTE

VIRGINIA ROHDE
VIOLIN

BARBARA ROHNERT (HAMPTON)
FLUTE

ROBERT KEVIN ROLAND
TUBA

BEN ROLFS
VIOLIN

SONDRA ROMAN
VIOLA

DEBORAH ROMEO (DEAN)
OBOE

PETER ROMEO
TROMBONE

MARIA JOSE ROMERO
VIOLIN

MISTY RONDEAU (THEISEN)
FLUTE

PAT (JOHN) ROONEY
CLARINET

ZACHARY NATHAN ROSE
TRUMPET

DORIS ROSENBAUM
VIOLIN

GERALD ROSENBAUM
VIOLIN

SIDNEY ROSENBAUM
CELLO

ALAN ROSENBERG
VIOLA

BARBARA ROSS
TRUMPET

JEANIE ROSS
TUBA

JUNE ROSS
VIOLIN

MAYER E. ROSS
VIOLIN

VINCENT ROSSE
PERCUSSION

KELLY BECKMAN ROTH
ORGAN

ROBERT ROUBOS
ORGAN

STEPHEN ROUSE
BASSOON

WEBSTER ROWAN
TROMBONE

JENNIFER ROWE

JONATHAN ROWE
TROMBONE

JAMES ROWELL
CONTRABASSOON

JUDY ROYALS
BASSOON

ART RUANGTIP
TROMBONE

D. RUNNELLS
BASS

MARTHA RUNNELS
TRUMPET

PAMALA RUNNELS
HORN

HAL RUNYAN
CELLO

SORANA RUS
HARP

CONNIE RUSHTON (WHEAT)
TROMBONE

JASON RUSK
CLARINET

LINDA RUSLING
PERCUSSION

CHERYL RUSSELL
BASSOON

THEODORE RUSSELL
CONDUCTOR/VIOLA

JENNIFER RYAN (DIAMOND)
OBOE

VIRGINIA RYAN
BASS

KEVIN KAI RYTTER
TENOR TUBA

BILL SADLER
TUBA

PABLO SAELZER
VIOLA

MARIA DOLORES SAENZ
CELLO

GILBERT SAETRE
VIOLIN/VIOLA/BASS

GRAZZIA SAGASTUME
VIOLA

NORMA ANGELICA (SUKY) SALAZAR (BLYTHE)
PIANO/VIOLA

ALEJANDRO SALGADO
VIOLA

MAURICE SALVANT
OBOE

ANTHONY SANCHEZ
FLUTE

ELDER SANCHEZ
BASS

RICHARD SANCHEZ
VIOLIN

THERESA SANCHEZ
PIANO

SERGIO EDUARDO SANDOVAL

MARY SANFORD
FLUTE

J. PAUL SANSING
TUBA

JULIE SARGEANT
CLARINET

ERIC SATTERWHITE
PERCUSSION

DAMION DEMETREOUS SAUCIER

THELMA SAUCIER
VIOLIN

RYAN SAUL
PERCUSSION

DEBORAH SAWYER (BLACKWELL)
HORN

KENNETH SAXON
TRUMPET

STEPHEN SAXON
VIOLIN

MARY ABBEY SAYLE
HARP

LUCAS SCALAMOGNA
VIOLIN

JOHN SCARBROUGH
CLARINET

CARLEIGH SCATES
PERCUSSION

CHRISTOPHER SCHAETZLY
TRUMPET

MICHAEL SCHALLOCK
TUBA

JOY SCHARMEN
TRUMPET

DAVID SCHELL
CLARINET

MATTHEW A. SCHICK
VIOLIN

SUSAN SCHIMELPFENIG (JOHNSON)
CELLO

MARGUERITE SCHMIDLEY (WOLFE)
BASS

WAYNE SCHMIDT
TUBA

CLARE SCHOLTZ
OBOE

MARY LEIGH SCHRAMKO

EDWIN SCHULTZ
VIOLIN

RAYMOND SCHULZE
VIOLIN

MOHAMAD SCHUMAN
PERCUSSION

LINDA SCHWARZ-MUGGENBURG
VIOLA

JAMES SCLATER
CLARINET

JACQUELINE SCOTT
HORN

MATTHEW JAMIL SCOTT

MOLLI SCOTT
HORN

RICHARD SCOTT
CLARINET

RICHARD SCOTT
VIOLA

SAMUEL SCOTT
CLARINET

CHARLOTTE SCURRY (SCHUENKE)
VIOLIN

NITA ANN SEE
PIANO

BLANCA SEGURA (BERDION)
VIOLIN

SANDRA SELING
BASSOON

ROMEKA NICOLE SELLERS

JEREMY SENECA
TRUMPET

ELLEN SESSIONS
VIOLA

DAVID SEVIER
CLARINET

ROBERT SEVIER
CLARINET

GLEN SEWELL
PERCUSSION

SUSAN SHACKELFORD
OBOE

E.A. SHAMBURGER
VIOLIN

MICHAEL SHAMBURGER
BASSOON

SCOTT SHANKS
TUBA

CAROLYN SHANNON (SAPER)
VIOLIN

JAMES SHANNON
VIOLIN

DAVID SHAW
PERCUSSION

TIMOTHY GAVIN SHAW
PERCUSSION

BARRY SHAW
PERCUSSION

NANCY SHEEHAN
TROMBONE

REGINALD SHELBY
BASS

ANNA SHELTON
PERCUSSION

MARY BUSH SHEPPARD
TRUMPET

HANNAH SHETLER
VIOLA

YUJI SHIBATA
TRUMPET

KARL GREEN SHIELDS
VIOLIN

STEVE SHIELDS
PERCUSSION

GENSHOKU (KEN) SHIMMURA
TRUMPET

KEVIN SHIRA
BASSOON

PHILIP SHIRLEY
BASSOON

NATHAN M. SHIVER
ELECTRIC BASS

ILYA SHPIGELMAN
VIOLA

IRINA SHPIGELMAN
VIOLIN

GAO SHULI
CELLO

JAMES SHUMATE
OBOE

JESSICA SICSU DE FRANCA
VIOLA

JOYCE SIDORFSKY
VIOLIN

CARMEL SIGNA
HORN

ALLEN KENT SILLS
TROMBONE/BASS

CHARLES SILLS
OBOE

KENT SILLS
DOUBLE BASS

HEATHER SIMMONS (FAIRCHILD)
FLUTE

JENNIFER SIMMONS
CLARINET

JUNE SIMMONS
OBOE

SHERRY SIMMONS
VIOLIN/VIOLA

TODD SIMMONS
PIANO

ELIZABETH SIMOLKE
BASS

JAMES SIMPSON
CLARINET

BECKY SIMS
CELLO

LARRY SIMS
PERCUSSION

SHERRY SIMS
VIOLIN

LINDA SINGLETARY
VIOLIN

DANA SKELTON
TRUMPET

CHRISTIE ANN SLADE

JEFFREY SLADE
TUBA

CLIFTON JERRAD SLATER
TRUMPET

SCOTT SLAUGHTER
BASS

DUDLEY SLAY
ALTO SAXOPHONE

GRACE SLAY
VIOLA

WILLIAM SLAYTON
TRUMPET

MARILYN SLIPETZ
VIOLIN

BENJAMIN SLOAN
PERCUSSION

ANNA SLOSS
HORN

SHANNON SLYFIELD
CLARINET

SHERRY SMIS

AMY SMITH
OBOE

ANGELA SMITH
TRUMPET

BETTY LOU SMITH
TRUMPET

BILL SMITH
TRUMPET

CYNTHIA SMITH
VIOLIN

DALTON SMITH
TRUMPET

DAVID SMITH
BASSOON

DAWN AVERY SMITH
VIOLA

DEBBIE K. SMITH
VIOLIN

DIANNE SMITH
FLUTE

GARY SMITH
CELLO

GORDON SMITH
CELLO/BASSOON

JENNY SMITH (GOTT)
FLUTE

KATIE ARNOLD SMITH
VIOLIN

KEN SMITH
TUBA

LAMAR SMITH

MRS. P.E. SMITH
VIOLIN

RICHARD SMITH
TROMBONE

RONALD SMITH
CLARINET

SABINA (TERRY) SMITH (IVY)
BASSOON

SAMANTHA SMITH
FLUTE

VIRGINIA SMITH
BAGPIPES

WILLIAM H. SMITH
HORN

GAYLA SMITHEY
PERCUSSION

JOHN SMOODY
BASS

BURDETTE SMYTHE
HORN

DAVID SNELL
TRUMPET

ETHEL SNODGRASS
ACCOMPANIMENT

BRAD SNOW
TRUMPET

DON SOHAN
TRUMPET

REGINA SOHRWIDE
OBOE

CAMILLA SOLEN
CELLO

FIDENCIO SOLIS
VIOLIN/VIOLA

ANA MARIA SOLIS
VIOLIN

SUZANNE SONNIER
CLARINET

GEORGINA SOTELO
OBOE

GILBERTO SOTO
BASS

PABLO SOTOMAYOR
PIANO

SARAH SOULEN
FLUTE

ARNIE SOWDEN
PERCUSSION

CHRISTINA SPAHMER
VIOLIN

JONATHAN SPANGLER
PERCUSSION

JOHN SPARKS
TROMBONE

DANIEL SPEER
CELLO

KLAUS SPEER
HARP/HARPSICHORD

CLINTON SPELL
TRUMPET

DAVID SPENCER
TRUMPET

GLENN SPILLER
TRUMPET

JOSEPH SPIRAKIS
TUBA

FELIX SPOONER
BASS

LOIS SPOONER
VIOLA

GREG DOUGLAS SPRINGER
TROMBONE

CONNIE SPRINKELL
PERCUSSION

DONALD SPURRIER
CLARINET

MARK ST. PIERRE
TRUMPET

PAUL ST. PIERRE
TUBA

LAURA STAFFANELL
VIOLIN

PAULA STAMBORSKI
VIOLIN

ELIZABETH STANFORD
CELLO

CHANDLER STAPLETON
BASSOON

AMANDA STEELE
OBOE

STEPHANIE STEELMAN (SMITH)
FLUTE

VICTOR STEEN
TROMBONE

BERRY STEINACKER
PICCOLO

TEMPERANCE BABCOCK STEISKAL
VIOLIN

LINDA STEJSKAL (STEVENS)
PIANO/CELESTE/PERCUSSION

DE ANN STEPHENS (MCLAURIN)
HORN

KAREN STEPHENS
HARP

BRIAN STEVENS
PERCUSSION

EMILY STEVENS
OBOE/ENGLISH HORN

FLOYD STEVENS
HORN

LYNDALL B. STEVENS
VIOLIN

MARY ANN STEWART
FLUTE

STACEY STEWART
BASS FLUTE

STEPHAN STEWART
TRUMPET

ALLAN STIFFLER
TRUMPET

BRIAN STIFFLER
HORN

BLYTHE STILES
CELLO

JEFF STILL
TROMBONE

WILLIAM STINE

RICHARD STOELZEL
TRUMPET

TODOR STOINOV
PIANO

TOMMY STOKES
CLARINET

BOB STOREY
TROMBONE

CHRISTOPHER STOREY
PERCUSSION

LEE ANN STOTT
FLUTE

ALMAN STRAIN
BASSOON

BILL STRAIN
CLARINET

CARRIE STRICKLAND
HORN

NAN STRICKLIN
VIOLIN

GEORGE STRINGER
BASS

MARY ANNE STRINGER
HARPSICHORD

RANDY STRINGER
TRUMPET

WILLIAM STROHM
OBOE

AMEY STRONG
FLUTE

BRIAN STRONG
HORN

JEB STUART
BASS

JOY STUART
CELLO

MARY STUART (HARMON)
VIOLIN

ROBERT STUMP
TROMBONE

BLYTHE STYLES

LUCIANA SUAREZ
HARPSICHORD

ANGELA SULLIVAN (KILCREASE)
OBOE/ENGLISH HORN

MARIE SUMNER-LOTT
CLARINET

JOSE SUNDERLAND
CELLO

ERNEST SUTER
BASS

KISHIKO SUZUMI
VIOLA/VIOLIN

PETER SWANN
TROMBONE

WAYNE SWANN
BASSOON

CHRISTIAN SWEATT
OBOE/ENGLISH HORN

MORRIS SWEATT
TROMBONE

CRYSTAL SWEPSON-BRITTON
HORN

GLENN SWIATEK
BASS

HENRY SWINDULL
FLUTE

CAROLYN SWITZER (TILLER)
CELLO

GINGER SWITZER
CELLO

JANA SWITZER
VIOLA

PAT TALLEY
HORN

KEN-ICHIRO TAMAYAMA
TRUMPET

ROCIO TAMEZ
VIOLIN

YAU AGNES TANG
VIOLIN

MATTIE SUE TERRY
VIOLIN

STELLA TARTSINIS
SAXOPHONE

KYRI TATE
VIOLIN

HELENA M. TAVAST
VIOLIN

ARLINE TAYLOR
VIOLIN

BROOKS TAYLOR
VIOLIN

CLIFTON TAYLOR
TROMBONE

MATTHEW TAYLOR
HORN

STEPHEN TAYLOR
PERCUSSION

THOMAS TAYLOR
PERCUSSION

ATICO TAZERA
VIOLIN

DASHA TEELIN
CLARINET

PAMELA TELLEJOHN
VIOLIN

IVY TERRY
HORN

GEORGE RAY THEAUX
PERCUSSION

ALAN THEISEN
SAXOPHONE

JAMES THEISEN
HORN

BENJAMIN THERRELL
VIOLIN

VALENCIA THEVENIN (COLLINS)
VIOLIN

SHIQUITA THIGPEN

CLIFF THOMAS
TRUMPET

DALISAY THOMAS

ELIZABETH THOMAS
ORGAN

EMMETT THOMAS
CORNET

GENERAL LEE THOMAS
VIOLA

JANET THOMAS
CLARINET

K. THOMAS THOMAS

KATHERINE ANNE THOMAS
HORN

LOUISE THOMAS
FLUTE

MOLLY THOMAS
VIOLIN

STEPHANIE V. THOMAS
CELLO

CHRISTOPHER THOMPSON
VIOLIN

CORY MATTHEW THOMPSON
CLARINET

DAN THOMPSON
VIOLIN

DOMINIQUE THOMPSON
TROMBONE

HARRY THOMPSON
VIOLIN

RICK THORLEY
CLARINET

NEAL (DONALD) TIDWELL
TUBA/DOUBLE BASS

KAREN TIEGREEN (CEMBALO)

INGRID TITHCHEVA
CELLO

CHRISTOPHER TILLEY
PIANO/CELESTE

KELLY J. TISDALE
PIANO

REBECCA TODARO
HARP

JOSEPH TOMEI
HORN

SUE TOMLIN
VIOLA

LORENA TOMSON
DIRECTOR/VIOLIN

LESLIE (NATALIE) TORRENCE
VIOLIN

GLADYS TORRES
VIOLIN

RENE B. TORRES
VIOLIN

JOEL EDGARDO TOSTA ALARCON
VIOLIN

KATHLEEN TOUCHSTONE (PEARSON)
VIOLIN

ANA LUIZA TOVO LOUREIRE
VIOLIN

RUTH TOWNSEND
BASSOON

DAVID TRAMMELL
TRUMPET

HELENA TRAVAST

SYMPHONY ORCHESTRA ALUMNI, CONTINUED

JAMES TRIBBLE
VIOLIN

ANDREW TRIMBLE
TRUMPET

L.A. TRIMBLE
VIOLIN

DANIEL TRINGOV
VIOLIN

CATHERINE TROUARD (WAGONER)
CLARINET

CHERI TRUE (WAITE)
FLUTE

JERRY TRUSTY
HORN

YAO-YU TSAI
CELLO

WILMA TUBBS

CLIFTON CRAIG TUCKER
TROMBONE

NORMA CAROL TUCKER
CELLO

KARLA TULEY
VIOLIN

MEME TUNNELL
PIANO/HARPSICHORD

MICHAEL TUNNELL
TRUMPET

JUDY TURNBULL
CELLO

JIMMY TURNER
BASS

LLOYD TURNER
TRUMPET

TRUDY TURNER
FLUTE

MARJORIE TYRE
HARP

ALEJANDRO ULLOA
VIOLA

BILLY ULMER
TRUMPET

SUSAN UNDERWOOD (BOWERS)
OBOE

JOHN UNGURIAT
BASS

ALEX MAURICIO URBINA
VIOLIN

SHERRI VALENTINE
VIOLIN

BARBI VAN HORN
HORN

EVA VAN HOUTEN
VIOLIN

SUSAN VAN WICK
HORN

BURT VANCE
HORN

JUNE ROSS VARDAMAN
VIOLIN

JUNE VARDAMAN
VIOLIN

FERNANDO VARGAS
CELLO

DARRYL VARNADO
OBOE

KELLY K. VARNER
BASSOON

HOMERO VASQUEZ
PERCUSSION

MICHAEL VAUGHN
VIOLIN

SUSAN VEGLIA (PURSLEY)
HORN

MAYARA N. VELAZQUEZ
CELLO

JOHN VENETTOZZI
CONDUCTOR

DAVID VERNON
PERCUSSION

ELEYNA VERNON (KARR)
CLARINET

MICHAEL VERNON
TROMBONE

JOHN VETTEL
VIOLIN/VIOLA

JOSE ROBERTO VIANNA
BASS

DENISE VIATOR
TROMBONE

AMANDA VIRELLES
PIANO

MARY VOLPE
VIOLA

TROY VUYOVICH
VIOLIN

DIMITRI VYCHKO
CELLO

ELIZABETH WADE

MARY ANN WADE
CLARINET

RAY WADENPFUHL
HORN

HAROLD (NICKY) WAGGONER
TROMBONE

ELLEN WAILS
VIOLIN

CHARLES WAITE
TROMBONE

CHERI WAITE (TRUE)
FLUTE

JOHN WAITE
TRUMPET

JACOB WALBURN
TRUMPET

FAYE WALDORF
FLUTE

JODY WALKER
PERCUSSION

JONATHAN WALKER
TRUMPET

KELLY WALKER

THOMAS WALKER
TROMBONE

DAMION WALLACE
VIOLIN

NORMAN WALLACK
VIOLA

CHRISTA L. WALLER
VIOLIN

AMY WALSH
FLUTE

ANN WALTERS
PERCUSSION

BARRY WARD
CLARINET

NAPOLEON WARDELL
BASSOON

SUSAN WARD-STEINMAN
FLUTE

BOBBY WARE
OBOE/ENGLISH HORN

CAROLYN WARE
BASSOON

JOE WARE
BRASS

RAY WARREN
CELLO

ROBERT WARREN

JANE WASSON
VIOLA

THOMAS WASSON
BASSOON

DONALD WATANABE
CLARINET

GAIL WATERS
VIOLA

JAMES WATKINS

LAUNIN WATROUS
VIOLA

FRANK WATSON
BASSOON

SAMUEL WATSON
CELLO

ROGER WATTAM
OBOE

TALMAGE WATTS
TRUMPET

CAROL WEATHERFORD (STANDLAND)
OBOE/ENGLISH HORN

JOANNE (JULIE) WEATHERLY
VIOLIN

JESSICA WEATHERMON
OBOE

ANNA WEAVER

JOHN GRAYSON WEAVER
TUBA

KATIE WEAVER (BRAY)
FLUTE

KRISTINE WEBB
FLUTE

KAREN WEBSTER
CELLO

PETER WEHNER
PERCUSSION

NORA WEISH
FLUTE

DAN WELBORN
HORN

KEVIN WELBORN
PERCUSSION

LLOYD WELLS
BASS

GRETCHEN WELSCH
VIOLA

NORA WELSH
FLUTE

KARLENE WEST
FLUTE

RHONDA WEST
FLUTE

JAMES WESTBROOK
FLUTE

JUDITH WESTBROOK

BENJAMIN WETHERBEE
TRUMPET

J ROBERT WHIDDON
PERCUSSION

ELIZABETH WHIREN (SHUHAN)
FLUTE

CAROL WHITE
CLARINET

DANA WHITE
CELLO

JUDY WHITE
CLARINET

RONNIE WHITE
VIOLIN

SUZANNE WHITE
CLARINET

WILLIAM WHITE
BASS

WILLIAM WHITE
HORN

TOMMY WHITEHEAD
HORN

SUZANNE WHITEHORN

CAROL WITHERSPOON

WILLIAM WITHERSPOON

TINA WHITWORTH
PERCUSSION

MARY KAY WHORTON
BASSOON

SUSAN VAN WICK

THURE WIDEGREN
VIOLIN

BARBARA WIEMAN
VIOLIN

CAITLIN WIENERS
BASSOON

JOHN STEVEN WIEST
TROMBONE

NANCY WIGGINS
HORN

LAURIE WILCOX
VIOLIN

RUSSELL WILEY
TRUMPET

JAMES WILKERSON
VIOLIN

BETTY WILLIAMS
VIOLA

CHARLES WILLIAMS

EDWARD WILLIAMS
TRUMPET

ELIZABETH WILLIAMS
FLUTE

ELLEN WILLIAMS
CELLO

JEFF WILLIAMS
VIOLIN

KAREN WILLIAMS
FLUTE

KAREN WILLIAMS
PERCUSSION

LEANN WILLIAMS
OBOE

LESLEY WILLIAMS
CLARINET

RANDY WILLIAMS
VIOLIN

REGGIE WILLIAMS
VIOLIN

RHODA WILLIAMS (BRECKENRIDGE)
VIOLA

ROBERT WILLIAMS
SAXOPHONE/PERCUSSION

ROGER WILLIAMS
VIOLIN

ROSEMARY A. WILLIAMS
HORN

STEPHANIE WILLIAMS

TRACY WILLIAMS
OBOE

HOWARD WILLIAMSON

REBECCA WILLIAMSON
HORN

MARGARET WILLS
CELLO

CRAIG WILSON
PERCUSSION

DAMION WILSON
VIOLIN

HERBERT WILSON
TROMBONE

JAMES WILSON
TROMBONE

JAMIE WILSON
VIOLIN

KAREN WILSON
PIANO

SEAN WILSON
VIOLIN

PAGE WINFIELD (WINSFIELD)
VIOLIN

PAT WINNEGE
CLARINET

DAVID WINSTEAD
BASS

JEREMY WINSTEAD
SAXOPHONE

LYNN WITHERSPOON
VIOLIN

JAMES WITTMAN
CLARINET

ANDREW WOLVERTON
HORN

CYNTHIA WOLVERTON (MATTHEWS)
CLARINET

ERNEST WOOD
VIOLIN

GERALD WOOD
HORN

MARY WOOD
HORN

NORMAN WOOD
CELLO

CARLA WOODMANSEE
CLARINET

NORMAN WOODRICK
CLARINET

NATHAN A. WOODS
TROMBONE

JETHRO WOODSON
BASSOON

DAVID L. WOODWARD
TROMBONE

JAMES WOOLLY
HORN

DANIEL WOOTEN
PERCUSSION

CHARLES WOOTON
BASS

CHRISTOPHER S. WORD
CLARINET/SAXOPHONE

DAVID WOZNIAK
SAXOPHONE/BASSOON

AL WRIGHT
CLARINET

BARBARA WRIGHT (WORKMAN)
HORN

CYNTHIA WRIGHT
VIOLIN

JEANETTE WRIGHT
VIOLIN

JENEE WRIGHT
VIOLIN

STEPHEN WRIGHT
VIOLIN

AMY WRISTERS

L.W. WYATT
BASS/VIOLIN

WILLIAM WYNN
TROMBONE

JOSHUA YAEGER
VIOLA

AI YAMAGUCHI
FLUTE

IL-OH YANG
VIOLIN

RYAN YARD
PERCUSSION

TSAI YASYU
CELLO

ROBERT L. YATES JR.
CELLO

PHYLLIS YONKO
OBOE

SOO YOO
CELLO

PAUL YORK
CELLO

ANNIE YOUNG
VIOLIN

MARY KAY YOUNG (WOOLLY)
OBOE

MARY YOUNG
VIOLA

RAYMOND YOUNG
TROMBONE

SCOTT YOUNG
HORN

TERESA YOUNG
HORN

MARIE ZAMBONI
FLUTE

CHARLES ZANICHELLI
CLARINET

JOANNE ZANINELLI
VIOLIN

OLGA ZIABRIKOVA
VIOLA

ALVARO ZUNIGA
CELLO

[1] THIS LIST ALSO INCLUDES SOME FACULTY, COMMUNITY MEMBERS AND GUEST PERFORMERS.

SYMPHONY ORCHESTRA REPERTOIRE FROM 1988 TO PRESENT

1988-89

BARBER, SAMUEL
CONCERTO FOR VIOLIN AND ORCHESTRA
JACQUELINE PERRY, VIOLIN

BEETHOVEN, LUDWIG VAN
SYMPHONY NO. 7 IN A MAJOR, OP. 92

DUKAS, PAUL
L'APPRENTI SORCIER

DVORÁK, ANTONIN
SYMPHONY NO. 5 (9) IN E MINOR, OP. 95 ("FROM THE NEW WORLD")

GIULIANI, MAURO G.
CONCERTO FOR GUITAR, STRINGS, AND TIMPANI
NATASA KLASINC, GUITAR

HANSON, HOWARD
SYMPHONY NO. 2, OP. 30 (ROMANTIC)

HAYDN, JOSEPH
CONCERTO IN C MAJOR FOR CELLO AND ORCHESTRA
COLLEEN MARCOU, CELLO

MOZART, WOLFGANG AMADEUS
DIE ZAUBERFLÖTE (COMPLETE)

OVERTURE TO *DIE ZAUBERFLÖTE*
JOE BARRY MULLINS, GUEST CONDUCTOR

NIELSEN, CARL
SAUL AND DAVID: PRELUDE TO ACT II

PUCCINI, GIACOMO
"QUANDO M'EN VO"
FROM *LA BOHÈME*

"SI, MI CHIAMANO MIMI"
FROM *LA BOHÈME*
MARYANN KYLE, SOPRANO

RAVEL, MAURICE
BOLERO

REVUELTAS, SILVESTRE
SENSEMAYÁ

SAINT-SAËNS, CAMILLE
PIANO CONCERTO NO.2, OP. 22, IN G MINOR
STANLEY WALDOFF, PIANO

WEBER, CARL MARIA VON
CONCERTO FOR BASSOON AND ORCHESTRA
JOHN BIVINS, BASSOON

ZANINELLI, LUIGI
LEXICON OF BEASTIES

1989-1990

BEETHOVEN, LUDWIG VAN
OVERTURE TO *FIDELIO*

COPLAND, AARON
THREE DANCES FROM "RODEO"

MAHLER, GUSTAV
LIEDER EINES FAHRENDEN GESELLEN
VIRGINIA DUPUY, MEZZO-SOPRANO

MASSENET, JULES
CENDRILLON (COMPLETE)

MOZART, WOLFGANG AMADEUS
SINFONIA CONCERTANTE IN E-FLAT MAJOR, K. 297B

PROKOFIEV, SERGE
SUITE FROM *LIEUTENANT KIJE*, OP. 60

RAVEL, MAURICE
CONCERTO FOR PIANO AND ORCHESTRA IN G MAJOR
LOIS LEVENTHAL, PIANO

SUITE FROM *MA MERE L'OYE* (MOTHER GOOSE)

RODRIGO, JOAQUIN
CONCIERTO DE ARANJUEZ FOR GUITAR AND ORCHESTRA
GIOVANNI DECHIARO, GUITAR

SAINT-SAËNS, CAMILLE
LE CARNAVAL DES ANIMAUX

SHOSTAKOVICH, DMITRI
FESTIVE OVERTURE

TCHAIKOVSKY, PIOTR
ROMEO AND JULIET: FANTASY OVERTURE (1880 VERSION)

THE NUTCRACKER (COMPLETE)
WITH BALLET MISSISSIPPI

VERDI, GIUSEPPE
OVERTURE TO *LA FORZA DEL DESTINO*

1990-91

BRAHMS, JOHANNES
VARIATIONS ON A THEME BY HAYDN

BEETHOVEN, LUDWIG
PIANO CONCERTO NO. 1 IN C MAJOR, OP. 15
DAVID HUGHES, PIANO

GRONDAHL, LAUNY
CONCERTO FOR TROMBONE AND ORCHESTRA
MARTA JEAN HOFACRE, TROMBONE

HANDEL, GEORG F.
MESSIAH (COMPLETE)

LALO, ÉDOUARD
CELLO CONCERTO IN D MINOR
JORGE PAULIN, CELLO

MAHLER, GUSTAV
LIEDER EINES FARHENDEN GESELLEN (SONGS OF A WAYFARER)
VIRGINIA DUPUY, MEZZO-SOPRANO

MOZART, WOLFGANG AMADEUS
LE NOZZE DI FIGARO (COMPLETE)

PIANO CONCERTO NO. 19, K. 459
LAURA MCGAVOCK, PIANO

ORFF, CARL
CARMINA BURANA

PROKOFIEV, SERGEI
PETER AND THE WOLF

ROSSINI, GIOACHINO
"UNA VOCE POCO FA" FROM *THE BARBER OF SEVILLE*
ROSEMARY CALDWELL, SOPRANO

TCHAIKOVSKY, PIOTR
ROMEO AND JULIET

VERDI, GIUSEPPE
OVERTURE TO *LA FORZA DEL DESTINO*

POPS IN THE PINEBELT

1991-92

BACH, JOHANN SEBASTIAN
CONCERTO FOR HARPSICHORD NO. 1 IN D MINOR
DANA RAGSDALE, HARPSICHORD

BARBER, SAMUEL
ADAGIO FOR STRINGS, OP. II

BERLIOZ, HECTOR
HUNGARIAN MARCH FROM *LE DAMNATION DE FAUST*

BERNSTEIN, LEONARD
OVERTURE TO *CANDIDE*

BRAHMS, JOHANNES
CONCERTO FOR VIOLIN AND ORCHESTRA, OP. 77
ALEXANDRE BRUSSILOVSKY, VIOLIN

BRITTEN, BENJAMIN
SERENADE FOR TENOR, HORN, AND STRINGS, OP. 31
DAVID HOLLEY, TENOR
DENNIS BEHM, HORN

DURUFLE, MAURICE
REQUIEM, OP. 9

GERSHWIN, GEORGE
CONCERTO FOR PIANO AND ORCHESTRA IN F
MARY ANN STRINGER, PIANO

MOZART, WOLFGANG AMADEUS
REQUIEM IN D MINOR, K. 626

PIANO CONCERTO NO. 20 IN D MINOR, K. 466
THERESA SANCHEZ, PIANO

NICOLAI, OTTO
DIE LÜSTIGEN WEIBER VON WINDSOR (COMPLETE)

RESPIGHI, OTTORINO
PINI DI ROMA

REVUELTAS, SILVESTRE
HOMENAJE A FEDERICO GARCIA LORCA

OCHO POR RÁDIO

PLANOS

1992-93

BARTOK, BELA
FIRST RHAPSODY (FOLK DANCES)
CARA PATRICK, CELLO

BERNSTEIN, LEONARD
"AMERICA" FROM *WEST SIDE STORY*

"TONIGHT QUINTET" FROM *WEST SIDE STORY*

BIZET, GEORGES
"HABANERA" FROM *CARMEN*

"MELONS, COUPONS" FROM *CARMEN*

"NOUS AVONS EN TETE UNE AFFAIRE" FROM *CARMEN*

"VOTRE TOAST, JE PEUX VOUS LE RENDER" *FROM CARMEN*

BORODIN, ALEXANDER
PRINCE IGOR: POLOVTSIAN DANCES

BRAHMS, JOHANNES
SYMPHONY NO. 2, OP. 73, D MAJOR

BRUCH, MAX
CONCERTO FOR CLARINET, VIOLA AND ORCHESTRA
WILBUR MORELAND, CLARINET
MICKEY DAVIS, VIOLA

CHÁVEZ, CARLOS
SINFONÍA DI ANTÍGONA (SYMPHONY NO. 1)

COPLAND, AARON
EL SALON MÉXICO

HONEGGER, ARTHUR
CONCERTO DA CAMERA FOR FLUTE AND ENGLISH HORN
PATTY MALONE, ENGLISH HORN
SHARON LEBSACK, FLUTE

KHACHATURIAN, ARAM
CONCERTO FOR PIANO WITH ORCHESTRA
JENNIFER HIGHT, PIANO

MOZART, WOLFGANG AMADEUS
PIANO CONCERTO NO. 20 IN D MINOR
TARA VANDEVENDER, PIANO

PUCCINI, GIACOMO
"O MIO BABBINO CARO" FROM *GIANNI SCHICCHI*
DIANA JACKSON, SOPRANO

"QUANDO M'EN VO" FROM *LA BOHÈME*
LEAH KELLY, SOPRANO

ACT I FINALE FROM *LA BOHÈME*
RHONDA HOOD, SOPRANO
MICHAEL POSEY, TENOR

ROSSINI, GIOACCHINO
GUILLAUMETELL: OVERTURE

"ECCO RIDENTE IN CIELO" FROM *IL BARBIERE DI SIVIGLIA*
WILLIAM PARSONS, TENOR

STRAUSS, JOHANN
ACT II FINALE FROM *DIE FLEDERMAUS*

VERDI, GIUSEPPE
REQUIEM

"AH, FORS E LUI AND SEMPRE LIBERA" FROM *LA TRAVIATA*
CONSTANCE ROBERTS, SOPRANO

WAGNER, W. RICHARD
WESENDOCK LIEDER
SUZANNE WIEHN, MEZZO-SOPRANO

ZANINELLI, LUIGI
FANFARE AND ALLELUIA (WORLD PREMIERE)

OPERA A LA CARTE

1993-94

BERLIOZ, HECTOR
HAROLD IN ITALY, OP. 16
ATAR ARAD, VIOLA

SYMPHONY ORCHESTRA REPERTOIRE, CONTINUED

BRAHMS, JOHANNES
EIN DEUTSCHES REQUIEM, OP. 45

DEBUSSY, CLAUDE
PREMIERE RAPSODIE
JAMES DAVID COVELLI, CLARINET

GILBERT AND SULLIVAN
THE MIKADO

HAYDN, JOSEPH
CONCERTO IN E-FLAT FOR TRUMPET, HOB. VIIE: 1
ALAN COX, TRUMPET

HÜE, GEORGES
FANTAISIE POUR FLUTE ET ORCHESTRE
AMY ELIZABETH WHIREN, FLUTE

MAHLER, GUSTAV
SYMPHONY NO. 1 IN D MAJOR

MILHAUD, DARIUS
LA CRÉATION DU MONDE

MONCAYO, PABLO
HUAPANGO

POULENC, FRANCIS
CONCERTO FOR ORGAN, TIMPANI, AND STRINGS, G MINOR
PAUL ANDERSEN, ORGAN

SCHUMANN, ROBERT
SYMPHONY NO. 4 IN D MINOR, OP. 120

SIBELIUS, JEAN
SYMPHONY NO. 2, D MAJOR, OP. 43

STRAVINSKY, IGOR
SYMPHONY OF PSALMS

TELEMANN, G.P.
CONCERTO IN D MAJOR FOR TRUMPET
TIMOTHY L. MCCOUL, TRUMPET

1994-95

BEETHOVEN, LUDWIG VAN
SYMPHONY NO. 5 IN C MINOR

PIANO CONCERTO NO. 3 IN C MINOR, OP. 37
ROBERTO BALDWIN, PIANO

BIZET, GEORGES
SYMPHONY IN C MAJOR

DVORÁK, ANTONIN
CONCERTO FOR VIOLONCELLO AND ORCHESTRA IN B MINOR
LESLIE PARNAS, CELLO

CELLO CONCERTO, OP. 104, *ALLEGRO*
AMY WIEGAND MCCOUL, CELLO

GOUINGUENÉ, CHRISTIAN
CONCERTO NO. 2 FOR TROMBONE AND ORCHESTRA (WORLD PREMIERE)
MARTA HOFACRE, TROMBONE

GOUNOD, CHARLES
"THE JEWEL SONG" FROM *FAUST*
GABRIELA PALIKRUSCHEVA, SOPRANO

GRIEG, EDVARD
SUITE FOR STRINGS

MENDELSSOHN, FELIX
SINFONIA VII IN D

MOZART, WOLFGANG AMADEUS
DON GIOVANNI (COMPLETE)

POULENC, FRANCIS
GLORIA
KIMBERLEY DAVIS, SOPRANO

CONCERTO IN D MINOR FOR TWO PIANOS
SARAH ELIZABETH HARDIN, PIANO
DANIEL BLYTHE, PIANO

SAINT-SAËNS, CAMILLE
SAMSON ET DALILA: BACCHANALE

STRAVINSKY, IGOR
L'OISEAU DE FEU (1919 SUITE)

TELEMANN, GEORG PHILIPP
CONCERTO FOR VIOLA AND STRING ORCHESTRA, G MAJOR
IGOR FEDOTOV, VIOLA

VERDI, GIUSEPPE
NABUCCO: OVERTURE
J. DAVID ARNOTT, CONDUCTOR

WILLIAMS, VAUGHAN
DONA NOBIS PACEM

1995-96

ADAMS, JOHN
A SHORT RIDE IN A FAST MACHINE

BEETHOVEN, LUDWIG VAN
CONCERTO FOR VIOLIN AND ORCHESTRA, OP. 6L
ITZHAK PERLMAN, VIOLIN

BENJAMIN, ARTHUR
CONCERTO FOR HARMONICA AND ORCHESTRA
ROBERT BONFIGLIO, HARMONICA

BRITTEN, BENJAMIN
WAR REQUIEM

DVORÁK, ANTONIN
SYMPHONY NO. 8 IN G MAJOR, OP. 88
JAVIER GARCIA VIGIL, GUEST CONDUCTOR

GLAZUNOV, ALEXANDER
CONCERTO FOR SAXOPHONE AND ORCHESTRA, OP. 109
STEFFEN HASS, ALTO SAXOPHONE

JONES, SAMUEL
NOW LET US PRAISE FAMOUS MEN

MARQUEZ, ARTURO
DANZON, NO. 2

MUSSORGSKY, MODEST
PICTURES AT AN EXHIBITION/ RAVEL PETROVITCH

RIMSKY-KORSAKOV, NIKOLAI
SCHEHERAZADE, OP. 35

SAINT-SAENS, CAMILLE
MORCEAU DU CONCERT
HECTOR J. RODRIGUEZ, HORN

SCHUMANN, ROBERT
KONZERTSTÜKE FOR FOUR HORNS AND ORCHESTRA, OP. 86
HECTOR RODRIGUEZ, PAUL MORMINO, MARY WOOD AND JOANNA DELAUNE, HORNS

SCLATER, JAMES
WITNESS TO MATTERS HUMAN AND DIVINE
(WORLD PREMIERE)
WILLIAM WARFIELD, NARRATOR
PAUL YORK, CELLO

STRAUSS, RICHARD
TOD UND VERKLÄRUNG, OP. 24

TOMASI, HENRI
CONCERTO FOR TROMBONE
TUCKER DULIN, TROMBONE

WILLIAMS, VAUGHAN
CONCERTO IN F MINOR FOR TUBA AND ORCHESTRA
THOMAS STEIN, TUBA

ZANINELLI, LUIGI
JUBILATE (WORLD PREMIERE)

SNOW WHITE, THE OPERA (WORLD PREMIERE)

1996-97

BRAHMS, JOHANNES
CONCERTO FOR VIOLIN, CELLO, AND ORCHESTRA, OP. 102
STEPHEN REDFIELD, VIOLIN
PAUL YORK, CELLO

BIZET, GEORGES
"LE FLEUR QUE TU MAVAIS JETES" FROM *CARMEN*
DON FRAZURE, TENOR

GRIEG, EDVARD
CONCERTO IN A MINOR (ALLEGRO MOLTO MODERATO)
ROSANGELA YAZBEC SEBBA, PIANO
SUSAN ECKERLE, CONDUCTOR

HINDEMITH, PAUL
DER SCHWANENDREHER (THE SWAN HANDLER)
ILYA SHPIGELMAN, VIOLA

LALO, ÉDOUARD
SYMPHONIE ESPAGNOLE, OP. 21
FIDENCIO SOLIS, VIOLIN
PABLO SAELZER, CONDUCTOR

MOZART, WOLFGANG AMADEUS
MASS, K. 317, IN C MAJOR (CORONATION)

SYMPHONY NO. 35, K. 385, IN D MAJOR (HAFFNER)

COSI FAN TUTTE (COMPLETE) AT SOUTHERN ARTS FESTIVAL

PUCINNI, GIACOMO
LE VILLI (COMPLETE)

SUOR ANGELICA (COMPLETE)

RAVEL, MAURICE
CONCERTO IN G MAJOR (ALLEGRAMENTE)
ELLEN PRICE, PIANO

SHOSTAKOVICH, DMITRI
SYMPHONY NO. 5, OP. 47, IN D MINOR

STRAUSS, JOHANN
OVERTURE TO *DIE FLEDERMAUS*

TCHAIKOVSKY, PIOTR
WALTZ FROM *EUGENE ONEGIN*

SWAN LAKE SUITE, OP. 20A

VERDI, GIUSEPPE
REQUIEM

GALA SEASON OPENER WITH DOC SEVERINSEN

MISSISSIPPI HOLIDAY SPECTACULAR JULY POPS CONCERT

1997-98

BACH, JOHANN SEBASTIAN
CONCERTO FOR FLUTE IN C MAJOR (RAMPAL ED.)
JEAN-PIERRE RAMPAL, FLUTE

ORCHESTRAL SUITE NO. 1, BWV 1066, C MAJOR

CONCERTO FOR FLUTE, STRINGS IN C MAJOR
JEAN-PIERRE RAMPAL, FLUTE

BERLIOZ, HECTOR
SYMPHONIE FANTASTIQUE, OP. 14

BIZET, GEORGES
CARMEN (COMPLETE)
DENYCE GRAVES, MEZZO-SOPRANO

BRAHMS, JOHANNES
EIN DEUTSCHES REQUIEM, OP. 45

HUNGARIAN DANCE NO. 5
NEIL GODWIN, CONDUCTOR

GOUINGUENÉ, CHRISTIAN
FANFARE FOR VERSAILLES (WORLD PREMIERE)

SPLENDORS OF VERSAILLES (WORLD PREMIERE)

GRONDAHL, LAUNY
CONCERTO FOR TROMBONE AND ORCHESTRA
LEE HARRELSON II, EUPHONIUM

HANDEL, GEORG F.
SUITE FOR TRUMPET IN D
JAMES JENKINS, TRUMPET

HUSA, KAREL
FRESQUE

ÉLÉGIE ET RONDEAU FOR SAXOPHONE AND ORCHESTRA
LAWRENCE GWOZDZ, SAXOPHONE
KAREN HUSA, GUEST CONDUCTOR

KOCH, ERLAND V.
SAXOFONKONSERT
JEREMY GOTT, ALTO SAXOPHONE

LULLY, JEAN BAPTISTE
LE TRIOMPHE DE L'AMOUR: BALLET SUITE

OFFENBACH, JACQUES
ORPHEUS IN DER UNTERWELT (COMPLETE)

RIMSKY-KORSAKOV, NIKOLAI
CAPRICCIO ESPAGNOL, OP. 34

STAMITZ, KARL PHILIPP
CONCERTO FOR FLUTE IN G MAJOR
JEAN-PIERRE RAMPAL, FLUTE

TCHAIKOVSKY, PIOTR
PIANO CONCERTO NO. 1 IN B-FLAT MINOR
JOHN BROWNING, PIANO

AN EVENING WITH JEAN-PIERRE RAMPAL

MISSISSIPPI HOLIDAY SPECTACULAR
JULY POPS CONCERT

SPLENDORS OF VERSAILLES
INTERNATIONAL ART EXHIBITION

1998-99

BARTOK, BELA
CONCERTO FOR VIOLA AND ORCHESTRA
CSABA ERDELYI, VIOLA

BEETHOVEN, LUDWIG VAN
EGMONT OVERTURE, OP. 84
NEIL GODWIN, STUDENT CONDUCTOR

SYMPHONY NO. 9 IN D MINOR, OP. 125
STEPHANIE GREGORY, SOPRANO
ULIANA ILIEVA, MEZZO-SOPRANO
J.R. WALLEY, TENOR
BENNO SCHOLLUM, BARITONE
TIMOTHY KOCH, GUEST CONDUCTOR

COPLAND, AARON
RODEO: FOUR DANCE EPISODES

DRAGONETTI, DOMENICO
PEZZO DI CONCERTO
MARCOS ALTAMIRANO, DOUBLE BASS
DAVID ROMINES, STUDENT CONDUCTOR

ELLINGTON, SIR EDWARD K. (DUKE)
SUITE FROM *THE RIVER*

GERSHWIN, GEORGE
CUBAN OVERTURE

SUITE FROM *PORGY AND BESS*

"SUMMERTIME"
CASSANDRA DEAN, SOPRANO

GOUNOD, CHARLES FRANCOIS
JE RIS DE MES VOIR

JONES, SAMUEL
SYMPHONY NO. 3 (PALO DURA CANYON)

MENDELSSOHN, FELIX
VIOLIN CONCERTO IN D MINOR
ALEXANDRE BRUSSILOVSKY, VIOLIN

MOZART, WOLFGANG AMADEUS
SERENATA NOTTURNA IN D MAJOR FOR STRINGS AND TIMPANI, K. 239

PROKOFIEV, SERGE
CONCERTO NO. 3 IN C MAJOR, OP. 26
ADONIS GONZALEZ, PIANO

RAVEL, MAURICE
SUITE FROM *ME MERE L'OYE*

TZIGANE FOR VIOLIN AND ORCHESTRA
JERRIE LUCKTENBERG, VIOLIN

ROSAURO, NEY
CONCERTO FOR MARIMBA AND ORCHESTRA
JOHN WOOTON, MARIMBA

SCHUBERT, FRANZ
OVERTURE TO *DIE ZAUBERHARFE*

TCHAIKOVSKY, PIOTR
SOUVENIR D'UN LIEU CHER

SÉRÉNADE MÉLANCOLIQUE

VALSE-SCHERZO
ALEXANDRE BRUSSILOVSKY, VIOLIN

VIVALDI, ANTONIO
IL QUATRO STAGIONE (THE FOUR SEASONS)
ALEXANDRE BRUSSILOVSKY, VIOLIN

AN EVENING WITH RAY CHARLES

THE MAGIC OF CHRISTMAS

1999-2000

BERLIOZ, HECTOR
LE CARNAVAL ROMAIN
LOUIS LANE, GUEST CONDUCTOR

BRAHMS, JOHANNES
SYMPHONY NO. 4, OP. 98, IN E MINOR

BRUCKNER, ANTON
SYMPHONY NO. 8 (1890 VERSION) IN C MINOR

CATALANI, ALFREDO
"EBBEN LONTANO" FROM *LA WALLY*

CHOPIN, FRÉDÉRIC
PIANO CONCERTO NO. 2 IN F MINOR, OP. 21
KEVIN KENNER, PIANO

CURNOW, JAMES
SYMPHONIC VARIANTS FOR EUPHONIUM
WILLIAM HESS, EUPHONIUM

FAURE, GABRIEL
REQUIEM
LOUIS LANE, GUEST CONDUCTOR

MOZART, WOLFGANG AMADEUS
LE NOZZE DI FIGARO

HORN CONCERTO NO. 3 IN E-FLAT MAJOR, K.447
MARY WOOD, HORN

POULENC, FRANCIS
CONCERTO FOR TWO PIANOS AND ORCHESTRA IN D MINOR
LOIS LEVENTHAL, PIANO
MARY ANN STRINGER, PIANO
LOUIS LANE, GUEST CONDUCTOR

PUCCINI, GIACOMO
TURANDOT:"NESSUN DORMA" AND "IN QUESTA REGGIA"

ROSSINI, GIOACCHINO
OVERTURE TO *LA SCALA DI SETA*
WILLIAM T. GOWER, GUEST CONDUCTOR

OVERTURE TO *IL BARBIERE DI SIVIGLIA*

SHOSTAKOVICH, DMITRI
CONCERTO NO. 1 FOR CELLO AND ORCHESTRA, OP. 107
YO-YO MA, CELLO

STRAUSS, RICHARD
HORN CONCERTO NO. 1 IN E-FLAT MAJOR, OP. 11
RAUL RODRIGUEZ, HORN

TCHAIKOVSKY, PIOTR
THE NUTCRACKER (WITH BALLET MISSISSIPPI)

VERDI, GIUSEPPE
"RITOURNA VINCITOR" AND "PACE, PACE" FROM AIDA

TRIUMPHAL MARCH FROM *AIDA*

OVERTURE TO *NABUCCO*

GLORIOUS VISTAS OF ITALIAN OPERA

2000-01

BARTOK, BELA
CONCERTO FOR VIOLA AND ORCHESTRA
CSABA ERDÉLYI, VIOLA

CHEETHAM, JOHN
PROPHETA LUCIS
STATE SENATOR RON FARRIS, NARRATOR
USM SYMPHONY CHORUS
USM CONCERT CHOIR
GREGORY FULLER, CONDUCTOR

DANKNER, STEPHEN
HURRICANE

FALLA, MANUEL DE
NOCHES EN LOS JARDINES DE ESPAÑA
THERESA SANCHEZ, PIANO

GRIEG, EDVARD
PIANO CONCERTO IN A MINOR,OP. 16
TODOR STOINOV, PIANO

HANDEL, GEORG F.
MESSIAH (PART ONE)

LISZT, FRANZ
HAMLET (SYMPHONIC POEM NO. 10)

MAHLER, GUSTAV
KINDERTOTENLIEDER
BENNO SCHOLLUM, BARITONE

MENDELSSOHN, FELIX
VIOLIN CONCERTO IN E MINOR, OP. 64
JORGE GONZALEZ, VIOLIN

ROSSINI, GIOACCHINO
IL BARBIERI DI SIVIGLIA (COMPLETE)

SCHUMAN, ROBERT
SYMPHONY NO. 3 OP. 97 IN E-FLAT MAJOR (RHENISH)

TCHAIKOVSKY, PIOTR
VIOLIN CONCERTO IN D MAJOR, OP. 35
ITZHAK PERLMAN, VIOLIN

PIANO CONCERTO NO. 1 IN B FLAT MINOR, OP. 23
GERARDO FERNANDEZ, PIANO

BRAVO BROADWAY III, WITH ORIGINAL MEMBERS OF *CATS*, *PHANTOM OF THE OPERA*, AND *LES MISERABLES*

MISSISSIPPI SOUNDS, A TRIBUTE TO MISSISSIPPI'S MUSICAL HERITAGE

2001-02

BERNSTEIN, LEONARD
CHICHESTER PSALMS
JAMIE HADAWAY, SOPRANO
BROOKE CARROLL, MEZZO-SOPRANO
RUDY GATLIN, TENOR/COUNTER TENOR
ARLANDRA HARVEY, BASS
GREGORY FULLER, CONDUCTOR

BOURGEOIS, DEREK
TROMBONE CONCERTO, OP. 114
LEROY BROWN, EUPHONIUM

DANKNER, STEPHEN
CONCERTO FOR SAXOPHONE AND ORCHESTRA
LAWRENCE GWOZDZ, SAXOPHONE

ELGAR, EDWARD
CROWN IMPERIAL MARCH, OP. 32

EWAZEN, ERIC
RHAPSODY FOR BASS TROMBONE AND STRING ORCHESTRA
CATHERINE ALGRIM, BASS TROMBONE

FAZZI (ARR.)
CARNIVAL OF VENICE

GRIEG, EDVARD
SUITE IM ALTEN STYLE (AUS HOLBERG'S ZEIT), OP. 40

HANDEL, GEORG F.
CONCERTO GROSSO IN D MINOR, OP. 6, NO. 10

JONES, SAMUEL
THE SHOE BIRD (WORLD PREMIERE)
LESTER SENTER, NARRATOR
THE MISSISSIPPI BOY CHOIR

LARSSON, LARS-ERIK
CONCERTO FOR SAXOPHONE AND STRING ORCHESTRA
CHRIS CONDON, ALTO SAXOPHONE

CONCERTINO, OP. 45, NO. 5, FOR HORN
MOLLIE PATE, HORN

MOZART, WOLFGANG AMADEUS
ADAGIO IN E MAJOR, K. 261, AND RONDO IN C MAJOR, K. 373 FOR VIOLIN AND ORCHESTRA
STEPHEN REDFIELD, VIOLIN

MURPHY, BILL
GYPSY PROPHET

NEWSON, TOMMY (ARR.)
SAINT LOUIS BLUES

PUCCINI, GIACOMO
"UN BEL DI" FROM *MADAMA BUTTERFLY*

REVUELTAS, SILVESTRE
LA NOCHE DE LOS MAYAS

REINEKE, STEPHEN (ARR.)
ODE TO DOC

SMITH, CLAUDE T.
RONDO CONCERTINO

SONDHEIM, STEPHEN
"SEND IN THE CLOWNS" FROM *A LITTLE NIGHT MUSIC*

TCHAIKOVSKY, PETER
SYMPHONY NO. 4 IN F MINOR

TYZIK, JEFF (ARR.)
GERSHWIN

WALTON, WILLIAM
BELSHAZZAR'S FEAST
GERALD DOULTER, BASS
HATTIESBURG CHORAL UNION

CROWN IMPERIAL

WILLIAMS, VAUGHAN
FANTASIA ON A THEME BY THOMAS TALLIS

THE LARK ASCENDING
ALEXANDRE BRUSSILOVSKY, VIOLIN

ZANINELLI, LUIGI
ARIA FESTIVA (WORLD PREMIERE)
DOC SEVERINSEN, TRUMPET

DOC SEVERINSEN AND NIGHT OF A THOUSAND TRUMPETS

VICKSBURG CELEBRATES AMERICA: JULY POPS CONCERT

SYMPHONY ORCHESTRA REPERTOIRE, CONTINUED

2002-03

BEETHOVEN, LUDWIG VAN
CONCERTO IN C MAJOR FOR VIOLIN, VIOLONCELLO, AND PIANO, OP. 56
ALEXANDRE BRUSSILOVSKY, VIOLIN
ALEXANDER RUSSAKOVSKY, CELLO
THERESA SANCHEZ, PIANO

SYMPHONY NO. 6, OP. 68, IN F MAJOR (PASTORALE)

CONCERTO IN D MAJOR, OP. 61
DANIEL TRINGOV, VIOLIN

BERNSTEIN, CHARLES HAROLD
INTERLUDE FOR ORCHESTRA

BOTTESINI, GIOVANNI
CONCERTO NO. 2 IN B MINOR FOR BASS AND ORCHESTRA
EDGAR MEYER, BASS

BRAHMS, JOHANNES
SYMPHONY NO. 2, OP. 73, IN D MAJOR

SYMPHONY NO. 3 IN F MAJOR, OP. 90

SCHICKSALSLIED, OP. 54, FOR CHORUS AND ORCHESTRA

DONIZETTI, GAETANO
DON PASQUALE: OVERTURE

"QUEL GUARDO IL CAVALIERI" FROM *DON PASQUALE*
ROBERTA PETERS, SOPRANO

FALLA, MANUEL DE
EL AMOR BRUJO

MENDELSSOHN, FELIX
A MIDSUMMER NIGHT'S DREAM: OVERTURE, OP. 21

MEYER, EDGAR
CONCERTO IN D MAJOR FOR DOUBLE BASS AND ORCHESTRA
EDGAR MEYER, BASS

MOZART, WOLFGANG AMADEUS
REQUIEM

EXULTATE JUBILATE, FOR SOLO VOICE AND ORCH., K. 165
ROBERTA PETERS, SOPRANO

OVERTURE TO *DON GIOVANNI*, K. 527

BATTI, BATTI FROM *DON GIOVANNI*

CONCERTO FOR TWO PIANOS IN E FLAT MAJOR, K. 365
RICHARD STEINBACH, PIANO
HOWARD HELVEY, PIANO
GREGORY FULLER, CONDUCTOR

REQUIEM, K. 626
THE HATTIESBURG CHORAL UNION
GREGORY FULLER, CONDUCTOR

"WER EIN LIEBCHEN HAT GEFUNDEN" FROM *THE ABDUCTION FROM THE SERAGLIO*, K. 384

ARIA: O ISIS UND OSIRIS FROM *THE MAGIC FLUTE*,K. 620

ARIA: IN DIESEN HEIL'GEN HALLEN FROM *THE MAGIC FLUTE*
RONALD MATTHEW GREEN, BASS

CONCERTO IN A MAJOR FOR VIOLIN AND ORCHESTRA NO.5 K. 219
ALBA VARINIA MADRID, VIOLIN

PROKOFIEV, SERGE
SUITE FROM ROMEO AND JULIET SUITE (COMBINATION OF SUITES NOS.1 AND 2)

RACHMANINOFF, SERGEI
PIANO CONCERTO NO. 2 IN C MINOR, OP. 18
KEVIN KENNER, PIANO

MISSISSIPPI, THE BIRTHPLACE OF AMERICA'S MUSIC

ROBERTA PETERS CONCERT

VICKSBURG CELEBRATES AMERICA: JULY POPS CONCERT

2003-04

ALBRECHTSBERGER, JOHANN
CONCERTO FOR ALTO TROMBONE AND STRINGS
JÖRGEN VAN RIJEN, TROMBONE

ARUTUNIAN, ALEXANDER
CONCERTO FOR TRUMPET
MICHAEL ELLZEY, TRUMPET

BEETHOVEN, LUDWIG VAN
SYMPHONY NO. 9, OP. 125, IN D MINOR

BERNSTEIN, ELMER
CONCERTO FOR GUITAR AND ORCHESTRA
CHRISTOPHER PARKENING, GUITAR

COPLAND, AARON
APPALACHIAN SPRING

CONCERTO FOR CLARINET AND STRING ORCHESTRA
MATT CARL, CLARINET
JUAN CARLOS PEÑA, CONDUCTOR

CORIGLIANO, JOHN
TO MUSIC

GRØNDAHL, LAUNY
CONCERTO FOR TROMBONE AND ORCHESTRA
JÖRGEN VAN RIJEN, TROMBONE

HANDEL, GEORG F.
MESSIAH

JONES, SAMUEL
JANUS
PABLO SAELZER, CONDUCTOR

MAURICE, PAULE
LES TABLEAUX DE PROVENCE
DAVID PARKS, SAXOPHONE

MOZART, WOLFGANG AMADEUS
SYMPHONY NO. 40 IN G MINOR, K. 550

MYER, STANLEY
"CAVATINA" FROM *THE DEER HUNTER*

RODRIGO, JOAQUIN
ADAGIO FROM *CONCIERTO DE ARANJUEZ*
CHRISTOPHER PARKENING, GUITAR

WAGNER, RICHARD
OVERTURE TO *TANNHÄUSER*

FROM *DER RING DES NIBELUNGEN*

DAS RHEINGOLD
"ENTRANCE OF THE GODS INTO VALHALLA"

DIE WALKÜRE
ACT 1- PRELUDE
ACT 1, SCENE 3 - "WINTERSTÜRME"
ACT 2, SCENE 1 - PRELUDE
ACT 3, SCENE 1 - OPENING (VALKYRIES RIDE)
ACT 3, SCENE 3 - WOTAN'S FAREWELL

SIEGFRIED
ACT 3, SCENE 1 - PRELUDE
ACT 1, SCENE 3 - SIEGFRIED'S FORGING SCENE
ACT 3, SCENE 2 - SIEGFRIED'S RISE TO SUMMIT
ACT 3, SCENE 3 - FINAL SECTION

GÖTTERDÄMMERUNG
ACT 3, SCENE 2 - SIEGFRIED'S FUNERAL MUSIC
ACT 3, SCENE 3 - BRÜNNHILDE'S IMMOLATION

TANNHÄUSER
OVERTURE

GLORY OF BAROQUE DRESDEN
INTERNATIONAL ART EXHIBITION

VICKSBURG CELEBRATES AMERICA: JULY POPS CONCERT

CUERDAS LATINAS, LATIN STRINGS

2004-05

BEETHOVEN, LUDWIG VAN
LEONORE OVERTURE NO. 3

SYMPHONY NO. 3 IN E-FLAT ("THE EROICA"), OP. 55

BERNSTEIN, LEONARD
CANDIDE: OVERTURE

"TONIGHT" FROM *WEST SIDE STORY*
PLÁCIDO DOMINGO, TENOR
ANA MARIA MARTINEZ, SOPRANO

BIZET, GEORGES
SUITE NO. 1 FROM *CARMEN*

CHAPI, RUPERTO
"CARCELERAS" FROM *LAS HIJAS DE ZEBEDEO*
ANA MARIA MARTINEZ, SOPRANO

CILEA, FRANCESCO
"LAMENTO DI FEDERICO" *FROM L'ARLESIANA*
PLÁCIDO DOMINGO, TENOR

CIMAROSA, DOMENICO
CONCERTO FOR TWO FLUTES
SIR JAMES AND LADY JEANNE GALWAY, FLUTES

DONIZETTI, GAETANO
"O MIO FERNANDO" FROM *LA FAVORITA*
PATRICIA RAMIREZ, MEZZO-SOPRANO

DVORÁK, ANTONIN
CARNIVAL OVERTURE

SERENADE FOR STRINGS, OP. 22

FLOYD, CARLISLE
SUSANNAH (COMPLETE)

GOUNOD, CHARLES FRANCOIS
"FAITES-LUI MES AVEUX" FROM *FAUST*
PATRICIA RAMIREZ, MEZZO-SOPRANO

"AH! JE VEUX VIVRE" FROM *ROMEO ET JULIETTE*
ANA MARIA MARTINEZ, SOPRANO

KORNGOLD, ERICH WOLFGANG
"MARIETTA'S SONG" FROM *DIE TOTE STADT*
ALLANDA SMALL, SOPRANO

LEHAR, FRANZ
"WALTZ DUET" FROM *THE MERRY WIDOW*
PLÁCIDO DOMINGO, TENOR
ANA MARIA MARTINEZ, SOPRANO

LOEWE, FREDERICK
"I COULD HAVE DANCED ALL NIGHT" FROM *MY FAIR LADY*
ANA MARIA MARTINEZ, SOPRANO

LUNA, PABLO
"D'ESPAÑA VENGO" FROM *EL NIÑO JUDIO*
ANA MARIA MARTINEZ, SOPRANO

MASSENET, JULES
"AH! TOUT EST BIEN FINI...O, SOUVERAIN, O JUGE, O PERE" FROM *LE CID*
PLÁCIDO DOMINGO, TENOR

MOZART, WOLFGANG AMADEUS
FLUTE, CONCERTO NO. 1 IN G MAJOR, K.313
SIR JAMES GALWAY, FLUTE

FLUTE CONCERTO NO. 2 IN D MAJOR, K.314
SIR JAMES GALWAY, FLUTE

EINE KLEINE NACHTMUSIK, K.525

PALMERIN, RICARDO
"PEREGRINA"
PLÁCIDO DOMINGO, TENOR
ANA MARIA MARTINEZ, SOPRANO

PUCCINI, GIACOMO
"IN QUELLE TRINI MORBIDE" FROM *MANON LESCAUT*
ALLANDA SMALL, SOPRANO

RAVEL, MAURICE
CONCERTO FOR LEFT HAND
LOIS LEVENTHAL, PIANO

RODGERS, RICHARD
"SOME ENCHANTED EVENING" FROM *SOUTH PACIFIC*
PLÁCIDO DOMINGO, TENOR
ANA MARIA MARTINEZ, SOPRANO

ROSSINI, GIOACHINO
"CRUDA SORTE!" FROM *L'ITALIANA IN ALGERI*
ROCIO TAMEZ, MEZZO-SOPRANO

SHOSTAKOVICH, DMITRI
FESTIVE OVERTURE, OP. 96

SOROBAZAL, PABLO
"NO PUEDE SER" FROM *LA TABERNERA DEL PUERTO*
PLÁCIDO DOMINGO, TENOR

SVENDSEN, JOHAN
ROMANZE FOR VIOLIN, OP. 26
STEPHEN REDFIELD, VIOLIN

TCHAIKOVSKY, PIOTR
POLONAISE FROM *EUGENE ONEGIN*

TORROBA, MORENO
"EN MI TIERRA EXTREMEÑA" FROM *LUISA FERNANDA*
PLÁCIDO DOMINGO, TENOR
ANA MARIA MARTINEZ, SOPRANO

VERDI, GIUSEPPI
OTELLO: GIA NELLA NOTTE
PLÁCIDO DOMINGO AND ANA MARIA MARTINEZ

LA FORZA DEL DESTINO: OVERTURE

"STRIDE LA VAMPA" FROM *IL TROVATORE*
ROCIO TAMEZ, MEZZO-SOPRANO

WILLIAMS, JOHN
CONCERTO FOR TUBA
RICHARD PERRY, TUBA

HOLIDAYS AND THE SAENGER

CARNEGIE HALL LINK-UP!

ONE VOICE, ONE ORCHESTRA, ONE NIGHT ONLY WITH PLÁCIDO DOMINGO

2005-06

BARBER, SAMUEL
ADAGIO FOR STRINGS, OP. II

BEETHOVEN, LUDWIG VAN
EGMONT OVERTURE, OP. 84
DARRYL E. HARRIS SR., CONDUCTOR

CHORAL FANTASY, OP. 80
GREGORY FULLER, CONDUCTOR

BERNSTEIN, LEONARD
WEST SIDE STORY (COMPLETE)

BRAHMS, JOHANNES
SCHICKSALSLIED, OP. 54
DONALD TROTT, CONDUCTOR

DANKNER, STEPHEN
CONCERTO FOR ALTO SAXOPHONE
MARCUS BALLARD, ALTO SAXOPHONE

DOPPLER, FRANCOIS
FANTAISIE PASTORALE HONGROISE, OP. 26
DENISSA RIVAS DE MUNGUIA, FLUTE
RAUL MUNGUIA, CONDUCTOR

DVORÁK, ANTONIN
SLAVONIC DANCES, OP. 46

NO. 4 IN F MAJOR

NO. 8 IN G MINOR
DARRYL E. HARRIS, SR., CONDUCTOR

MENDELSSOHN, FELIX
HEBRIDEN, DIE (FINGAL'S CAVE) OVERTURE, OP. 26
DARRYL E. HARRIS, SR., CONDUCTOR

RACHMANINOFF, SERGEI
CONCERTO NO. 2 FOR PIANO IN C MINOR, OP. 18
AMANDA VIRELLES, PIANO

SAINT-SAËNS, CAMILLE
INTRODUCTION, RONDO AND CAPRICCIOSO, OP. 28
ISABEL ESCALANTE, VIOLIN

TCHAIKOVSKY, PYOTR
CONCERTO FOR VIOLIN AND ORCHESTRA IN D MAJOR
JOSHUA BELL, VIOLIN

SYMPHONY NO. 6 IN B MINOR, OP. 74 ("THE PATHÉTIQUE")

TORROBA, FEDERICO MORENO
"AMOR, VIDA DE MI VIDA" FROM *MARAVILLA*
DALAND JONES, TENOR
RAUL MUNGUIA, CONDUCTOR

VERDI, GIUSEPPI
LA TRAVIATA (COMPLETE)

IL POVERETTO

WEBER, CARL MARIA VON
CONCERTINO FOR HORN AND ORCHESTRA, OP. 45
WILLIAM FARMER, HORN

WILLIAMS, VAUGHAN
LORD, THOU HAST BEEN OUR REFUGE
RICHARD WATERS, CONDUCTOR

RICKY SKAGGS –SYMPHONIC BLUEGRASS

SPIRIT OF MISSISSIPPI: A CONCERT OF HOPE (DEDICATED TO THE VICTIMS AND HEROES OF HURRICANE KATRINA)

TANGO VALENTINO
ALEJANDRO DRAGO, CONDUCTOR

THE NOT-CRACKER

HOLIDAYS ON BROADWAY, THE SOUTHERN OPERA AND MUSICAL THEATRE COMPANY

2006-07

BIZET, GEORGES
CARMEN (COMPLETE)

BERLIOZ, HECTOR
RÁKÓCZY MARCH, FROM LA DAMNATION DE FAUST, OP.24

BORNE, FRANCOIS FANTASIE
BRILLANTE ON BIZET'S *CARMEN*
SIR JAMES GALWAY, FLUTE

BRAHMS, JOHANNES
PIANO CONCERTO NO. 2
KEVIN KENNER, PIANO
THERESA SANCHEZ, PIANO

HOLST, GUSTAV
THE PLANETS, SUITE FOR A LARGE ORCHESTRA, OP. 32

MANCINI, HENRY
BABY ELEPHANT WALK FROM *HATARI*
SIR JAMES GALWAY, FLUTE

PENNYWHISTLE GIG FROM *THE MOLLY MAGUIRES*
SIR JAMES GALWAY, FLUTE

PINK PANTHER FROM *THE PINK PANTHER*
SIR JAMES GALWAY, FLUTE

OVERTON, DAVID
THE MAGIC FLUTES
SIR JAMES GALWAY, FLUTE
LADY JEANNE GALWAY, FLUTE

STRAVINSKY, IGOR
SYMPHONY OF PSALMS
GREGORY FULLER, CONDUCTOR

LE SACRE DU PRINTEMPS

WAGNER, RICHARD
VORSPIEL ZU DIE MEISTERSINGER VON NÜRNBERG

CHARLEY PRIDE, THE PRIDE OF MISSISSIPPI

UNITED IN SONG: A TRIBUTE TO THE MUSIC OF TENA CLARK FEATURING PATTI LA BELLE, DIONNE WARWICK, PATTY AUSTIN, ANN NESBY, AND VESTA WILLIAMS

GODSPELL, JOHN MICHAEL TEBELAK AND STEPHEN SCHWARTZ

TANGO VALENTINO

2007-08

BARBOSA, ARTURO
VIOLIN CONCERTO (WORLD PREMIERE)
JEAN REIS, GUEST CONDUCTOR
ALEJANDRO DRAGO, VIOLIN

BRUCH, MAX
VIOLIN CONCERTO NO. 1 IN G MINOR, OP. 26
NADJA SALERNO-SONNENBERG, VIOLIN
JULIA BUSHKOVA, VIOLIN

DEBUSSY, CLAUDE
NOCTURNES

KHACHATURIAN, ARAM
SUITE NO. 1 FROM *GAYNEH*

SUITE NO. 3 FROM *GAYNEH*

SUITE FROM *MASQUERADE*

MENDELSSOHN, FELIX
SYMPHONY NO. 4 IN A MAJOR, OP. 90 ("THE ITALIAN")
JEAN REIS, GUEST CONDUCTOR

MOZART, WOLFGANG AMADEUS
LE NOZZE DI FIGARO (COMPLETE)

NEPOMUCENO, ALBERTO
SUITE ANTIGA
JEAN REIS, GUEST CONDUCTOR

SAINT-SAËNS, CAMILLE
REQUIEM

DANSE MACABRE

STRAUSS, RICHARD
DON JUAN

WEIGEL, JAY
RENAISSANCE FOR NEW ORLEANS (WORLD PREMIERE)

ATLANTIS GALA WITH THE CIRQUE DE LA SYMPHONIE

POINTER SISTERS IN CONCERT

GUYS AND DOLLS, FRANK LOESSER

HOLIDAY CHORAL SPECTACULAR, HATTIESBURG CHORAL UNION
JOHN FLANERY AND GREGORY FULLER, CONDUCTORS

2008-09

BACH, JOHANN SEBASTIAN
BRANDENBURG CONCERTO NO. 4, BWV 1049, G MAJOR

BEETHOVEN, LUDWIG VAN
PIANO CONCERTO NO. 4
AMBER NICHOLSON

BOTTESINI, GIOVANNI
FANTASIA FOR BASS

BRITAIN, JOSEPH
SUITE FROM *SHANGRI-LA* (WORLD PREMIERE)

COPLAND, AARON
FANFARE FOR THE COMMON MAN

DEBUSSY, CLAUDE
LA MER

DVORÁK, ANTONIN
SYMPHONY NO. 8, OP. 88, G MAJOR

GOUNOD, CHARLES
FAUST: SALUT DEMEURE
DAVID LOMELÍ, TENOR

IBERT, JACQUES
CONCERTO FOR FLUTE
CARLOS FELLER, FLUTE

LISZT, FRANZ
LES PRÉLUDES

MÁRQUEZ, ARTURO
DANZÓN, NO. 2

MASGAGNI, PIETRO
INTERMEZZO FROM *CAVALLERIA RUSTICANA*

MASSENET, JULES
"MÉDITATION" FROM *THAIS*

MOZART, WOLFGANG AMADEUS
CONCERTO FOR PIANO AND ORCHESTRA, NO. 23, IN A MAJOR, K. 488

ORFF, CARL
CARMINA BURANA

PROKOFIEV, SERGE
SYMPHONY NO. 1, *CLASSICAL SYMPHONY*

ROSSINI, GIOACCHINO
LA GAZZA LADRA: OVERTURE

INTRODUCTION, THEME AND VARIATIONS
MARY EVELYN CLARK, CLARINET

SAINT-SAËNS, CAMILLE
REQUIEM

SCHUMANN, ROBERT
CONCERTSTÜCK FOR FOUR HORNS IN F MAJOR, OP. 86
JONATHAN GLOVER, HORN
CARLOS LOPEZ, HORN
JESSICA POGUE, HORN
MATT TAYLOR, HORN

SIERRA, ROBERTO
FOLIAS
MANUEL BARRUECO, GUITAR

VERDI, GUISEPPI
AIDA: TRIUMPHAL MARCH

VIVALDI, ANTONIO
CONCERTO IN D MAJOR FOR GUITAR AND ORCHESTRA
MANUEL BARRUECO, GUITAR

OPERISSIMO WITH DAVID LOMELÍ

OVER THE RAINBOW, A CONCERT OF ORIGINAL SYMPHONIC JAZZ

SANDI PATTY, THE VOICE OF CHRISTMAS

SHANGRI-LA GALA WITH THE CIRQUE DE LA SYMPHONIE

2009-10

BACH, JOHANN SEBASTIAN
BRANDENBURG CONCERTO NO. 3, BWV 1048, G MAJOR

BARNEA, URI
HOMAGE A BACH

BRAHMS, JOHANNES
SYMPHONY NO. 1, OP. 68, C MINOR

SYMPHONY ORCHESTRA REPERTOIRE, CONTINUED

DVORÁK, ANTONIN
RUSALKA, "MESICKU NA NEBI HLUBOKEM" (SONG TO THE MOON)
RENÉE FLEMING, SOPRANO
MARYANN KYLE, SOPRANO

FROLOV, IGOR A.
FANTASY ON GERSHWIN'S *PORGY AND BESS*, OP. 19
ALEXANDRE BRUSSILOVSKY, VIOLIN

GERSHWIN, GEORGE
PORGY AND BESS, "SUMMERTIME"
RENÉE FLEMING, SOPRANO
MARYANN KYLE, SOPRANO

GIORDANO, UMBERTO
SIBERIA, "NO! SE UN PENSIER... NEL SUO AMORE RIANIMATA"
RENÉE FLEMING, SOPRANO
MARYANN KYLE, SOPRANO

GRUSIN, DAVE
TWO RIVERS
RENÉE FLEMING, SOPRANO
MARYANN KYLE, SOPRANO

HINDEMITH, PAUL
SYMPHONIC METAMORPHOSIS ON THEMES OF CARL MARIA VON WEBER

HUMMEL, JOHANN NEPOMUK
CONCERTO IN Eb FOR TRUMPET AND ORCHESTRA
BRUNO LORENSETTO, TRUMPET

JOLIVET, ANDRE
CONCERTO FOR FLUTE AND STRING ORCHESTRA
LINDSEY KEAY, FLUTE

KANDER, JOHN
LETTER FROM SULLIVAN BALLOU
RENÉE FLEMING, SOPRANO
MARYANN KYLE, SOPRANO

LARSON, LARS-ERIK
CONCERTO FOR SAXOPHONE AND STRING ORCHESTRA
THOMAS GILES, SAXOPHONE

LEONCAVALLO, RUGGERO
LA BOHÈME, "MIMI PINSON, LA BIONDINETTA"
RENÉE FLEMING, SOPRANO
MARYANN KYLE, SOPRANO

"MUSETTE SVARIA SULLA BOCCA VIVA"
RENÉE FLEMING, SOPRANO
MARYANN KYLE, SOPRANO

I PAGLIACCI (COMPLETE)

MAHLER, GUSTAV
"DAS HIMMLISCHE LEBEN" FROM SYMPHONY NO. 4 IN G MAJOR
RENÉE FLEMING, SOPRANO
MARYANN KYLE, SOPRANO

MASCAGNI, PIETRO
"INTERMEZZO" FROM *CAVALLERIA RUSTICANA*

MENDELSSOHN, FELIX
D MINOR VIOLIN CONCERTO
STEPHEN REDFIELD, VIOLIN

PENHORWOOD, EDWIN
AN AMERICAN REQUIEM (WORLD PREMIERE)

PUCINNI, GIACOMO
GIANNI SCHICCHI (COMPLETE)

"DONDE LIETA USCI" FROM *LA BOHÈME*
RENÉE FLEMING, SOPRANO
MARYANN KYLE, SOPRANO

"VISSI D'ARTE" FROM *TOSCA*
RENÉE FLEMING, SOPRANO
MARYANN KYLE, SOPRANO

RIMSKY-KORSAKOV, NIKOLAI
SCHEHERAZADE, OP. 35

SCHUMANN, ROBERT
CELLO CONCERTO IN A MINOR, OP. 129
JOSHUA ROMAN, CELLO

SMETANA, BEDRICH
"DOBRÁ! JÁ MU JE DÁM! ... JAK JE MI?" FROM *DALIBOR*
RENÉE FLEMING, SOPRANO
MARYANN KYLE, SOPRANO

STRAUSS, RICHARD
TILL EULENSPIEGELS LUSTIGE STREICHE, OP. 28

TCHAIKOVSKY, PYOTR
"POLONAISE" FROM *EUGENE ONEGIN*

TURINA, JOAQUIN
EL POEMA DE UNA SANLUQUEÑA
ALEXANDRE BRUSSILOVSKY, VIOLIN

WAGNER, RICHARD
OVERTURE TO *TANNHÄUSER* (DRESDEN VERSION; 1854)

ZANINELLI, LUIGI
THE BEAUTY OF THE EARTH (WORLD PREMIERE)

VOICE OF THE CENTURY WITH RENÉE FLEMING, INAUGURAL USM CENTENNIAL EVENT

HOLIDAY CHORAL SPECTACULAR

THE UNIVERSITY OF SOUTHERN MISSISSIPPI SYMPHONY ORCHESTRA MISSION STATEMENT

THE MISSION OF THE UNIVERSITY OF SOUTHERN MISSISSIPPI SYMPHONY ORCHESTRA IS TO (1) SERVE AS THE MAIN EDUCATIONAL DEVELOPMENT ENSEMBLE FOR THE STUDENTS IN THE ORCHESTRA AT THE UNIVERSITY OF SOUTHERN MISSISSIPPI IN HATTIESBURG AND (2) SERVE AS A CULTURAL PROVIDER FOR THE GENERAL PUBLIC IN SOUTH CENTRAL MISSISSIPPI. IN CONCERT WITH THE MISSION OF THE UNIVERSITY, THE ORCHESTRA FOSTERS LEARNING AMONG STUDENTS IN WAYS THAT PREPARE THEM TO BECOME PROFESSIONAL PERFORMERS AND EDUCATORS, AS WELL AS CONTRIBUTING CITIZENS AND LEADERS IN A GLOBAL SOCIETY.

Through our annual concert season which offers programs with classical music, popular music, operas and musicals, large combined choral/symphonic works and world-class guest artists, the orchestra strives to fulfill its goal of serving not only the university community, but also the larger community of south Mississippi. The core values of The University of Southern Mississippi Symphony Orchestra, which enable us to develop artist/teachers of the future and to serve the community, state, nation, and world, are

ARTISTIC QUALITY
To present programs of uncompromising quality and excellence that reflect the education and the artistic abilities of the musicians in an international ensemble from diverse backgrounds

REPERTOIRE
To perform works of diverse styles and periods, as well as new works

PERFORMANCE
To prepare all repertoire to the exacting level required for a high-quality public performance

AUDIENCE DEVELOPMENT
To increase the partnerships and participation of the communities we serve through balanced and diverse repertoire, guest artists and symphony volunteers

ORGANIZATIONAL DEVELOPMENT
To give orchestra members and music students in the university opportunities to showcase their talents through the annual concerto competition and smaller ensembles as well as interaction with other businesses and musical organizations in the region

EDUCATIONAL AND COMMUNITY OUTREACH
(1) To serve as an educational outreach organization for students in grades K through 12 through various educational programs designed to introduce young audiences to orchestral instruments, musical theatre, jazz and opera and (2) to serve as a community outreach organization by providing high-quality performances for all citizens in our community

OPERA AND MUSICAL THEATRE PRODUCTIONS FROM 1948 TO PRESENT[1]

* DENOTES COLLABORATIVE PRODUCTION WITH DEPARTMENT OF THEATRE AND DANCE

THE BARTERED BRIDE (SMETANA)
1948
LLOYD PATTEN, DIRECTOR

ROBIN HOOD (DEKOVEN)
1949
LLOYD PATTEN, DIRECTOR

DOWN IN THE VALLEY (WEILL)
1950

TRIAL BY JURY
(GILBERT AND SULLIVAN)
1950
ROBERT WATERSTRIPE, DIRECTOR
FRANK EARL MARSH, MUSIC DIRECTOR

THE CHOCOLATE SOLDIER
(STRAUSS)
1952
LEONARD STOCKER, DIRECTOR

TRIAL BY JURY
(GILBERT AND SULLIVAN)
1952
LEONARD STOCKER, DIRECTOR

NAUGHTY MARIETTA (HERBERT)
1953
LEONARD STOCKER, DIRECTOR

MARRIAGE BY LANTERN LIGHT
(OFFENBACH)
1954
LEONARD STOCKER, DIRECTOR

SUMMER OPERA WORKSHOP
1954
MARRIAGE BY LANTERN AND *TRIAL BY JURY*
LEONARD STOCKER, DIRECTOR

HEY DAZE
1955
ORIGINAL PRODUCTION
ROBERT HAYS, COMPOSER
THOMAS LONG, RICHARD JOHNSON, PATRICIA HAYS, JACQUELINE LONG, AND ROBERT HAYS, BOOK AND LYRICS
CARL SQUITIERO, DIALOGUE
WILLIAM SEAY, CHOREOGRAPHY

THE RED MILL (HERBERT)
1955
LEONARD STOCKER, DIRECTOR

CUMBERLAND FAIR
(SUNDGAARD)
1955
LEONARD STOCKER, DIRECTOR

OPERA CONCERT
1956
THE MARRIAGE OF FIGARO, THE BARTERED BRIDE, LA BOHÈME, HANSEL AND GRETEL, DIE FLEDERMAUS
LEONARD STOCKER, DIRECTOR
HARRIS CROHN, MUSIC DIRECTOR

THE MIKADO
(GILBERT AND SULLIVAN)
1956
LEONARD STOCKER, DIRECTOR
HARRIS CROHN, MUSIC DIRECTOR

SUNDAY EXCURSION (WILDER)
1956
LEONARD STOCKER, DIRECTOR

OPERA EXCERPTS
1957
THE MAGIC FLUTE, FAUST, COSI FAN TUTTE, DON GIOVANNI, MARTHA, DIE FLEDERMAUS, THE GONDOLIERS
LEONARD STOCKER, DIRECTOR
HARRIS CROHN, MUSIC DIRECTOR

THE OLD MAID AND THE THIEF
(MENOTTI)
1957
LEONARD STOCKER, DIRECTOR
HARRIS CROHN, MUSIC DIRECTOR

COX AND BOX
(GILBERT AND SULLIVAN)
1957
LEONARD STOCKER, DIRECTOR
HARRIS CROHN, MUSIC DIRECTOR

BRIGADOON
(LERNER AND LOEWE)
1958*
RAYMOND MANNONI, GILBERT HARTWIG,
AND ROBERT TRESER, DIRECTORS
ROBERT HAYS, MUSIC DIRECTOR

THE MERRY WIDOW (LEHAR)
1958
LEONARD STOCKER, DIRECTOR
HARRIS CROHN, MUSIC DIRECTOR

THE WHISTLER (PRESSER)
1959
ORIGINAL PRODUCTION FOR SOUTHERN OPERA
LEONARD STOCKER, DIRECTOR
HARRIS CROHN, MUSIC DIRECTOR

GUYS AND DOLLS (LOESSER)
1959*
LEONARD STOCKER, DIRECTOR
HARRIS CROHN, MUSIC DIRECTOR

DIE FLEDERMAUS (STRAUSS)
1959
ROBERT MESROBIAN, DIRECTOR

OKLAHOMA! (ROGERS AND HAMMERSTEIN)
1960*
GILBERT HARTWIG, ROBERT HAYS, AND ROBERT TRESER, DIRECTORS

GIANNI SCHICCHI AND
LA BOHÈME (PUCCINI)
1960
LEONARD STOCKER, DIRECTOR
HARRIS CROHN, MUSIC DIRECTOR

THE WHISTLER (PRESSER) AND
H.M.S. PINAFORE
(GILBERT AND SULLIVAN)
1960
LEONARD STOCKER, DIRECTOR
HARRIS CROHN, MUSIC DIRECTOR

OPERA CONCERT
1961
THE MAGIC FLUTE, LA TRAVIATA, MADAME BUTTERFLY, THE DAMNATION OF FAUST, FAUST, THE YEOMEN OF THE GUARD, THE LANTERN MARRIAGE
LEONARD STOCKER, NARRATOR
HARRIS CROHN, PIANIST

DAMN YANKEES
(ADLER AND ROSS)
1961*
GILBERT HARTWIG, STAGE DIRECTOR

SUSANNAH (FLOYD)
1961
FEATURING GUEST ARTIST NORMAN TREIGLE IN THE ROLE OF OLIN BLITCH
LEONARD STOCKER, DIRECTOR
HARRIS CROHN, MUSIC DIRECTOR

THE BOY FRIEND (WILSON)
1961*
GILBERT HARTWIG, DIRECTOR
ROBERT TRESER, MUSIC DIRECTOR

THE GONDOLIERS
(GILBERT AND SULLIVAN)
1961
ERNESTINE FERREL, DIRECTOR
THEODORE RUSSELL, CONDUCTOR

AN EVENING OF OPERA EXCERPTS
1962
THE MARRIAGE OF FIGARO, CARMEN, TALES OF HOFFMANN, THE BALLAD OF BABY DOE, RIGOLETTO
CLIFFORD REIMS, DIRECTOR

AN EVENING ON BROADWAY
1962
KISS ME KATE, SONG OF NORWAY, CAMELOT, MOST HAPPY FELLA, CAROUSEL
CLIFFORD REIMS, DIRECTOR
LEONARD STOCKER, ASSOCIATE

THE MERRY WIVES OF WINDSOR
(NICOLAI)
1962
CLIFFORD REIMS, DIRECTOR
HARRIS CROHN, CONDUCTOR
LEONARD STOCKER, ASSOCIATE

THE STUDENT PRINCE (ROMBERG)
1962
CLIFFORD REIMS, DIRECTOR
HAROLD AVERY, CONDUCTOR

PAINT YOUR WAGON
(LERNER AND LOEWE)
1962
CLIFFORD REIMS, DIRECTOR
THEODORE RUSSELL, CONDUCTOR

AN EVENING OF OPERA
1962
GALANTRY, THE CLOAK
CLIFFORD REIMS, DIRECTOR

THE CRUCIBLE (WARD)
1963
CLIFFORD REIMS, DIRECTOR
HAROLD AVERY, CONDUCTOR

DON GIOVANNI (MOZART)
1963
CLIFFORD REIMS, DIRECTOR
HAROLD AVERY, CONDUCTOR

THE TELEPHONE (MENOTTI)
1963

SWEET BETSY FROM PIKE (BUCCI)
1963
KAREN MANNONI, DIRECTOR

LITTLE MARY SUNSHINE
(BESOYAN)
1963
FRANCIS MONACHINO, DIRECTOR AND PRODUCER
ROBERT HAYS, CONDUCTOR

IN THE GARDEN (KUPFERMAN)
1963

THE MEDIUM (MENOTTI)
1963
FRANCIS MONACHINO, DIRECTOR AND PRODUCER
LEONARD STOCKER, ASSOCIATE DIRECTOR

DON GIOVANNI (MOZART)
1963
WILLIAM GOWER, MUSIC DIRECTOR
HATTIESBURG CIVIC OPERA PRODUCTION FEATURING GUEST ARTIST
NORMAN TREIGLE

THE KING AND I
(ROGERS AND HAMMERSTEIN)
1964
FRANCIS MONACHINO, DIRECTOR
WILLIAM GOWER, CONDUCTOR

THE MAGIC FLUTE (MOZART)
1964
FRANCIS MONACHINO, DIRECTOR AND PRODUCER
WILLIAM GOWER, CONDUCTOR

HANSEL AND GRETEL
(HUMPERDINCK)
1964
FRANCIS MONACHINO, DIRECTOR
WILLIAM GOWER, CONDUCTOR

MARDI GRAS (KAYDEN)
1965
FRANCIS MONACHINO, DIRECTOR

DIE FLEDERMAUS (STRAUSS)
1965
WILLIAM GOWER, MUSIC DIRECTOR
HATTIESBURG CIVIC OPERA PRODUCTION

THE CONSUL (MENOTTI)
1965

CAROUSEL
(ROGERS AND HAMMERSTEIN)
1965
FRANCIS MONACHINO, DIRECTOR

DRAGENFUT GIRL (KUPFERMAN)
1965
FRANCIS MONACHINO, DIRECTOR

DIDO AND AENEAS (PURCELL)
AND LA SERVA PADRONA
(PERGOLESI)
1965
FRANCIS MONACHINO, DIRECTOR

THE MUSIC MAN
1966
FRANCIS MONACHINO, DIRECTOR
WILLIAM GOWER, CONDUCTOR

AMAHL AND THE NIGHT VISITORS
(MENOTTI)
1966
FRANCIS MONACHINO, DIRECTOR AND PRODUCER
WILLIAM GOWER, CONDUCTOR

THE MEDIUM (MENOTTI)
1967

GIANNI SCHICCHI (PUCCINI)
1967
FRANCIS MONACHINO, DIRECTOR AND PRODUCER
WILLIAM GOWER, MUSICAL DIRECTOR

OPERA SCENES
1967
CLIFTON WARE, TENOR
MARIE MELICHAR, SOPRANO

THE MIKADO
(GILBERT AND SULLIVAN)
1967
CLIFTON WARE, DIRECTOR
WILLIAM GOWER, CONDUCTOR

CAVALLERIA RUSTICANA
(MASCAGNI)
1968
CLIFTON WARE, DIRECTOR
WILLIAM GOWER, CONDUCTOR

THE MIKADO
(GILBERT AND SULLIVAN)
1968
(FIVE-CITY TOUR)
WILLIAM GOWER, CONDUCTOR

THE OLD MAID AND THE THIEF
AND THE TELEPHONE (MENOTTI)
1968
CLIFTON WARE, DIRECTOR

THE THREE PENNY OPERA (WEILL)
1969
CLIFTON WARE, DIRECTOR

OPERA SCENES
1969
AIDA, THE CLOAK
CLIFTON WARE, DIRECTOR

FLOWER DRUM SONG
(RODGERS AND HAMMERSTEIN)
1969
JACK DONOVAN, DIRECTOR
WILLIAM GOWER, CONDUCTOR

OPERA HIGHLIGHTS AND
GALLANTRY (MOORE)
1969
ROBERT MESROBIAN, DIRECTOR

COSI FAN TUTTE (MOZART)
1970
ROBERT MESROBIAN, DIRECTOR

VOYAGE TO THE MOON
(OFFENBACH)
1970
ROBERT MESROBIAN, DIRECTOR
WILLIAM GOWER, CONDUCTOR

GIANNI SCHICCHI (PUCCINI)
1970
ROBERT MESROBIAN, DIRECTOR
JAMES YESTADT, CONDUCTOR

LA BOHÈME (PUCCINI)
1971
ROBERT MESROBIAN, DIRECTOR
WILLIAM GOWER, CONDUCTOR

A FUNNY THING HAPPENED
ON THE WAY TO THE FORUM
(SONDHEIM)
1971*
BLAINE QUARNSTROM, DIRECTOR
WILLIAM GOWER, CONDUCTOR

OPERA AND MUSICAL THEATRE PRODUCTIONS, CONTINUED

L'INFEDELTA DELUSA (HAYDN)
1972
ROBERT MESROBIAN, DIRECTOR
WILLIAM GOWER, CONDUCTOR

THE BARBER OF SEVILLE (ROSSINI)
1972
ROBERT MESROBIAN, DIRECTOR
WILLIAM GOWER, CONDUCTOR

A MIDSUMMER NIGHT'S DREAM (BRITTEN)
1972
ROBERT MESROBIAN, DIRECTOR
WILLIAM GOWER, CONDUCTOR

BORIS GODOUNOV, CONCERT VERSION (MUSSORGSKY)
1973
FEATURING GUEST ARTIST NORMAN TREIGLE
JAMES YESTADT, GUEST CONDUCTOR
DAVID FOLTZ AND JACK DONOVAN, CHORAL CONDUCTORS
WILLIAM GOWER, ORCHESTRA CONDUCTOR

YOU'RE A GOOD MAN, CHARLIE BROWN (GESNER)
1973*
BLAINE QUARNSTROM, DIRECTOR
SHERMAN HONG, MUSIC DIRECTOR

DIE FLEDERMAUS (STRAUSS)
1974
ROBERT MESROBIAN, DIRECTOR
WILLIAM GOWER, CONDUCTOR

FIDDLER ON THE ROOF (BOCK)
1974*
BLAINE QUARNSTROM, DIRECTOR
JOE BARRY MULLINS, CONDUCTOR

WEST SIDE STORY (BERNSTEIN)
1975*
LARRY MULLICAN, DIRECTOR
JOE BARRY MULLINS, CONDUCTOR

SUOR ANGELICA AND IL TABARRO (PUCCINI)
1976
PATRICIA HAYS, DIRECTOR
VERNON RAINES, CONDUCTOR

AMAHL AND THE NIGHT VISITORS (MENOTTI)
1978
PATRICIA HAYS, DIRECTOR
WILLIAM PRESSLEY, CONDUCTOR

AN EVENING OF OPERETTA
1979
PATRICIA HAYS, DIRECTOR

PATIENCE (GILBERT AND SULLIVAN)
1980
PATRICIA HAYS, DIRECTOR
DAVID ZEPEDA, MUSIC DIRECTOR

GREAT SCENES FROM OPERAS
1981
COSI FAN TUTTE, CARMEN, THE MARRIAGE OF FIGARO, THE CONSUL, THE ABDUCTION FROM THE SERAGLIO
KARL BROCK, DIRECTOR AND PRODUCER

THE TELEPHONE (MENOTTI)
1986
DAVID HOLLEY, DIRECTOR

HANSEL AND GRETEL (HUMPERDINCK)
1987
DAVID HOLLEY, DIRECTOR

SUSANNAH (FLOYD)
1988
DAVID HOLLEY, DIRECTOR

AN EVENING OF ONE ACTS AND SCENES
1988
THE MAGIC FLUTE, CARMEN, A HAND OF BRIDGE, THE IMPRESARIO
DAVID HOLLEY, DIRECTOR

THE MAGIC FLUTE (MOZART)
1989
DAVID HOLLEY, DIRECTOR AND PRODUCER
JAY DEAN, MUSIC DIRECTOR

AN EVENING OF ONE ACTS AND SCENES
1989
THE BARTERED BRIDE, HANSEL AND GRETEL, LA RONDINE, HIN UND ZURÜCK, LA BOHÈME
DAVID HOLLEY, DIRECTOR

CENDRILLON (MASSENET)
1990
DAVID HOLLEY, DIRECTOR AND PRODUCER
JAY DEAN, CONDUCTOR

AN EVENING OF OPERA WORKSHOP SCENES
1990
LE NOZZE DI FIGARO, DON GIOVANNI, CARMEN, ROMEO ET JULIETTE, DIALOGUES DES CARMELITES, COSI FAN TUTTE
DAVID HOLLEY, DIRECTOR

THE MARRIAGE OF FIGARO (MOZART)
1991
DAVID HOLLEY, DIRECTOR AND PRODUCER
JAY DEAN, CONDUCTOR

THE MERRY WIVES OF WINDSOR (NICOLAI)
1992
DAVID HOLLEY, DIRECTOR AND PRODUCER
JAY DEAN, CONDUCTOR

OPERA A LA CARTE, LE MENU
1993
JAY DEAN, DIRECTOR AND PRODUCER

THE MIKADO (GILBERT AND SULLIVAN)
1994
MARCIA ORBISON WEINERT, DIRECTOR
JAY DEAN, MUSIC DIRECTOR AND PRODUCER

SIDE BY SIDE BY SONDHEIM (SONDHEIM)
1994
ROB MULHOLLAND, DIRECTOR
JOSEPH BRITAIN, MUSIC DIRECTOR
JAY DEAN, PRODUCER

DON GIOVANNI (MOZART)
1995
ROB MULHOLLAND, DIRECTOR
JAY DEAN, MUSIC DIRECTOR AND PRODUCER

SNOW WHITE (ZANINELLI)
1996
ROB MULHOLLAND, DIRECTOR
JAY DEAN, MUSIC DIRECTOR AND PRODUCER

AN EVENING OF PUCCINI
1997
LEVILLI, SUOR ANGELICA
ROB MULHOLLAND, DIRECTOR
JAY DEAN, MUSIC DIRECTOR AND PRODUCER

ORPHEUS IN THE UNDERWORLD (OFFENBACH)
1998
ROB MULHOLLAND, DIRECTOR
JAY DEAN, MUSIC DIRECTOR AND PRODUCER

CARMEN, CONCERT VERSION (BIZET)
1998
FEATURING DENYCE GRAVES
SOUTHERN ARTS FESTIVAL OPERA
ROB MULHOLLAND, DIRECTOR
JAY DEAN, CONDUCTOR AND PRODUCER

YOU'RE A GOOD MAN, CHARLIE BROWN (GESNER)
1998
ROB MULHOLLAND, DIRECTOR
JOSEPH BRITAIN, MUSIC DIRECTOR
JAY DEAN, PRODUCER

THE TENDER LAND (COPLAND)
1999
ROB MULHOLLAND, DIRECTOR AND PRODUCER
TIM KOCH, CONDUCTOR

THE FANTASTIKS (SCHMIDT)
1999
ROB MULHOLLAND, DIRECTOR
JOSEPH BRITAIN, MUSIC DIRECTOR
JAY DEAN, PRODUCER

JOSEPH AND THE AMAZING TECHNICOLOR DREAMCOAT (WEBBER)
1999
ROB MULHOLLAND, DIRECTOR
JOSEPH BRITAIN, MUSIC DIRECTOR
JAY DEAN, PRODUCER

THE MARRIAGE OF FIGARO (MOZART)
2000
ROB MULHOLLAND, DIRECTOR
CHRISTOPHER WHITE, CONDUCTOR
JAY DEAN, PRODUCER

GLORIOUS VISTAS OF ITALIAN OPERA
2000
ROB MULHOLLAND, DIRECTOR
JAY DEAN, MUSIC DIRECTOR AND PRODUCER

THE BARBER OF SEVILLE (ROSSINI)
2001
ROB MULHOLLAND, DIRECTOR
FIORA CONTINO, CONDUCTOR
JAY DEAN, PRODUCER

THE SOUNDS OF RICHARD RODGERS
2002
CONSTANCE ROBERTS, DIRECTOR
JAY DEAN, PRODUCER

CARMEN (BIZET)
2003
MARYANN KYLE, DIRECTOR AND PRODUCER

INTO THE WOODS (SONDHEIM)
2003
OBRA QUAVE, DIRECTOR
CONSTANCE ROBERTS, CONDUCTOR
MARYANN KYLE, PRODUCER

THE MAGIC FLUTE (MOZART)
2004
MARYANN KYLE, DIRECTOR AND PRODUCER
PABLO SAELZER, CONDUCTOR

A GRAND NIGHT FOR SINGING (RODGERS AND HAMMERSTEIN)
2004
MARYANN KYLE, DIRECTOR AND PRODUCER
JUAN CARLOS PEÑA, MUSIC DIRECTOR

A TOAST TO BROADWAY
2004
MICHAEL LOPINTO, DIRECTOR
JAY DEAN, PRODUCER

SUSANNAH (FLOYD)
2005
MARYANN KYLE, DIRECTOR AND PRODUCER
JAY DEAN, CONDUCTOR

A TOAST TO BROADWAY 2
2005
MICHAEL LOPINTO, DIRECTOR
JAY DEAN, PRODUCER

LA TRAVIATA (VERDI) (COLLABORATIVE PRODUCTION WITH MISSISSIPPI OPERA)
2005
ALAN MANN, DIRECTOR
JAY DEAN, MUSIC DIRECTOR
MARYANN KYLE, PRODUCER

WEST SIDE STORY (BERNSTEIN)
2006
ROB MULHOLLAND, DIRECTOR
JAY DEAN, MUSIC DIRECTOR
MARYANN KYLE, PRODUCER

GODSPELL (SCHWARTZ)
2006
ROB MULHOLLAND, DIRECTOR
KIM CARGILE AND DARRYL HARRIS, CONDUCTORS
MARYANN KYLE, PRODUCER
JAY DEAN, MUSICAL SUPERVISOR

CARMEN (BIZET) (COLLABORATIVE PRODUCTION WITH MISSISSIPPI OPERA)
2007
ALAN MANN, STAGE DIRECTOR
JAY DEAN, MUSIC DIRECTOR
MARYANN KYLE, GENERAL DIRECTOR

GUYS AND DOLLS (LOESSER)
2007
ROB MULHOLLAND, DIRECTOR
KIM CARGILE, MUSIC DIRECTOR
JAY DEAN, PRODUCER

THE MARRIAGE OF FIGARO (MOZART) (COLLABORATIVE PRODUCTION WITH MISSISSIPPI OPERA)
2008
WENDY TAUCHER, DIRECTOR
JAY DEAN, MUSIC DIRECTOR AND PRODUCER

COMPANY (SONDHEIM)
2008
ROB MULHOLLAND, DIRECTOR
TAMMY MANSFIELD, MUSIC DIRECTOR
JAY DEAN, PRODUCER

THE MERRY WIDOW (AND OTHER STUFF!)
2009
MARYANN KYLE, DIRECTOR AND PRODUCER
JEAN REIS, CONDUCTOR

I PAGLIACCI (LEONCAVALLO) AND GIANNI SCHICCHI (PUCCINI)
2009
ROB MULHOLLAND, DIRECTOR
JAY DEAN, MUSIC DIRECTOR AND PRODUCER

THE PIRATES OF PENZANCE (GILBERT AND SULLIVAN) (THE PREMIER STAGE PRODUCTION OF FESTIVALSOUTH)
2010
ROB MULHOLLAND, DIRECTOR
JAY DEAN, MUSIC DIRECTOR AND PRODUCER

LA BOHÈME (PUCCINI)
2010
ROB MULHOLLAND, DIRECTOR
JAY DEAN, MUSIC DIRECTOR

[1] LEONARD STOCKER (MUSIC FACULTY, 1953-74) COMPILED A BRIEF HISTORY OF MUSICAL THEATRE AT SOUTHERN MISS THROUGH 1977 WHICH WAS OF INVALUABLE ASSISTANCE IN COMPILING THIS HISTORY.